The Art of Decision Making

The Art of Decision Making

Mirrors of Imagination, Masks of Fate

Helga Drummond

JOHN WILEY & SONS, LTD
Chichester · New York · Weinheim · Brisbane · Singapore · Toronto

For Sheena

Science reassures, art disturbs
(Proverb)

Contents

Acknowledgements

This book was prompted by an invitation to teach risk and decision making on the Manufacturing Leaders' course of the Department of Engineering at the University of Cambridge. I am grateful to Peter Webster and Robin Daniels for their enthusiasm and encouragement.

Elizabeth and Stuart Rayner (who may have been magnolia for thirty years) helped more than they realised by listening to my comparisons between their task of converting a barn and mine of writing a book. Chapters, like oak floors, need sanding down, and material, like staircases, sometimes refuses to fit. I at least had the consolation of not having to worry about whether the plumber or the electrician would turn up as promised – the ultimate in uncertainty.

My commissioning editor ('you want it when?') Diane Taylor went beyond the call of duty in reading material and contributing suggestions. But for her willingness to take a chance there would have been no book.

My colleagues in Liverpool have been good-humoured and supportive. Laura McAllister read substantial parts of the text and saved me from many errors. Janet Beale proofread the manuscript and helped with part of the research. I am grateful to Sheena Waitkins for directing me to the Aberdeen Typhoid Report and for much, much else besides.

Introduction

'Well, here's another fine mess' (Laurel and Hardy)

The poet Robert Burns warns us that our best-laid schemes frequently go awry. It is hilarious when Laurel and Hardy find themselves embroiled in 'another fine mess', rather less so when it happens in real life.

Moreover, for all our technical sophistication, we only have to open a newspaper to find yet another 'fine mess' – the Millennium Dome that promised so much and ended in ignominy, the BSE saga, the Internet trading companies that fell to earth. Some decision failures are so serious that the word 'mess' is inadequate. The patients murdered by their trusted doctor, Harold Shipman, died because potentially ominous evidence was misinterpreted. The victims of the Concorde disaster died because a potentially catastrophic risk went unrecognised.

In our personal lives we also sometimes make decisions that 'gang aft a-gley'. We may find ourselves trapped in a career or a relationship and wonder how we got there. We may do something exactly 'by the book' and fail miserably yet succeed brilliantly when we act upon intuition and impulse. The central question this book tries to answer is *how* and *why* decisions go awry. There are many books that treat decision making as a science. This is emphatically not one of them. There are no probability statistics, no mathematical models, no spreadsheets, and no techniques of risk analysis. Although such tools have their place, they can lull us into a false sense of security as they imply that risk is something that can be managed and controlled. If so, why did the collapse of markets in the Far East in 1998 take analysts by surprise?[1] More recently, the risk of 'foot and mouth' disease seemed so remote that by early 2001, when the disease reappeared, many farmers in the UK had stopped insuring against it.

My theme is *uncertainty*. Consider the board game 'Monopoly'. We can improve our chances of winning by taking a strategic approach to decision making. We can compute the probability of landing on Mayfair, or drawing the card marked 'Go to jail'. Yet the ultimate arbiter is a roll of the dice.

Almost all decisions are a gamble. No matter how carefully we research and plan, there is always the risk that things will turn out differently from what we expect. Laptop computers were expected to oust the larger desktop machines – a prediction that has yet to be fulfilled. Although the forecast upsurge in sales of mobile telephones has materialised, the unexpected twist is that expansion has largely favoured the 'pay as you go' sector.

Decision makers must not only confront uncertainty about the future, ambivalence also surrounds the past and present. During the summer of 2000, analysts debated the significance of the upsurge in house prices. Did it signal the start of another boom similar to that of the late 1980s, or were we witnessing an isolated event that would soon give way to a market correction?[2] In October 2000, an express passenger train was derailed at Hatfield killing four people. The immediate cause of the accident was a broken rail. A more important question is what that broken rail signified.

Did the accident reflect Railtrack's alleged policy of 'sweating assets' being pushed too far? Was the subsequent decision to embark upon a full-scale programme of track checking that delayed rail services for months an over-reaction, or did it prevent other accidents?

Act II of the play *Rosencrantz and Guildenstern Are Dead* ends with the words, '. . . anything could happen yet'. We cannot make a decision without formulating some idea of what the future may hold. Yet for all our techniques of forecasting and scenario planning, the future remains hidden. AT&T, the US telecoms carrier, foresaw the convergence of telecoms and computing and how it would transform our lives and their business. However, they were not to know that the Internet would be the vehicle of convergence, and that their decision to merge with NCR, the US business machine manufacturer, in anticipation of developments would be a waste of time, money and opportunity.[3]

Even when we guess the future correctly, the dividing line between success and failure can be slender. In the late 1980s the Reichmann brothers began the Canary Wharf project. The plan was to construct 12 million square feet of office space in London's then derelict Docklands. The brothers believed that London would soon require modern office buildings with spacious floors for service companies. Yet this massive venture was launched with almost no transport infrastructure in the area. Consequently, City firms in search of office space dismissed Canary Wharf as a fringe development. In 1992, as the property market collapsed, and office rents plummeted, construction halted. Canary Wharf was placed in administration with only 4.5 million of the intended 12 million square feet of office space complete.

In 1995, Paul Reichmann succeeded in buying Canary Wharf back from the banks. The *Financial Times* was not impressed, predicting that the venture might remain an expensive 'white elephant' as the prospective release of 7.5 million square feet of office space would create an increase in supply likely to limit the recovery in office rents.[4]

The question now is will the story of Canary Wharf end happily? In 1995 rents were £80.73 a square metre. Five years later, in July 2000, with the Docklands Light Railway in service and the Jubilee Line extension finally complete, rents have more than trebled to £269.10p a square metre, prompting Paul Reichmann to predict that the site would be fully occupied within eighteen months.

The upsurge in Canary Wharf's fortunes has been the recent expansion and merging of multinational firms such as Citigroup, Credit Suisse and First Boston. In the late 1980s Reichmann predicted that it would take ten to fifteen years for Canary Wharf to realise its potential.[5] He may have been right but it surely counts as a 'close-run thing'.

Luck plays a part in decision making. When the volunteer workers of the Peak Rail organisation decided to hire engine 4472 *Flying Scotsman* for nine days in the summer of 2000 they knew they were taking a risk as the costs of staging the event might far outweigh the revenues. The decision must have seemed ill-starred when the lorry carrying the engine to Derbyshire burst a tyre on the main road near Rowsley. Yet the event generated £100 000 (the equivalent of a year's turnover), a figure boosted by the free publicity generated as motorists passed the stranded transporter.[6]

Sometimes we are luckier than we deserve to be. Text messaging generates more profit for mobile telephone operators than calls. Yet the facility was added to mobile telephones largely as an afterthought.

What we do know is that if we get it wrong, we have to live with the consequences. Unlike the fictional *Beggar's Opera* no one is going to insist that 'the piece must end happily'. Metaphorically speaking, if we finish up in the condemned cell there is no reprieve, unless we are incredibly lucky.

The Questions

My fascination with decision making dates from when I was about seven years old. I read a book that said history was all about blunders, lost opportunities, and failed gambles. So is decision making.

The specific questions this book tries to address are as follows:

1. Why are danger signs often missed? (Chapters 1, 4, 5, 7)
2. How do decision makers become committed to a course of action without apparently having made a decision? (Chapters 2, 3, and 10)
3. Why is it that decisions that were absolutely right can suddenly seem completely wrong? (Chapters 2, 6, 9)
4. Are decision makers completely at the mercy of chance? (Chapters 3, 6, 8, 10)
5. Decision fiascos frequently take us by surprise, yet in retrospect were inevitable. If something is unexpected it cannot be inevitable. How do we explain that paradox? (Chapters 8, 10)
6. All decisions have unintended consequences. Yet sometimes decisions produce the complete opposite of what was intended. How does this happen? (Chapters 2, 8, 10, 11)

7. When decision makers are confronted by failure they frequently make matters worse by 'throwing good money after bad' – why? (Chapters 7, 9, 10)
8. Why do crises occur? (6, 11)
9. Why are problems sometimes ignored until they become crises? (Chapters 6, 7, 9 and 11)
10. What can we do to 'get lucky'? (Chapter 12, 13)

Ambiguity Lurks

Decision science assumes that we live in a world where two and two equal four and where problems arrive on decision makers' desks one at a time, neatly labelled and marked 'for attention'. In contrast, an important theme of this book is that ambiguity always lurks. Decisions are rarely clear. Feedback tends to be slow to arrive, and is invariably equivocal. Moreover, the people on whom we rely for our information may exaggerate, dissimulate and even tell lies.

The Imagined World

The problem of ambiguity runs deeper than that, however. Decision science treats reality as something that exists 'out there' waiting to be discovered. In contrast, another important theme of this book is that reality exists as we define it.

Our freedom to define reality implies contradictory things. On the one hand, we can escape *from* reality by retreating into fantasy. Conversely, we can *change* reality by viewing the world from a different viewpoint. While we risk missing danger signs when we retreat into an unreal world, our freedom to define our realities also means that we are not entirely at the mercy of chance. Our problems are a figment of our imagination. This is not to suggest that we are deluded, only that there are many different ways of seeing and indeed, many different realities.

The Rutted Road

Decision science teaches that the correct approach in decision making is to choose whatever course of action promises maximum benefit. Yet a basic dilemma of decision making is that we can never be sure of the consequences of our actions.

A more important issue is how we resolve that dilemma in practice. Experience suggests that there are no good or bad decisions as such. More specifically, decisions succeed or fail according to whether they command support.

According to our textbooks this suggestion is nonsense. The textbook approach to decision making requires us to make rational choices. In this view, rationality acts as a guide. I suggest that it is safer to see rationality as an *achievement*, forged from all the arguments, counter-arguments, claims and counter-claims of the day. Most decisions can be made to look good on paper. The only valid test is the rutted road of reality.

Shifting Tides

The word 'decision' means 'to cut', implying a clear and volitional choice between alternatives. I suggest that scientific perspectives place too much emphasis upon the notion of decision at the expense of considering other aspects of the process.

First, until we can make sense of a situation there is no decision to make. Second, we are faced with the problem of implementing our decisions. Our management textbooks suggest that implementation is simply a matter of monitoring progress and taking corrective action where necessary. This mechanistic prescription can leave us feeling inadequate as decision makers because it is insensitive to the shifting tides of organisation, the oblique twists and turns whereby best-laid plans can go awry.

Decision science further assumes that things happen because somebody, somewhere makes a decision. This perspective ignores how destiny may be shaped by *indecision* and *inaction*.

The Ripening of Events

Decision science rests upon taking the risk out of uncertainty by pre-emptive planning and forecasting. The art of decision making stresses reflection, imagination and insight.

While decision science suggests we can eliminate surprise, the art of decision making involves reflecting upon the ripening of events, assessing what the future may bring, where the weaknesses lie and preparing to be surprised.

Yet events are not always random. Frequently what appears to be a chance misfortune is the product of an underlying force. Although nothing need be inevitable, the tensions inherent in a situation can produce a fiasco. At other times our efforts to avoid a fiasco may create the situation we were trying to prevent.

'All is Human'

Decision science depicts the decision maker as analytical, devoid of feeling. Yet just as the feudal barons destroyed castles out of greed, fear and jealousy, are we any different? Our educational sophistication may enable us to hide our darker impulses beneath a veneer of managerial language but they still exist.

All decisions are driven by emotion. Moreover, we can only work to the limits of our own mental processing capacities. The so-called 'human factor' can undermine our judgement, not least by driving us to persist with decisions that are clearly hopeless. It can also work in the opposite direction. Our feelings, our intuition, and even hallucinations can sometimes tell us more than our so-called 'hard information.'

Are You Competent or Lucky?

A merchant banker once received over 200 applications for one vacancy. Determined to lighten the task of shortlisting, the banker threw half of the forms into the waste bin without even looking at them. When a colleague protested at the waste of human potential, the banker replied, 'You wouldn't want to work with someone who was unlucky would you?'

Indeed when Napoleon was recruiting generals he is reputed to have said, 'never mind whether he is competent, is he lucky?' *Competence* in decision making is about increasing one's power through better forecasting, a more thorough search for options, more rigorous analysis, better monitoring and control. My purpose in writing this book has been to try to offer insight into the realities of decision making. Chapter 12 suggests how we can confront those realities in order to improve the prospects of success. The most important suggestion is that *luck* starts with humility. The message is that real power derives from being able to sense the limits of one's power. There is no Chapter 13 for that might be unlucky but there are some closing words.

Read on: anything might yet happen.

Chapter 1

The clock that struck thirteen: the challenge of sense making

'We see but we do not observe' (Sherlock Holmes)

Friday 5 July 1991 was just another day for Ahmed Al-Shari. At lunchtime he left his wife in charge of their corner shop in Bradford and journeyed to the city centre to bank his takings. The journey was uneventful. His mission complete, Ahmed tucked the deposit slip into his wallet and turned for home. The time was 12.57.

Like many Asian shopkeepers, Ahmed banked with BCCI (Bank of Credit and Commerce International). Unknown to Ahmed, in banking circles BCCI was known as the Bank of Crooks and Cocaine International. Three minutes after Ahmed had left the building, at 1 pm precisely, the regulators suddenly closed BCCI down. Accounts in no fewer than sixty-nine countries were immediately frozen. One of those accounts held Ahmed's life savings.

The subsequent investigation showed that BCCI had indeed lived up to its nickname:

BCCI was a giant hall of mirrors; money that didn't exist, customers who didn't exist, money that went round in circles, money that vanished and money that simply popped up out of nowhere.[7]

A question mark had existed over BCCI almost from the start. In 1980 the Bank of England declined to grant BCCI a full UK banking licence because of its dubious credentials. In 1985, BCCI's external auditors, Price Waterhouse (as they were then known), discovered that BCCI had used highly questionable accounting methods in order to disguise losses. Price Waterhouse, however, attributed the error to incompetence rather than fraud. By 1990 bankers knew that BCCI was struggling to obtain credit in the main money market because of its association with drug dealing and money laundering. In January 1991 Price Waterhouse discovered that vital information on problem credits appeared to be missing from BCCI's accounts. Furthermore, loans involving hundreds of millions of pounds were being 'parked' with other banks in order to conceal their existence. Three months later, in April 1991, a former employee of BCCI called Mr Rahman told the Bank of England about possible false accounts and some $300 million being diverted through shell companies – money that subsequently vanished.

Mr Rahman's allegations were extremely serious, yet another three months passed before the regulators acted. From the Bank of England's point of view closing down a bank was a momentous step. Robin Leigh-Pemberton, then governor of the Bank of England, subsequently told the House of Commons Treasury select committee, 'If we closed down a bank every time we found an instance of fraud, we would have rather fewer banks than we do at the moment'.[8]

Besides, Mr Rahman was a man with a grievance against BCCI. How seriously should his allegations be taken? An official of the Bank of England said, 'It was like seeing two dead fish floating down a river … You did not know how serious a problem you were looking at.'[7]

'Two Dead Fish'

Decision science is about making the right choice. Yet as the story of BCCI shows:

> Until we can make sense of a situation, there is **no** decision to make.[9]

Sometimes making sense of a situation is fairly straightforward. It did not take the captain of the *Titanic* long to realise that the ship was sinking and to order the boats to be lowered accordingly. When the IRA warned that a bomb had been planted in Manchester city centre the police soon grasped the seriousness of the situation and by their prompt and apposite actions averted disaster.

It is not always so easy to make correct sense of things, however. We can be good at decision making and yet fail because of deficient sense making. In the early 1990s the classical music industry thought it had struck gold with *Nessun Dorma* and so decided to capitalise upon its success by becoming more commercially orientated. Record companies set targets and invested heavily in making new recordings. The outcome was a disaster because the projected upsurge in sales never happened. Instead the industry discovered that there was no point in releasing another Beethoven symphony unless the recording happened to be highly distinctive.

Decision making is about asking clear questions and obtaining clear and definite answers, for example, 'where should we go?' 'What options have we got?' 'What should we do?' and 'What should our strategy be?' and so on. Once the regulators recognised that BCCI was corrupt they moved swiftly and decisively. One option was to close down the bank at a stroke – a drastic move with potentially far-reaching political consequences. The second option was to wind the bank down – a less drastic move but one which would give the fraudsters time to flee.

No one criticised the regulators' decision to close down the bank at a stroke. Complaints centred upon the length of time it took for the regulators, and the Bank of England especially, to recognise the extent of the problems within BCCI.

The problem is that in sense-making the waters are invariably muddied. Questions are inevitably vague, answers are inevitably flimsy. Our information is almost invariably equivocal to some extent. Often all we have to go on are small cues, 'two dead fish' that may be significant or coincidental. The dilemma is that we can never be sure. On the one hand, we risk overreacting, shutting down a bank every time an instance of fraud is discovered. Yet if we wait for the full picture to emerge, we may discover we have a BCCI on our hands.

One day, Christine, a solicitor, took lunch with a colleague in another firm. Christine was depressed, having become emotionally involved with a client for whom she had acted in divorce proceedings. The client had protested at the size of the bill and threatened to report Christine to the Law Society. He had also written a satirical letter to a magazine. As a consequence of this episode Christine felt exposed and vulnerable practising alone. Her colleague suggested that they go into partnership as he was feeling 'fed up' with his firm. The prospects were good as Christine explains:

> ... he [the prospective partner] was very competent and had got quite a good following. He had in his practice a young solicitor ... a very personable young man who was also 'fed up' with his firm. We thought he could take some of the low-level work off me. We decided we would keep both offices for the time being ... and gradually build up the practice. It seemed like an ideal situation.

The first dead fish floated down the river on day one. Christine tried to telephone her partners at 3 pm. There was no reply. She subsequently learned that they had taken the staff from their office to a champagne lunch. Christine was angry:

> It was my practice. These people were out at my expense ... time that they should have been in the office ... You would have thought that on day one they would have been very keen ... getting things sorted out.

Christine began sending her bookkeeper on trumped-up errands to her partners' office. It soon became clear that long lunches were the norm. Christine said:

> As days went by, my bookkeeper ... never seemed to find any of them there. People used to phone up and say, 'I can't get any reply from your office in ....' This is at 3.30 in the afternoon.

Alarmed by these developments, Christine began making her own spot checks. Sometimes the partners were in when she called, though they never returned from lunch before 3 pm.

Whenever Christine mentioned this to either of her partners, however, the response was, 'Oh we got back at . . . [sic].' It would usually be ten minutes after I had tried to contact them.

One day the bookkeeper arrived to find the partners' premises deserted apart from a client who had clearly been waiting for some time. When Christine telephoned, the secretary had returned and assured her that one of the partners was due back shortly. When Christine telephoned again ten minutes later the partner had returned and was seeing the client. 'I thought well, its probably a one-off, I know I am sometimes delayed unavoidably if I am down in court or whatever.' Yet Christine felt uneasy:

> I thought the Law Society could get involved and say there was something seriously amiss with the office . . . . I would lose my reputation that I had worked hard to build up . . . I would lose my client base. It did cross my mind that they could have been taking money out [stealing from the practice].

The firm had been in existence for six weeks when Christine received a telephone call from the senior partner of a large City law firm. The caller said that he had been trying unsuccessfully to call one of Christine's partners. The caller threatened that unless he received a reply within half an hour, he would report the matter to the Law Society. Christine said, 'I thought if I don't do something quickly I am going to lose everything.'

When the partners returned from lunch Christine summoned them to her office. She told them what had happened and then said, 'It's not working out is it?' From that moment the practice was dissolved.

Dissolving a practice after six weeks might seem like a drastic course of action. Yet Christine's interpretation of events proved to be correct as she subsequently discovered shoals of 'dead fish' relating to her erstwhile partners' work including misplaced documents, clients' money in the wrong place, cases neglected, documents not filed on time and failing to keep an appointment in court for which Christine subsequently incurred liability. Christine said:

> I think they thought they were out for an easy ride. They knew I had a good practice. I think they thought that they would just . . . pick up the cheque at the end of the month without putting any substantial effort in.

As for Christine's former partners:

> They were without a job. . . . There was no way they could have survived on their own because they just hadn't got a client base. They went back cap in hand [to their old firm] and said, 'We find ourselves available, we come as a pair and have you got any jobs?'

Interestingly Christine's flash of fear that her partners might have been stealing money from the practice was by no means completely unfounded. A few months later the personable young man was struck off for stealing £20 000 from an elderly client.[10]

Hanged in the Middle of the Play

Christine ended up risking her livelihood for the benefit of a pair of freeloading incompetents. Notice, however, that at the beginning of the story Christine's prospective partner had a good following, yet by the end of it was incapable of standing on his own two feet. Did he deceive Christine?

A more likely possibility is that Christine deceived herself. Imagine someone getting hanged in the middle of a play. The audience boos and jeers because it is not believable. It is not believable because it is not what the audience expects.[11] Sir Thomas Beecham said the same thing in a different language when he told an orchestra, 'Start together and finish together, the audience doesn't give a damn what goes on in between'. The point is:

Expectations may determine what we see and hear.

We shall see later in this book that it can be dangerous to make a decision in an emotionally charged state of mind. Suffice be it here to note that Christine may have decided that her prospective partner had a good following because that was what she expected to see, for it enabled her to rationalise her decision to go into partnership when the real reason for her decision was that she feeling depressed and vulnerable. Christine missed an important cue when her prospective partner said he was 'fed up' in his existing firm as was the personable young assistant. If they were so successful why were they 'fed up'? There may have been a valid reason. The point is, Christine's state of mind was not conducive to making any form of objective analysis or rigorous questioning.

The surest way to send a confidential communication in an organisation is via the internal mail in an open re-usable envelope. No one will think of looking inside it because no one expects such packets to contain anything other than routine communications. Jack the Ripper may have evaded capture by turning round and running towards his pursuers. The pursuers missed their quarry because they expected him to be running away from them.

'We see but we do not observe', said Sherlock Holmes. The

difference between seeing and observing lies in being able to appreciate the *significance* of what we see. For instance, people have been known to walk into a room where someone has hanged themselves and leave again without noticing anything amiss. To be more precise, they see the dangling corpse but fail to register what they see because it is not what they expect. As a university discovered to its cost, one way to steal a valuable painting is to slip the canvas out of the frame and substitute wrapping paper. Despite the fact that people walked past the painting every day, six weeks elapsed before the theft was discovered, as everyone continued to see what they expected to see.

Most of us go through life expecting our share of misfortune. Yet how many of us imagine that we might one day be wrongly convicted of murder? On 6 December 1949 a group of children playing in St Mark's Road, London, discovered a human skull in a blitzed house. The skull could not be identified as teeth and hair were completely missing. The coroner presumed it to be that of a victim of the air-raid that had destroyed the house in 1940 and ordered it to be burnt.

St Mark's Road is about half a mile from 10 Rillington Place, where a lorry driver named Timothy Evans lived. On 30 November 1949 at ten minutes past three in the afternoon, Evans walked into Merthyr Vale police station. He told the astonished officer on duty 'I have disposed of my wife. I have put her down a drain'[11] The police subsequently discovered the dead body of Evans' wife and his baby daughter Geraldine in the washhouse. Both had been strangled and had been dead for several days.

Evans subsequently changed his story and accused another resident of 10 Rillington Place, a man called John Reginald Halliday

Christie, of both crimes. The allegations were dismissed by the prosecution as 'bosh' and Evans was hanged.

Three years later, in March 1953, Christie left the flat at 10 Rillington Place. A new tenant called Beresford Brown moved in:

> He did a bit of cleaning up and looked round for a place to fix a bracket for his wireless. He tapped a wall and it sounded hollow, so he tore off some ragged wallpaper. Through a gap in the rough boards behind, which proved to be part of a door to what had once been a coal-cupboard, he saw a woman's naked back . . .[12]

The police discovered three dead bodies in the alcove. When they lifted the floorboards of Christie's former living room, the body of Mrs Christie was revealed, encased in rubble. A search of the garden yielded fragments of bones and teeth, a mass of hair, complete with a kirby grip plus a piece of newspaper dated 19 July 1943. In fact, two bodies had been buried there, Ruth Freust and Muriel Eady, reported missing in 1943 and 1944 respectively. The skull was missing from Eady's skeleton. The police also discovered a femur being used as a garden stick. The bone had been visible when the police inspected the garden during their investigation into Evans' confession.

Christie confessed to all six murders and to murdering Mrs Evans. He pleaded guilty but insane. The jury decided, however, that a man who altered the date on a letter written by his wife shortly before he strangled her, who subsequently forged her signature in order to claim the contents of her bank account, and who took to sprinkling Jeyes Fluid in the passages and down the drains after everyone else in the building had gone to work was sane enough to hang.

In those days a person could only be tried for one murder.

Evans was actually convicted of murdering the baby – the one crime Christie denied committing. The prosecution nevertheless maintained that both crimes were a single transaction, that is, whoever had killed one had killed the other.

We will never know whether an innocent man was hanged. One factor that told heavily against Evans was that he confessed to the murder. In fact, he said he had 'disposed' of his wife which may have meant that he helped to hide her body. The point is, would the jury have felt as confident about Evans' guilt if they had known about the existence of the two mouldering skeletons in the garden? The evidence was not discovered because the police failed to look beyond the obvious. The discovery of the skull provided a clue. Christie claimed that his dog had dug it up when the police were examining the wash-house, and that he hid it in his raincoat and subsequently pushed it through the open window of the house where it was later discovered. The police failed to make sense of the skull because they did not expect a connection between a long-dead body and two that were almost newly dead. They failed to notice the human bone stuck in the ground because they were not expecting to see it.

The Clock That Struck Twelve?

Expectations may not only determine what we see, they also influence what we hear. The clock that strikes thirteen is significant because it casts doubt on all that has gone before. It holds the potential to alert us to impending danger but only if we hear it. The trouble is, when the clock strikes thirteen we may hear it striking twelve, because that is what we expect to hear.

People often tell us what we want to hear. They sometimes tell us what we expect to hear. We are at our most vulnerable if what they tell is what we want *and* expect to hear.

On 27 March 1977, KLM flight 4805, a 747 en route from Amsterdam to the Canary Islands, and Pan Am 747 en route from Los Angeles to the Canary Islands were diverted to Tenerife along with a number of other aircraft because of a security alert at Las Palmas. Tenerife airport, which had only one runway, was consequently extremely crowded. When the Pan Am flight heard that Las Palmas airport was clear for landings, the captain decided to leave but was prevented from doing so by the KLM flight that was in the middle of refuelling and stood between the Pan Am plane and the runway. Eventually, air traffic control instructed the KLM plane to taxi down the runway, turn round, and await permission to take off. Meanwhile, the Pan Am plane was instructed to taxi down the runway, leave at the third taxiway and report when it was clear of the runway.

Tenerife airport is subject to sudden and unpredictable weather changes. Just as the KLM plane was about to turn round at the end of the runway, a cloud descended, lowering visibility to barely fifty yards. The sudden mist and rain caused the crew of the Pan Am plane to miss the taxiway they had been instructed to go to. However, the crew saw the next one along and made for that instead. As the Pan Am plane was being manoeuvred into position, air traffic control instructed the KLM flight to proceed to the runway for take-off and await further instructions.[13]

Thirteen seconds later, the KLM flight took off without clearance and collided with the Pan Am plane, killing 583 people in one of the worst disasters in aviation history.

The KLM crew were killed, so their decision to take off without permission remains a mystery. It is easy to imagine, however, the mounting stress and tension in the cockpit. The flight was running late. The crew were almost at the end of the flight. Yet unless they left soon they would be stranded as they had almost exhausted their flying hours. The captain was very irritated, he had called numerous times to get information about when he could leave. His behaviour towards his crew was overbearing, he was not communicating or interacting with them very well. Added to that was the strain of being diverted and needing to manoeuvre the plane in the cloud, mist and difficult physical conditions of Tenerife airport. The tired and frustrated crew's one aim would have been to leave as quickly as possible. Finally, the KLM pilot said, 'We go,' whereupon 'the co-pilot blurted out, in an anxious and highly stressed voice, "We are uh ... taking off," an odd pronouncement not called for by procedures.'[13]

The crew were expecting and wanting take-off clearance, when the control tower issued the following message:

Okay, stand by for takeoff, I will call you,

The message the crew probably heard was:

OK, take off.

Disaster might have been averted when the KLM flight replied:

We are now at takeoff

except that since the control tower was not expecting the plane to take off, the message was heard as:

We are now at takeoff position.[14]

The Clock That Really Did Strike Thirteen

Even when something is staring us in the face we may not see it for what it is. This is because:

We rationalise what we see to fit our expectations.

Once a tentative explanation has taken hold in our minds, information to the contrary may produce not corrections but elaborations of the explanation. Alternatively, having invested time and effort in finding a solution, we may prefer to distort reality rather than abandon the solution.

This explains incidentally why deception can be a powerful tactic in war. That is, provided the deception contains just enough truth to be credible it is likely to be swallowed. Moreover, once a deception is swallowed, fantastic blind spots tend to develop for evidence to the contrary.[15,16]

What this means is that once we form a view of a situation we rarely alter it as new evidence emerges. Instead what tends to happen is that we change our information to fit our expectations. In other words, even if we hear the clock striking thirteen we would probably say to ourselves and to others, 'Don't worry, it meant twelve.'

When Christine's partners failed to return from lunch she rationalised the facts to fit her expectations. That is, she told herself they were probably delayed in court just as she sometimes is.

The same thing happens in organisations day in, day out. When a computer prints out reams and reams of 'gobbledegook' the usual response is to throw it into a box and then take a felt-tip pen and write 'GARBAGE' across the box in large letters. The box is then pushed into a corner and forgotten. In other words, because we expect nothing better from the IT department we rationalise what we see to fit our expectations. It never occurs to us that we may be looking at the outcroppings of fraud.

In 1949 a sixteen-man fire crew was summoned to a forest fire at Mann Gulch in the USA. The crew were told to expect a so-called 'ten o'clock' fire, that is, one that would be surrounded and under control by ten o'clock the following morning. In fact, the fire, which was probably caused by lightning striking a dead tree, was much more serious. The crew's subsequent behaviour shows the blind spots that can develop once expectations are formed. The fire crew travelled to Mann Gulch by helicopter. As they marched towards the scene the crew became uneasy. The distant flames flapping back and forth did not make sense.

"'Then Dodge saw it!' What he saw was that the fire had crossed the gulch just 200 yeards ahead and was moving toward them.'[17] Dodge (the leader) lit a fire in front of his crew, ordered them to drop their tools and lie down in the area it had burned. The panic-stricken crew ignored the instruction and continued running up the ridge. Only two plus Dodge the leader survived.

The firecrew died because of a failure of sense making. To give some idea of the scale of that failure it subsequently took 450 men five days to bring the fire under control. The fundamental mistake was rationalising everything they saw to fit the expectation of a 'ten o'clock' fire until it was too late. Consequently nothing made sense. As events made less and less sense, the group became progressively disorientated. We tend to think of panic as demolishing organisational coherence. For example, if passengers on a burning aircraft panic it become impossible to effect orderly evacuation procedures.

Yet it can happen the other way round. That is, organisational disintegration may precipitate panic. Incidentally there are two types of panic. One is where people run amok charging towards emergency exits. The other is a frozen panic where people become immobilised blocking gangways and emergency exits.[13]

In the case of the Mann Gulch firecrew, a deadly sequence was set in motion. As the fire made less and less sense the group became more and more stressed. As the crew became stressed the social organisation began to disintegrate. Then, as the group became progressively incoherent panic set in. Panic prevented the crew from making sense of the one thing that would have saved them, that is, the escape fire.

Interestingly the three who survived kept some semblance of organisation around them. The leader Dodge survived because his first priority was the safety of his crew and that kept his own fear under control. Dodge continued to see a group even though it had disintegrated. The other two crew members, Rumsey and Sallee, probably survived because they stuck together. By doing this Rumsey and Sallee kept each other's fears under control thus enabling them to think more clearly. They escaped through a crack in the ridge which their colleagues either failed to see or assumed was too small for them to squeeze through. Moreover, when Rumsey collapsed 'half hysterically' into a juniper bush where he would have perished:

> His partner Sallee stopped next to him, looked at him coldly, never said a word, and just stood there until Rumsey roused himself, and the two then ran together over the ridge and down to a rock slide.[17]

In despair, his colleague merely looked at him coldly. This pitiless response prompted him to get up and continue running.

The Perils of Experience

Expectations can determine not only what we see and hear, but also how we *act*. Airline pilots know from experience that most electrical faults on planes are trivial, a loose wire on a coffee pot, for example. Likewise, a doctor knows from experience that a sore throat is rarely serious.

Experience makes us efficient at our jobs and prevents us from over-reacting. It becomes a liability, however, if it blinkers us to more ominous possibilities. On 2 December 1984 there was an explosion at a chemical plant at Bhopal in India. The final death toll has never been established but is estimated to have been anywhere between 1800 and 100000 people plus 200000–300000 injured, to say nothing of the effects on animals and the environment. The immediate cause of the accident was a leak of a highly toxic gas. An important contributory factor was the lack of staff training in chemical engineering.[18] More specifically, supervisors at the plant believed that 90% of the variances observed in the gauges were caused by fluctuations in the electricity supply. Consequently when the gauges began to signal danger they were ignored. The crisis was well advanced before they began to question whether this assumption might be seriously wrong.[19]

Interestingly another possible cause of the Tenerife disaster was the KLM pilot's earlier experience as training captain. Stress creates tension and tension creates emotional turbulence. Emotional turbulence limits our ability to respond to situations. In consequence, we may regress to our earliest learned behaviour. Regression can be very positive when it is necessary to act immediately. Aesop's cat eluded the hunters because it did not have to stop and think what to do whereas the fox with its wide repertoire of tactics was caught and killed while still making up his mind.[20]

Regression can also prove disastrous, however. It may explain the behaviour of the Mann Gulch firecrew in that the primitive response of 'flight' is learned before more sophisticated behaviours such as lying down in an escape fire. Returning to the Tenerife disaster, training captains do not require permission for takeoff. The tired and stressed KLM pilot may have regressed to his first learned behaviour and given himself permission to take off.[14]

Turning a Drama into a Crisis

Common sense suggests that we think and then act. In this view, accidents happen when people act without thinking. Another possibility is that:

> *We think by acting.*[19]

Action generates information and feedback and so enables us make sense of events. Yet by acting we also become part of the crisis. We now know that President Kennedy was not killed by a single bullet. Three shots hit the president, only the third of which was fatal. If the president's driver had pressed the accelerator when the first shot was fired, history might have been different. Instead, he slowed down momentarily, and then:

> The First Lady, in her last act as First Lady, leaned solicitously towards the President. His face was quizzical. She had seen that expression so often, when he was puzzling over a difficult press conference question. Now, in a gesture of infinite grace, he raised his right hand, as though to brush back his tousled chestnut hair. He had been reaching for the top of his head. But it wasn't there any more.[21]

It is often our initial response to the critical sign that determines the trajectory of the crisis. We can turn a drama into a crisis because when we act we bring events and arrangements into existence that would not otherwise be there.[19] If Kennedy's driver had not slowed down momentarily the motorcade would have been further along the road when the third and fatal shot was fired.

An event does not have to be a drama to become a crisis. The most mundane action can trigger disaster. By dint of good maintenance, many aircraft in commercial service are flying long past their planned retirement age, carrying millions of passengers every year. A particular problem with ageing aircraft is that the insulating material on the wiring eventually rubs away through vibration. Since almost 75% of it is inaccessible, it cannot be tested for faults. The first sign of trouble is usually when a circuit breaker blows.

Recall, we think by acting. When a circuit breaker blows the pilot's first response is to reset it to see if the problem rectifies itself. Many ageing aircraft are fitted with an insulating material called Kapton. Although Kapton has many good properties it is prone to accelerated ageing. Moreover, under certain stresses it can explode into searing heat.

On 22 June 1998 a Boeing 757 had just taken off from Larnaca in Cyprus bound for Manchester with 217 people when there was a small explosion on board. A gantry of red 'out of order flags' lit up as the plane lost nearly all electrical power. A subsequent investigation discovered that the Kapton insulation on two wires had been damaged where they had rubbed against a support blanket. On this occasion the pilot managed to return to the airport safely. The 230 passengers on TWA flight 800 were not so lucky, as none survived when their plane came down off the coast of Long Island in 1996.

Although the cause of the disaster remains a mystery, the most likely possibility is an explosion caused by faulty wires inside a fuel tank.

Kapton has been taken out of military aircraft though it was installed in commercial planes as late as 1993. Every time a pilot resets a circuit breaker on one of these 'flying bombs' as they are known in aviation circles, they add to the stress on the wiring and may create the conditions for a much more serious failure.[22]

Moreover, having acted in accordance with our expectations, we may well see the results of our actions as *confirming* our expectations. The crisis then escalates as we take another inappropriate action and so on.

This may explain how unwanted attentions escalate into sexual harassment. That is, the harasser initially expects that their attentions are welcome. So they make some gesture that is consistent with that expectation. They then rationalise the response to fit with their expectations thus encouraging them to bolder gestures.

'It Can't Be'

Our sense-making abilities are ultimately limited by the power of our imagination. As the philosopher Wittgenstein said:

> *What we cannot think we cannot say. We cannot therefore say what we cannot think.*

The Bank of England was expecting bad apples within BCCI. It had never occurred to them, however, that the barrel itself was rotten. To mix metaphors, they saw the two dead fish and wondered whether there might be more. However, they never imagined that a whole ocean might be hopelessly polluted because such things were unprecedented.

On 19 December 1997, Silkair flight MI185 carrying 97 passengers and 7 crew was on a routine flight to Singapore when it suddenly went into a steep dive. Two minutes later the plane hit the ground at over 700 miles per hour. There were no survivors. There was no 'mayday' signal and no evidence to suggest a bomb or mechanical failure. A strange feature of the crash was that both the flight data recorder and the cockpit voice recorder had been switched off approximately 3 minutes before the plane crashed.

Another dictum of Sherlock Holmes is that when all other possibilities have been eliminated the explanation we are left with *must* be correct however fantastic or unthinkable it may seem. Did the pilot commit suicide and take a planeload of people with him?

Surely not, yet how significant is it that the pilot, Captain Tsu Way Ming, was in the clutches of Singapore's notorious loan sharks and that he had taken out a large life insurance policy immediately before the crash? Moreover, in 1997, two complaints had been filed against Tsu. One concerned flying to unsafe limits. The second involved an aborted landing where the first officer assumed command. After the plane had been landed safely, Tsu promptly erased the voice recorder.[23]

We can only make sense of things if we are willing to contemplate them in the first place. Ultimately it may not be our powers of imagination that prevent us from making correct sense of things so much as the limits we impose upon our imagination. Did Captain Oates really say 'I may be gone for some time' or was he murdered by his fellow explorers because he was ruining their chances of survival? The question is rarely asked because we want to believe the story of altruistic suicide.

A question that has puzzled historians of the Nazi Holocaust is why victims apparently preferred the certainty of death to the slim chance of escaping. The answer may simply be that the hapless men, women and children walked quietly to the gas chambers because, despite all the rumours and stories in circulation, they did not believe—could not believe—that humanity would be capable of such crimes.

It was suggested earlier that a sore throat is rarely anything to worry about. A doctor who treated his young wife for this condition said 'I saw the signs of cancer but I could not believe it in someone so young'.

When we are faced with evidence of an extreme situation we tend to exercise a form of self-censorship. We see, or hear or sense what is happening yet say to ourselves:

'It can't be, therefore, it isn't'.[9]

This is precisely what the doctor told himself until his wife's condition became inoperable. The Tenerife air disaster could have been averted if the co-pilot of the KLM flight had intervened. The faltering speech captured on the cockpit voice recorder suggests that he may have realised that something was wrong yet he failed to act upon his suspicions. One possible explanation for his behaviour is that the idea of a senior colleague taking off into the path of another plane was so inconceivable that he dismissed the evidence of his eyes, ears and senses. The collapse of Barings Bank (see page 92) might have been prevented if the external auditors had questioned possible evidence of fraud. The facts are as follows.

In early January 1995, Coopers & Lybrand, Barings' external auditors in Singapore, discovered a £50 million discrepancy in the accounts. Nick Leeson claimed that the outstanding £50 million represented an uncollected debt from a US firm of brokers known as Spear, Leeds and Kellogg (SLK). The auditors accepted Leeson's explanation subject to receipt of supporting documentation including confirmation of the transaction directly from SLK.

In fact, there was no sum of money owing. The 'hole' in the balance sheet reflected part of Leeson's losses arising from his unauthorised trading. Leeson subsequently forged the requisite letter from SLK. In order to make it look as if the letter had been sent directly from SLK, Leeson then faxed the letter to the external auditors from his own home.

The document that reached the auditors bore an imprint reading 'From Nick and Lisa'. This clearly meant that the document could not have come directly from SLK. It is a matter of record that the auditors did not question the fax.[24] Barings collapsed before the audit was completed. It is possible, therefore, that Leeson's malfeasance might have been exposed sooner. Again, we see but we do not observe. The imprint 'From Nick and Lisa' was unmistakable. The auditors must have seen it. Whether they observed it is another question. Since the auditors were expecting a fax from SLK, they may have unconsciously screened out the discordant imprint. In other words, although they saw the words 'From Nick and Lisa' the significance of what they saw may not have registered. Yet even if they had seen it they might not have acted upon their information. Until Barings collapsed, malfeasance on a massive scale was virtually unprecedented. Paradoxically, whereas a discrepancy of £100 000 or even £1 million might have alerted suspicion, a £50 million fraud was almost unthinkable. Barings rationalised other signs of malfeasance such as a reconciliation problem of £100 million in Leeson's accounts as evidence of a busy trader working flat out to exploit a bubble of profit but neglecting his administrative duties in the process. Interestingly it was not the missing monies that finally prompted alarm but Leeson's disappearance. Here was something that could not be rationalised.

Such self-censorship also partly explains why Dr Harold Shipman escaped detection for so long. Shipman was convicted of murdering no fewer than fifteen of his patients though the actual number of victims may be much higher. Many of those murdered died in Shipman's surgery. People rarely die in doctors' surgeries, and the undertakers who removed the dead bodies noted the exceptionally high mortality rate. In addition, doctors from the other practice in the neighbourhood realised they were countersigning an unusual number of death certificates for Shipman. Yet no one suspected murder. Only when Shipman forged a patient's will did questions begin to be asked. Even then, it was a long time before Shipman was arrested not least because the police were initially incredulous.

Shipman murdered because he enjoyed wielding the power of death. As human beings, we have a taste for power. The question that we are reluctant to ask is, how many more Shipmans are there? Some health trusts have acknowledged the possibility and have begun scanning their records for statistical evidence of unusual death rates. Others have so far been unwilling to contemplate the possibility. It is like hearing the message 'We are the *Titanic* sinking. Please have your boats ready'. The natural reaction is 'It can't be . . .'

Chapter 2

The morning after

'Life is lived forward and evaluated backwards.' (Kierkegaard)

In September 2000 a well-organised group of hauliers and farmers blockaded the UK's oil refineries in protest at the taxation on fuel prices. Within three days, the whole country ground almost to a halt.

Yet what had happened *exactly?* Was the fuel shortage a throwback to wartime shortages and rationing? Was it a new form of industrial action – like a virus that had jumped species from the unionised labour to the self-employed? Was it a chilling display of our reliance upon fossil fuels, an ominous dress rehearsal for the real crisis yet to come?

What we call decision making is often concerned less with making choices and more with deciding what has already happened. Notice I did not say 'is happening'.

The present time may be ours. There may be no time like the present, but the present is so fleeting that it is impossible to make sense of it. The fuel crisis was not made up of one event but a whole series of events, petrol pumps running dry, supermarket shelves starting to empty, hospitals becoming denuded of staff, schools closing, panic buying and so forth unfolding day by day, hour by hour. Was there ever a crisis? If so, when did it become a crisis? What was it before it was a crisis, and what is it now? Likewise, 'total quality management' was the managerial imperative of the 1990s – but what was the so-called 'quality movement'? Did it signify a profound shift in the forces of economic competition, or was it just a fad?

The poet John Gay's epitaph reads:

Life is a jest and all things show it,
I thought so once; but now I know it.[25]

Notice that certainty only arrives right at the end. The poet may have suspected life is a joke but it is only as he nears the end and looks back that he is able to make sense of it.

The play *The Roses of Eyam* tells the story of how in 1665 the plague of London reached the remote Derbyshire village of Eyam in a box of cloth sent to the tailor George Vicars. The cloth arrived damp and so he dried it before the fire, thus helping to spread the infection it carried. As the villagers begin to succumb to the plague, the rector and former rector of the village persuade the remaining inhabitants to enclose the village. They draw a boundary of stones and resolve that until the plague has finished, no villager will go out, nor will any stranger come in. As the news sinks in and the villagers leave the meeting, the two rectors look at one another, 'What have we done?'[26]

The Lantern and the Mirror

As decision makers we need both a lantern and a mirror. The lantern enables us to see where we are going. The mirror is just as

important because it tells us where we have been. More specifically, we need the mirror because:

*All sense-making comes from a **backwards** glance.*[27]

All knowledge, all meaning, all insight and all understanding come
from looking backwards. We may get drunk at the office party. Yet
it is only the morning after, when we look back, that we realise
what we have done. In the ghost scene in Shakespeare's *Richard
III*, Richard's eleven victims reappear in the order in which they
were murdered. Their purpose is to confront their murderer with
the enormity of his deeds, to show Richard what he has done, to
be in his mind, weighing down his spirit, sapping his energies and
driving him to despair on the eve of the Battle of Bosworth, 'Let
me sit heavily on thy soul tomorrow'.

To be more precise we are only ever conscious of what we have
done and never of doing it. Although we may think we know what
we are doing when we decide to do something, we only know
what have done, after we have done it. In Charles Dickens' *Oliver
Twist* the beadle Mr Bumble decides to marry Mrs Corney, the
women's superintendent of the workhouse, in order to qualify for
promotion to master of the workhouse. His decision is also made
with an eye to Mrs Corney's worldly goods. Two months later,
however, he sits moodily in the workhouse parlour, eyes fixed on
the cheerless grate musing upon events:

A great change had taken place. The laced coat and the cocked hat;
where were they? .... Mr Bumble was no longer a beadle.

There are some promotions in life, which independent of the
more substantial rewards they offer, acquire a peculiar value and the
dignity from the coats and waistcoats connected with them. ... Strip

the bishop of his apron or the beadle of his cocked hat and gold lace, what are they? Men, mere men. . . . Mr Bumble had married Mrs Corney, and was master of the workhouse. Another beadle had come into power. On him the cocked hat, gold laced coat, and staff, all three had descended. . . .

'I sold myself for,' said Mr Bumble '. . . six teaspoons, a pair of sugar tongs, and a milk pot; with a small quantity of second-hand furniture and twenty pound in money. I went very reasonable. Cheap, dirt cheap!'[28]

All decisions are gambles. Technically a decision succeeds if expectations are met. What is interesting about Bumble's predicament, however, is that decision has turned out as expected. His gamble in marrying Mrs Corney has paid off. Bumble is *exactly* where he wants to be, that is, master of the workhouse. Moreover, he always knew that upon attaining promotion he would have to surrender the cocked hat. Nor has Mrs Corney misled him about the value of her possessions. Bumble gets *exactly* what he expects, that is, six teaspoons, a pair of sugar tongs, and a milk pot; with a small quantity of second-hand furniture and twenty pound in money. So why is he unhappy?

'Oh *What* Have You Done?'

In fact, for Bumble worse was to come. Degraded and humiliated in front of the paupers by his shrewish wife, he is eventually dismissed from his post after being held responsible for her dishonest behaviour. Reduced to great indigence and misery, Bumble ends up as a pauper in the very workhouse where he once lorded over others.

Bumble might have thought twice about his ill-fated decision to marry Mrs Corney if he had realised that:

*knowing **why** we are doing something is not the same as knowing **what** we are doing.*

The two rectors in *The Roses of Eyam* knew exactly why they wanted to impose a curfew around the village. The play explores the significance of that decision, that is, the doubts, the tensions and the suffering as 277 villagers out of a population of about 350 die.

The oil companies knew exactly why they wanted to build supertankers. Quite simply, it is much cheaper to ship double the quantity of oil in one large tanker than it is to ship the same quantity in two small tankers. It is even more economical to use one tanker in place of five smaller ones. In other words, the doubling or even quintuplicating of tonnage was seen as a straightforward solution to a problem. There followed a series of disasters in daylight and calm seas, and explosions at the least likely moment, that is, when ships were travelling to the loading terminals while the crew were busy cleaning the empty holds with seawater. Gradually the oil companies began to realise that these supertankers behaved differently from their smaller predecessors, notably in their steering ability. As they looked back they saw that what they had actually done was to create something *else*.[29]

In the mid-1980s the City of London witnessed a bonanza as huge sums were offered to attract staff and even whole firms as banks scrambled for a share of the securities industry in anticipation of deregulation, known as the Big Bang. In the end, they bought lemons. For instance, hundreds of thousands of pounds were lavished upon 'golden hellos' to analysts and researchers who were then poached by other firms within months of their arrival. Moreover, merging organisations created huge and unresolvable cultural clashes between brokers, jobbers and bankers resulting in debilitating conflicts that would reverberate endlessly.

One such 'lemon' was Barclays' investment division known as BZW. BZW was formed from Stock Exchange firms, that is, de Zoete and Bevan and Wedd Durlacher, in 1986. The purpose of the merger was clear – to enable Barclays to turn itself into a major investment bank. There followed a ten-year civil war between the high-flying deal-chasing investment bankers and Barclays' staid domestic bankers.

The two cultures proved utterly incompatible. By 1997 it had become obvious to Barclays that the dream of becoming a world leader in investment banking had failed. Accordingly Barclays began selling parts of BZW.

In 1998, Barclays decided to dispose of BZW altogether. Again, the rationale was clear. Barclays had discovered that although domestic banking is unglamorous it was proving to be a much more profitable activity than investment banking and so Barclays decided to lead from strength. Consequently, BZW was seen as an incoherent organisation that no longer fitted with Barclays' strategy.

Initially the prospects seemed bright. Analysts were suggesting that the sale should net at least £300–500 million and might realise as much as £2.5 billion. Barclays appointed Goldman Sachs to handle the sale. From that moment, however, matters began to slide. What had Barclays done?

> The appointment of Goldman was seen afterwards as a fundamental mistake. 'Never auction a people business,' observed one veteran corporate financier. 'It's not like real estate.' The only way to have

made the deal work satisfactorily would have been to ask [BZW] to sell themselves.[30]

Having hoisted the 'for sale' sign, Barclays discovered that the market for second-hand investment banks was flat. Like a car rusting on a garage forecourt, BZW became a wasting asset as key staff moved to competitors rather than face an uncertain future. Barclays grew increasingly embarrassed as a succession of potential buyers walked away.

Eventually only one buyer remained interested, Credit Suisse First Boston (CSFB). When CSFB learned of this, they too withdrew. It was a brilliant negotiating ploy. A former BZW corporate finance director said:

> The whole BZW sale was an absolutely howling cock-up.... The only hope of screwing a reasonable price out of CSFB was to keep Bankers Trust [another potential buyer] in play. It would have been worth offering them a five million fee just to pretend they were still interested. That would have been wholly unethical of course, but a really talented corporate financier might have found a way to get away with it.[30]

When CSFB returned to the negotiating table they offered £100 million for BZW minus payments to retain certain staff and to make others redundant. Ultimately Barclays paid CSFB an estimated £200 million to take BZW off their hands.

Ostensibly the demolition contractors of the slum-clearance programmes of the 1960s demolished bricks and mortar and rid us of homes unfit for human habitation. What emerged, however, as people were dispersed to high-rise flats and 'overspill' areas on the fringe of cities was the destruction of communities. Moreover, it was not only houses that vanished but also a way of life characterised by the strong social bonds and social support that living in rows of terrace houses enabled.

Rolls Meets Royce

Sense making comes not so much from the facts of a situation but the *significance* that we attach to them. In Oscar Wilde's play *The Importance of Being Earnest* Jack is observed smoking. Mrs Bracknell replies that it is good that a man should have an occupation. More seriously, the facts of a car crash may amount to a fortnight off work due to a dislocated shoulder and an insurance 'write-off'. The incident assumes a particular significance, however, if it prompts a job or career change in order to work nearer home. Indeed, small things can turn out to be enormously significant. A small selfish action in a relationship can prompt the other party to rewrite the whole experience.

In 1998 an earthquake struck Turkey, killing 144 people and injuring hundreds more. About one third of the buildings in the cities of Adann and Ceyhan were either destroyed or rendered uninhabitable. Yet what really came tumbling down was an era of jerry building facilitated by political corruption. Buildings collapsed because contractors had used poor-quality reinforcing bars and skimped upon cement. Moreover, they had ignored advice cautioning against erecting high-rise buildings in areas prone to earthquakes. The fact that schools and hospitals were among the buildings worst hit added to the suggestion that politicians had taken bribes to award contracts and then been unable to enforce building regulations for fear of their activities being exposed.[31]

Time alone reveals the significance of events.

In July 2000 I took afternoon tea at the Midland hotel in Manchester. I sat near to the spot where Messrs Rolls and Royce met in 1904 to discuss the prospect of going into partnership. It was a weekday and the hotel lounge was host to several meetings. One young man was earnestly describing his skills and experience to a consultant from a recruitment agency. The consultant responded with textbook nods and gestures of encouragement in between making notes with a Cross ballpoint. On the settee next to me, a brightly attired American was examining tapes and illustrations while his companion slowly and patiently pushed down the obstinate lid on the coffee pot. The fleeting image of a Red Admiral butterfly caught my attention as snatches of a conversation drifted over, 'these could be really useful . . . we were with a company . . . even signed declarations of intent – and then they went out of business.'

Were they Rolls meeting their Royces? Will the consultant end up keeping the ballpoint as a souvenir of a very special day? Will the discussion over the tapes and illustrations mark a turning point in a seemingly unlucky project? Or were they wasting their time? Only the ripening of events can reveal the meaning of those encounters.

Divorce Your Husband Without Him Noticing

As we saw in the previous chapter, certain situations and events have only one meaning and our interpretations are either right or they are wrong. Indeed, our old images of decision making depicted the world in black and white. In this view, what we see, hear and experience must be either one thing or another. We are either dealing with love or hate, obedience or defiance, sorrow or joy, success or failure.

Rarely is anything so simple. As decision makers we must grapple with ambiguity. Ambiguity means capable of more than one meaning. A couple sold their house in order to enable her to buy a studio flat in the city and him to take a small cottage in the country where they could be together for weekends. The reason for the decision was that the wife had grown tired of commuting. Had she also, consciously or unconsciously, grown tired of her husband? The weekends together might become fewer and fewer with the wife finding excuses to remain in the city. Eventually the story might be entitled 'how to divorce your husband without him noticing'.

As decision makers our realities are more like shot silk. The colours are many and changing as hues interact with one other and with the light to produce subtle and sometimes shifting effects. In the days that followed the sinking of Russian submarine *Kursk* in August 2000 we went about our business believing that there were men trapped under the sea who might be saved if only the rescuers could reach them in time. As the Russians' own attempts to rescue survivors repeatedly failed, public opinion grew impatient with the Russians' apparent intransigence in accepting international help. Then it emerged that the accident had happened sooner than the reports from Russia initially stated. Moreover, for all the stories about the severely damaged hatch hampering rescue efforts, the Norwegian team of divers opened it with little difficulty. Finally, there was the press photograph of a distraught mother of one of the crew being forcibly injected with a sedative.

Those images reflected many levels of meaning. On one level the sinking of *Kursk* was a military accident, a reminder that even in peacetime, danger lurks. On another level flitted the spectre of nuclear power shot with a demonstration of incompetence and all it implies. On yet another level the incident revealed that although the Cold War is officially over, it is still being fought. Then we realised that the ghost ship carried one survivor after all – Stalin. The point is, the incident was not one thing or another. It was many things *simultaneously*.

The greatest gift, says the poet Robert Burns, is too see ourselves as others see us. One of the risks of decision making is the significance that others may attach to our actions. For instance, in 1999 the former MP Neil Hamilton sued Mohammed Al-Fayed for libel over the so-called 'cash for questions' affair whereby Hamilton was alleged to have accepted payment in return for raising questions in parliament. The case was going well when defending counsel George Carman delivered a bombshell. Did Mrs Hamilton recall an occasion when she and her husband had stayed at the Ritz hotel in London at Al-Fayed's expense? Carman then described the '"four courses of Desperate Dan mountains of food" every night' eaten by the Hamiltons before asking Mrs Hamilton whether she and her husband normally drank two bottles of vintage champagne between them at dinner. '"Do you not think you were a bit greedy,"' he said?

Hearing her conduct *re*presented in this way Mrs Hamilton tearfully declared, '"I wish we had never set foot over the threshold of that beastly hotel"'.[32]

Sentence First, Verdict Later

'Funny,' said an estate agent 'but when we look back at our records, the houses that people buy are often nothing like what they said they were looking for.' You might say, surely only fools behave in such an illogical fashion? Yet many of our decisions end up as nothing like as planned and yet we are perfectly happy with them. Conversely, we saw earlier that we can achieve our objectives and yet be miserable.

This is because we *discover* our preferences through action. Indeed, one of the limitations of the 'total quality management' philosophy with its emphasis upon consulting the customer is that it assumes customers know what they want. Yet how many of us knew we wanted remote control devices on our televisions? Yet imagine having to get up and walk across the room to change channels! How many of us know that we want infra-red connections on our electrical equipment? Yet once they become a commercial possibility, who will want to revert to trailing cables?

We may think that we would prefer a south-facing study until we step into the room on a sunny day and find the heat unbearable and the computer screen almost invisible. Conversely, we may discover that certain features of a house that we thought we would dislike are actually quite pleasant.

This may seem like common sense, that is, as nothing more than a willingness to change our minds in the light of new information. I suggest that the process is more subtle. More specifically, common sense suggests that we do things for a reason. I suggest that it may sometimes be the other way round. That is:

We act and then invent a reason for acting.

In a fascinating experiment two supervisors were instructed to check the work performance of two subordinates. Conditions were then manipulated so that one supervisor had to spend more time watching one employee rather than the other. The actual performance of the two subordinates was carefully controlled and almost identical. Yet when the supervisor was asked to evaluate the two employees, he reported that one was untrustworthy and so required extra supervision in order to force them to perform. In other words, this biased perception of the subordinate's performance arose in order to enable the supervisor to make sense of the time spent watching the subordinate.[33]

This experiment explains why marital couples who split up often spend hours going over the past, trying to make sense of what has happened. For example:

'We grew out of each other . . .'
  'I was only twenty when we met . . . I thought I was missing something . . . .'
  'I regret the way it happened, but it would have happened anyway.'

We need to decide upon a reason in order to justify our actions to ourselves and to other people. Yet ultimately we can never know exactly why we did something.

The Ghosts of Christmas

More rarely, understanding comes from being visited by the Ghost of Christmas Yet to Come – the phantom that shows us shadows of things that have not yet happened but will happen in the time before us. When Scrooge sings and dances for joy on Christmas morning he explains to his astonished housekeeper that he has not taken leave of his senses but has come to them. The ghost of Christmas Yet to Come has shown Scrooge his own death. He sees his fellow businessmen scraping for volunteers to go to his funeral. 'What was the matter with him?' says one. 'God knows', comes the reply. 'I don't mind going if a lunch is provided . . .' says another.[34]

Then Scrooge sees the housekeeper pawning the curtains from his bed – robbing the corpse that lies there – the ghost of Christmas Yet to Come shows Scrooge the neglected grave bearing his name.

The journey into the future is an exercise in sense making because it confronts Scrooge with the implications of the life he *presently* leads. In other words, our understanding of where we are today may depend upon where we believe we will be tomorrow. In consulting our horoscope we hope to learn about what the future has in store. What we are really doing, however, is trying to make sense of the present. If the stars predict fabulous wealth then our present poverty appears as a transitory phase, something to be endured en route to somewhere else. The real value of opinion polls is that they tell governments where they are *now*.

We all know that memory tells us what has happened. There is another intriguing possibility however, namely:

*Memory tells us what is **going** to happen.*

A theme of this book is that we cannot predict the future. Yet sometimes prophesy is sometimes uncannily accurate. One possible explanation for this apparent contradiction is that what we remember and how we remember makes the future for us. The ghosts that rise on the eve of the Battle of Bosworth sap Richard

III's energy and his will to win. By the time he mounts his horse he is as good as beaten and he knows it. Yet where do those ghosts reside but in his memory?

The Magnolia Years

'We've been magnolia for thirty years,' said a wife peering doubtfully into the tins of lemon and raspberry paint. We have painted our walls in magnolia for thirty years – that much is certain, but *what* have we been?

Life may be lived forwards and evaluated backwards but that does not mean that every time we look back we reach the same conclusion. Hindsight is said to be the only exact science known to us. Experience certainly teaches, but the proverb assumes that the past is set in stone.

Yet the past may be just as elusive as the present. The decade and a half that preceded the First World War has come to be seen as an epoch characterised by stability and certainty. Yet that is because of the shattering that followed. In other words,

Our view of the past shifts according to what the future brings.

The title of Marilyn Monroe's last film *Something's Got to Give* seems ominous in the light of her subsequent death and the mystery surrounding it. The magnolia years may be seen as an era of certainty and stability if the switch to lemon and raspberry paint ushers in ill-health, marital tension or other misfortune. Conversely, if the change to lemon and lemon and raspberry is followed by spiralling fortune and a social whirl, the magnolia years will be seen as a boring waste.

The same applies to our decisions. Time can transform success into failure and failure into success. In the year 2000 Barclays' sale of BZW is seen as a 'howling cock-up'. By, say, 2002, it may seem that Barclays was wise to have disposed of BZW at any price.

Politicians were resolved that when the contract to run the UK's National Lottery expired they would part company with Camelot, the existing operators. Although Camelot had run the lottery efficiently their contracted share of the profits had attracted criticism and allegations of 'fat cats'. The probity of one of Camelot's suppliers had also been questioned.

Yet when politicians had taken time to reflect upon the implications of Richard Branson's bid to run the so-called Peoples' Lottery there was a palpable shift in attitudes towards Camelot. Camelot had accepted criticism – Branson might well be more vociferous. Branson would certainly give the lottery a high profile, but where might that lead? Then there were the questions over the financial structure of Branson's business empire and his allegedly colourful private life. The last thing the government wanted was a scandal involving the lottery. Consequently, when Camelot won its court case enabling it to remain in the competition thus reopening the whole issue just as the lottery had seemed to be within Branson's grasp, perhaps the politicians were not too sorry after all.

The Lantern Flickers

This still leaves unanswered the question of why something that seems the logical, sensible way forward at time a, can appear reckless or foolhardy at time b. For instance, in 1968 oil was discovered under the North Slope of Alaska. The discovery prompted a scheme to build an 800-mile pipeline underground to the relatively ice-free port of Valdez. From there the oil could be pumped into tankers.

The scheme aroused considerable controversy, particularly as regards the environmental implications and the risks of a major spillage. After four years of argument over the costs and benefits, construction was finally authorised on the understanding that environmental effects would be minimised and that oil shipping operations at Valdez would be 'the safest in the world'.[35]

A crucial element of safety was the plan for a 'clean-up' opera-tion in the event of a spillage. Since an independent report estimated that the likelihood of a major oil spillage was only once in 241 years, it seemed sensible to plan for a more probable scenario. Shortly after midnight on 24 March 1989, the fully loaded supertanker *Exxon Valdez* collided with rocks as it was leaving port, spilling 11 million gallons of oil into the sea, that is, an incident 175 times worse than that which had been planned for.

Suddenly all the disputed estimates over risk appeared in a new light. Past warnings about slippages in safety standards that had been dismissed as the work of troublemakers now appeared 'certain and ominous' and managers callously indifferent to environmental safety. The plan that had seemed entirely adequate was now dubbed 'the greatest work of maritime fiction since *Moby Dick*'.[35]

According to decision science, we are guided by the lamp of rationality. Our task is to weigh the pros and cons objectively and choose accordingly. Yet this is exactly what the port authorities thought that they had done. Indeed, when the accident was reported the response was, 'That's impossible. We have the perfect system'.[35]

One of the iconic images of the new century is the picture of Concorde with smoke and flames pouring from its wing seconds before it crashed near Paris in July 2000. Fifty-five seconds into the flight when the plane was travelling at 220 mph, the control tower told the pilot that flames were streaming from the back of the plane. Almost simultaneously engine number two failed and engine number one was losing power. The undercarriage failed to retract and burning fuel was streaming from the fuel tank.

It was too late to abort the take-off. Concorde was already airborne when, seconds later, a second call from the control tower told the pilot that the flames were now much larger. There followed a second drop in power in number one engine. Concorde banked to the left and then stalled in mid-air.[36]

Air France immediately grounded its fleet of Concordes whereas British Airways continued flying the plane until the authorities withdrew Concorde's certificate of airworthiness weeks later. The certificate was withdrawn because the crash investigation confirmed earlier speculation that the primary cause of the accident was a burst tyre. Debris from the burst then ruptured a fuel tank, causing a fire followed by engine failure.

Concorde was grounded because the fact that a tyre could cause a catastrophic failure rendered the aircraft unfit for commercial service. Yet there had been reports of tyre problems with Concorde dating back twenty years, including a near-catastrophic failure as early as 1979. Why was nothing done then?

What the *Exxon Valdez* spillage and Concorde catastrophe teach us is that what is rational, sensible and an acceptable level of risk does not exist 'out there' as an objective entity but as we define it. What we call rational is not a guide but an achievement[37] forged from all the arguments and counter-arguments of the day. Like the *Exxon Valdez* spillage, when it emerged that the Concorde crash resulted from a burst tyre, earlier incidents that were rationalised away suddenly appeared in a new and very ominous light.

In short, we may be right, we may be wrong. Time will tell and retell. Winston Churchill put it most eloquently when he led the parliamentary tributes to Neville Chamberlain:

> It is not given to human beings, happily for them, otherwise life would be intolerable, to foresee or predict to any large extent the unfolding of events. In one phase men seem to have been right, in another they seem to have been wrong. Then again, a few years later, when the perspective of time has lengthened, all stands in a different setting. There is a new proportion. There is another scale of values. History with its flickering lamp stumbles along the trail of the past, trying to reconstruct its scenes, to revive its echoes.[38]

Chapter 3

The dark side of the moon

'War is not tragedy but life giving revelation.' (Heidegger)

On 15 April 1989 Liverpool and Nottingham Forest had played just six minutes of an FA Cup semi-final at Sheffield's Hillsborough stadium when a Liverpool supporter darted onto the pitch:

> Sprinting up to Ray Houghton, the Liverpool midfielder, the Liverpool fan gesticulated wildly towards the Leppings Lane end of the ground. 'Ray, Ray, they are dying in there,' he yelled. . . . Before anyone had time to react, ninety-five Liverpool fans had literally been crushed to death against security fencing designed to stop hooligans invading the pitch.[39]

Just twelve minutes earlier, fans arriving to watch the match were filing through the turnstiles when a roar went up from the crowd already inside the stadium as the players arrived on the pitch. There followed a sudden stampede by Liverpool fans to get into the ground. They made for the nearest entrance, that is, the middle section, that was already full. As the fans continued pushing their way into the middle section, those at the front of the crowd toppled forwards and disappeared under the tramping mass.

We will never know precisely what happened during those twelve minutes from when the stampede started at 2:54 until the game was stopped at 3.06. and whether lives could have been saved if the police had summoned medical help sooner. By then it was too late for 15-year-old Kevin Williams:

> The boy had been dragged out of the crush and carried across the pitch by men who knew that he was still alive. The policewoman tried to pump his heart and give him mouth to mouth resuscitation. She worked on him for at least twenty-five minutes .... 'I said to him, "You are not going to die. You can't die". I remember holding him, and he actually opened his eyes and stared at me. He made a noise and I thought: "I've got him. I have actually got him alive". He opened his eyes again and looked straight ahead at me and said: "Mum". Then he just slipped back into my arms and died.'[39]

The popular image of football resonates multi-million-pound transfer deals, lucrative sponsorship, celebrities, trophies and triumph. Lord Justice Taylor's subsequent inquiry into the Hillsborough disaster turned the spotlight on the darker corners of the industry:

> The ordinary provisions to be expected at a place of entertainment are not merely basic but squalid. At some grounds lavatories are primitive in design, poorly maintained and inadequate in number. This not only denies the spectator a facility he is entitled to expect. It directly lowers standards of conduct. The practice of urinating against walls has become endemic and is followed by men who would not behave in that way elsewhere. The police, who would charge a man for urinating in the street, either tolerate it in football

grounds or do no more than give a verbal rebuke. Thus crowd conduct becomes degraded and other misbehaviour seems less out of place.[40]

As for the food:

> The refreshments available to supporters are often limited and of indifferent quality. They are sold in surrounding streets from mobile carts and inside many grounds from other carts or from shoddy sheds. Fans eat their hamburgers or chips standing outside in all weathers. There is a prevailing stench of stewed onions. Adequate bins for rubbish are often not available; so wrappings and detritus are simply dropped. This inhospitable scene tends to breed bad manners and poor behaviour.[40]

Many fans, says Taylor, are content to eat on the hoof but why can the food not be decent, clean and wholesome?[40]

Lord Justice Taylor's report proved to be a watershed in the history of football. By highlighting an image of the industry hitherto largely hidden by the glamour, it showed that the problem of soccer violence was not just a matter of controlling bad behaviour, but was also a reflection of how the football industry treated fans.

An *Imagined* World

We will return to the Taylor report later in this chapter. For now the key point to note is image. As decision makers we invoke images in order to make sense of our world.[41] For example, John Major's premiership has been referred to as a 'coma' between the eras of Margaret Thatcher and Tony Blair. Imposing a stealth tax is said to be like plucking a goose. The aim is to garner as many feathers as possible without causing the bird to squawk. The Holocaust may be seen as a 'window'.

Decision making is rich in imagery. We refer to the 'fault line' in a plan, issues hit 'the fan', we get 'stabbed in the back', our systems 'crash', our decisions return to 'haunt' us.

We can best understand why we need images by trying to do without them! For instance, we can say 'power is like power' but we are no wiser. Whereas if we say power is like love, impossible to define but easy to recognise, we can gain some idea of what power is like. To say 'software is like software' tells us nothing. Whereas if we describe software as like the 'engine' that drives the computer, the image enables us to understand what software does. We can see AIDS as an illness, an economic problem, a social problem, as divine retribution or as a virus. Yet however we see AIDS, we must always see AIDS as something else in order to understand it.

Images both reveal and conceal.

Imagine writing your autobiography. What would you call it? Former cabinet minister Barbara Castle called hers *Fighting all the Way*. Her colleague James Callaghan called his *Time and Chance*. Robert Graves' account of his early life is entitled *Goodbye to All That*.

Choosing a title may be a difficult task because it forces you to consider all the twists and turns of fate, all the highways and byways travelled, all the heroes and all the villains of the story and reflect the whole experience in one pithy statement that then becomes your defining image. The trouble is, however apt the title may be it leaves out as much as it includes.

The same applies to any image. No matter how much our images reveal, there is always something that is hidden from view. For instance, to see the mind as a machine highlights the mind's reasoning and analytical capabilities while eclipsing the mind's intuitive and creative powers.[42] To see the organisation as like 'one big happy family' highlights unity but conceals division. Prior to the Taylor report the glamorous image of football eclipsed the dingy side of the industry.

As decision makers we are constantly reducing complex multi-levelled issues to pithy statements. Moreover, like a doctor with a surgery full of patients awaiting attention, we seldom have the luxury of agonising over definitions. Indeed, we are only useful as decision makers if we can make sense of a situation quickly. Yet the very skill that enables us to work effectively is also a potential liability.

Received Images

The first danger of misjudging a situation is that we become so used to our images that we end up taking them literally. We 'know' what the First World War was like because we have seen photographs of troops, wagons and horses, bogged down in mud and slime. We have listened to the poet 'guttering, choking, drowning'; we can picture the wagon that they flung him in. Yet our knowledge is an illusion because we are not seeing the war itself but only the conventional images through which the war has become known.

Most of us, when we think of time, automatically think of a clock. Yet the clock upon the wall is not time. The clock is merely an image that depicts time in a particular way. Linking time with the clock implies regularity. It encourages us to see events as cohering in time and space. Yet this may be exactly what does *not* happen in a crisis. Moreover, if we behave in a critical situation as if events unfold neatly in time and space, we may transform a crisis into a disaster.[19]

The images that we should be most careful of in decision making are those that seem so obvious we seldom if ever think about them. Our management textbooks invite us to *imag*ine responsibility as something that can be allocated to people like allocating packs of butter to a supermarket. Obviously it is important that lines of responsibility are clearly communicated. Yet communication alone is not enough. The police have well-established procedures for dealing with casualties at the scene of a crime or an accident. Moreover, police officers are carefully trained in the precise nature of their responsibilities at all stages of attending an incident. Yet the murdered black teenager Stephen Lawrence died surrounded by experienced police officers who did nothing for him except check his pulse and see that he was breathing. Lawrence had been stabbed yet the police officers present at the incident all assumed that someone else was attending to him.[43]

In other words, no matter what the organisation chart may say, no matter how frequently duties are affirmed and reaffirmed, responsibility exists only where it is *accepted* and operated. Moreover, unless responsibility is accepted, there is no responsibility.

The same applies to authority. Our management texts suggest that authority is something that we possess, to have and to hold whenever we occupy a particular position. Again, no matter what the organisation chart may say, authority is a *relationship*. To be more precise, authority ultimately rests upon the quality of a relationship. If one party puts their selfish interests above those of the other party, the relationship is soon destroyed. When that happens, authority fails.[44] No matter what authority an organisational risk and compliance unit has on paper, it is only effective if that authority is respected by other people in the organisation. Danger enters in when checks and balances that exist in theory become ineffective in practice because the authority of those involved has been undermined.

The Dark Side of the Moon

No image can reveal everything about a particular entity otherwise it would be redundant. We would be back to 'power is like power' and 'software is like software'. One of the joys of invoking new images is that it can lead to new insight. We may doubt the idea of war as a health-giving revelation but it does at least show us a different way of thinking about war. What is blackmail? According to the novelist Helen Dunmore[45] it is always an inside job:

> Somebody in the house has left that little window open .... The person who leaves the window open doesn't know why. Or else doesn't want to know why.
> Some blackmailers just want money.... The others put on pressure without letting you know what they want.... They steer you where you don't want to go, but in a way that's so intimate you have to give in.... The pressure comes from what they don't say. They wait and wait until you can't wait any more, and you'll do anything to know why they've come.

We shall return to this unconventional image of blackmail later in this chapter. All I need to say now is that I found it unsettling and not just because it forced me to think again about blackmail.

The danger is that our images become so familiar that we forget about what is hidden. We get so used to *imag*ining the bottle as half-empty, that we forget it is also half-full. We get so used to the image 'Guinness' that we forget that we are not drinking the sumptuous product brewed in Ireland but actually something else. It is so obvious that fuel tanks are empty that we forget that they are full of vapour.

The image of the clock depicts time as moving forwards. Part of Stephen Hawking's contribution to knowledge has been to reconceptualise time, *imag*ining it moving backwards as well as forwards – hence the 'discovery' of so-called 'black holes'.[46]

You may say this is interesting for physicists and astronomers but somewhat remote from the practical realities of decision making. Yet possibly the most 'taken for granted' image is the notion of decision. We automatically assume that things happen because somebody somewhere makes a decision. Again, it is not what this perspective reveals that is important but what it conceals. More specifically it conceals two important dimensions of organisational reality namely:

- Things that happen without anyone apparently having made a decision, and
- Decisions that are made and then nothing happens.

The key is recognising that the notion of decision is a trick of language that we invoke to explain outcomes. Like any image the notion of decision both reveals and conceals. More specifically, the notion of decision allows us to see volitional choices made between alternatives but conceals everything else that happens (or does not happen) to shape outcomes. We can best see 'everything' else if we forget about decisions and instead imagine everything existing in a constant state of flux and transformation. In other words, as forever *becoming*.[47]

The notion of becoming highlights the subtle shifts, the ruptures, the twists and turns, the shoving and hauling whereby one state of affairs gives way to another. In this view, the implementation phase of decision making is basically a state of becoming. Implementation is the juncture where vision meets reality. It is the point where corners are cut, compromises are made, concessions granted, ideals are watered down. The notion of becoming helps us to understand how and why decisions can become blown off-course slowly, almost imperceptibly.

Decision making is often overshadowed by conflict. We tend to see conflict as obstacle, that is, as something that we could well do without. Conflict can certainly be exhausting. It can also be de-stabilising and even destructive. Indeed, one of the key characteristics of Peters and Waterman's 'excellent' organisations was a marked absence of conflict. Yet that may explain why those organisations did not retain the appellation for very long.

Conflict arises partly because many 'pies' are finite, and, since there is never enough to go round, people inevitably fight over who gets what. Another important reason for conflict is the sheer uncertainty that attends decision making. If everyone knew exactly what to do all the time there would be no conflict.[48]

Conflict is not an obstacle but a transaction.[49]

Conflict can be a vital part of the sense-making process. This is because when all the arguments of the day are aired about whether to go 'this way' or 'that way' decision makers are actually exchanging perspectives. In other words, conflict can improve decision making because it means that claims relating to the pros and cons of a particular course of action are challenged, estimates of risk are contested and so forth.

Love is Like . . . ?

Who says power is like love? There are no rules when it comes to choosing images. The most that can be said is that some images are more useful than others because they allow us to see more of what is there. We can say 'a car is like a tube of toothpaste' but it does not lead us very far because the connections are few and very tenuous. In contrast, the notion of a computer as having a 'virus' is a useful image because it encapsulates the potentially contagious and debilitating nature of electronic sabotage. The image breaks down, however, because most computer viruses can be reversed, whereas there is no cure for a medical virus.

Our freedom to choose has important implications for decision making because:

*Our images determine **what** we see and **how** we see.*

A famous *Punch* cartoon depicts a group of Daleks at the foot of a flight of stairs. The caption reads 'This certainly buggers our plans to conquer the universe'. The cartoon gains its humour from the juxtaposition of opposites – the tin-can terrors of the universe thwarted by something as mundane as a flight of stairs. In other words, the cartoon shows us the limits of power. To be more precise, the limits of a particular image of power. In the world of the Daleks, power resonates machine-like efficiency and destruction. We see power as encased in metal, as laden with weapons. It is 'what is not' about this image of power that is instructive. The Daleks portray power as pitiless, as devoid of emotion. The transcending power of art, music, love and laughter cannot help the Daleks up the stairs, for all their fearful power they are well and truly 'buggered'. Stephen Hawking could have taught the Daleks a lesson. When asked whether he liked music, Hawking had the humility to reply that he could not have lived if there had been only physics in his life. That surely says something about the nature of power.

Our choice of image shapes the decision premises which in turn determines how we see the solution. If we *imag*ine a race riot as a threat to social stability the image suggests containment as the solution to the problem. Alternatively, if we ·imagine a riot as an explosion of the frustration felt by unemployed youth, the image suggests liberating creative potential as the solution to the problem.

As decision makers we can become so adept at thinking on our feet that we are no longer thinking but engaging in reflex action. When that happens our frame of vision narrows, our perceptions become polarised until we are no longer seeing the wider picture. Yet we believe we are in touch with reality when in fact the blinkers are becoming more and more tightly drawn.

Danger enters in:

To see something one way is not to see it another.

When the first cases of AIDS were reported in America, effective action was slow in coming because everyone thought they understood the problem:

> The federal government viewed AIDS as a budget problem, local health officials saw it as a political problem, and the news media regarded it as a homosexual problem that wouldn't interest anyone else. Consequently, few confronted AIDS for what it was, a profoundly threatening medical crisis.[50]

Hidden Possibilities

Our scientific models of decision making assume that problems exist 'out there'. In this view the most important thing is to muster sufficient information about the problem in order to select the most appropriate solution. For instance, what information would we need to decide how to treat someone who is mad?

In contrast, the art of decision involves recognising that:

Our problems are a figment of our imagination.

I am not suggesting that we are deluded. A new product that fails in service presents a very real problem, just as crime and traffic jams are a problem. What I am saying, however, is that because we can we can choose how we *imag*ine a problem, much of what seems concrete and real is actually of our own invention.

We might say that someone who goes about their daily business dressed in the style of a seventeenth-century Cavalier replete with armour, pike and horse is mad. Madness is commonly seen as illness – a problem in other words, and one that implies drugs, therapy and incarceration. Yet why shouldn't someone dress up if they want to and enter into another world? If we adopt a different image, that is, see madness as an extreme form of social distance, we see 'the problem' of our Cavalier differently.

Our pictures of the mud and poppies of the First World War are more accurately described not as images of war but as *received* images of war. The fact that an image is received does not make it right. Again, the trouble is our images can become so deeply ingrained that they seem incontrovertible. Until recently, the practice of medicine was so influenced by mechanical imagery that hospitals continued monitoring the temperature, pulse and urine of patients who were clearly dying while denying them any form of human comfort.

Recall, to see something one way is not to see it another. To see the disease is not to see the suffering person. Consider Julie a 28-year-old, terminally ill patient, too frightened to go to sleep in case she died. One image of medicine points to administering a sedative and walking away. The distinctive contribution of the hospice movement and the Macmillan nursing organisation has been to reach out to patients like Julie emotionally as well as clinically, listening, talking, just being there, that is, becoming involved in a manner that would once have been considered grossly unprofessional.

Our freedom to choose images means that as decision makers we are not entirely at the mercy of chance. More specifically, conventional perspectives of decision making depict organisations as responding to threats and opportunities that exist 'out there' in the environment. Another possibility, however, is that we create the environment in our own heads and then act as if our creation is forcing us to – which it eventually does![27]

Ultimately our choice of image dictates how we *experience* reality.[49] Imagine painting your life story in abstract colours. Anyone who then views the picture experiences you in a particular way. Do you *imag*ine a sculptor as chiselling an image into stone or releasing energy from stone?

Playing with images can enable us to see the familiar differently. We get so used to seeing the people we work with that their images have become etched upon our consciousness. Supposing we imagine them differently. What might be revealed? If your colleagues were a group of officers on the Western Front in the First World War who are the honest grapplers who are going to get killed trying to do a decent job? How does the office 'loudmouth' react under fire? Who is the emotionally unstable one who suddenly rushes at the guns in a pointless and suicidal attack? Who are the heroes who risk their lives trying to rescue wounded comrades? Is the leader the sort who engages in open confrontation with hierarchical superiors, or the lackadaisical type who orders the men to fire a few shots over the heads of the enemy to keep the HQ happy? In what role do you cast yourself?

From Hell

As there are no rules when it comes to choosing images we cannot be sure that the images other people select are the same as our own. Indeed, our reality is frequently very different from someone else's. Perhaps that explains why hell is other people. For instance, a patient growing tired of making endless visits to hospital complained, '. . . every time I go they bring out the same old file.' 'I should hope they do,' muttered the medical records clerk.

Our problem as decision makers is reminding ourselves that other people may see things differently from how we see them. You may see a table whereas a physicist sees a collection of atoms. You only have to look through a copy of the newspaper *Farmer's Guardian* to see a very different perspective on mobile phone telephone masts, battery-hen production and the role of chemical fertilisers from that promulgated by other sections of the media. When the London Ambulance Service commissioned a new computer system, management saw the project as an important step towards improving operational efficiency. In contrast, staffs saw it as a veiled attempt to impose control. The new system faltered shortly after it was installed partly because of technical deficiencies and mismanagement, but ultimately because the will to make it work was non-existent.

According to the management texts, good communication can rid us of all this nonsense about multiple realities. In this view, all the management of the London Ambulance Service needed to do was to make a better job of explaining the new system to staff.

Communication is important. I believe that a good many problems could be avoided if decision makers took more trouble to communicate. My point, however, is that communication will take us only so far. If an organisational restructuring or the introduction of new technology spells redundancy for someone, no amount of communication will change that dimension of reality.

Strangled by a Dish of Eels

More importantly, our management texts suggest that ambiguity can be eradicated just as smallpox and other deadly diseases have been declared extinct. I suggest that no matter how much trouble we take to communicate, no matter how carefully the rules are spelled out:

Ambiguity always lurks.

'A decision,' said the sagacious Sir Humphrey in the popular television series *Yes, Minister*, 'is only a decision if it's the decision you want. Otherwise it's a setback.' Getting someone to implement a decision can be like grappling with a dish of live eels.

Ambiguity means capable of more than one meaning. Scientific approaches to decision making see reality in black and white. In this view a given entity is either one thing or it is another. Something is either an act of resistance or of compliance. It cannot be both. In contrast, the art of decision making involves recognising that compliance can also involve resistance.

Victoria Baths and Wash-house (a pseudonym) was opened in 1910. Victoria is located in one of the poorer districts of a former manufacturing city in Britain. The facilities consist of swimming pools, bath cubicles and a meetings room. The building, a huge brick and glass structure was impossible to heat effectively. At ground level gas fires burned even in summer while the temperature in the roof void frequently soared above 90 degrees. Keeping the building clean was equally problematic. The joke among staff was that anyone entering the building at night always waited a few seconds before switching on the lights to allow the beetles and cockroaches to scuttle back into hiding.

Most serious from the council's point of view were the maintenance costs. The roof consisted of an enormous iron and glass structure over a 100 feet high. One day, just as a group of children were about to enter the pool, an attendant heard a slight 'plopping noise' in the water. The attendant shouted to the children to return to the changing cubicles. Seconds later the whole roof structure came roaring down. The roof was repaired but required constant attention thereafter. Victoria was never intended to make a profit but expenditure became increasingly disproportionate to income. Finally, a financial crisis persuaded the council to close the pool.

Unlike other parts of the city where the bulldozers had destroyed communities, there had been little slum clearance near Victoria. A cohesive community still existed, including a pensioners' swimming club that had been meeting at Victoria for over 70 years. Indeed, apart from a nightclub there were no other local amenities. Moreover, although housing conditions had improved since 1910, there were still people living in the locality in houses without bathrooms and who regularly used the facilities at Victoria.

The community was outraged by the council's insensitivity. 'We know the building's decrepit,' said one pensioner, 'By all means build us a new swimming pool, but please don't take away our only facility.' The area manager Philip (a pseudonym) who had worked at Victoria for 30 years was instructed to announce the impending closure. He was equally incensed, 'I was just supposed to go and say, "We're shutting."' Philip continues:

> There was a terrific upsurge of feeling in the community.... People wanted to do something. I was asked to attend a few meetings like ... they [the clients] needed someone to organize it a bit, to put their point of view. I said to people, 'I will be your spokesman'.

As area manager, an important part of Philip's brief was to foster relations with the local community. Philip turned the brief to advantage by directing the subsequent protest. Local school-children printed posters on the theme of 'Save our swimming pool'. Philip said 'I put them up all over the place, in the corridors, everywhere. It gave them [the children] a chance to air their views. They [management] could have over-ruled me but they didn't.'

Philip also encouraged the pensioners to raise a petition and to march to the town hall to present it. Next, Philip obtained management's permission for them to hold a jumble sale at the pool. Philip recounts:

> They [the pensioners] made £200 – it went nowhere with running costs but it was symbolic, it showed commitment. I could see it would make a good story .... They asked me what I thought they should do with the money and I said the best thing would be if you could actually go down there and give it to him [the leader of the council], which they did.

The leader of the council was impressed by the gesture and the pool was eventually reprieved. Notice what happens. Philip's job description required him to foster community relations. Yet his actions are highly ambiguous. On the one hand, he can claim that he is doing his job. On the other, compliance serves as a cloak for resistance and a very effective one at that.[51]

All That Jazz

To understand why ambiguity always lurks we need to step back a little and consider another 'taken for granted' image, namely structure. We tend to *imag*ine structure as like a garden fence, that is, clear, tangible and inflexible. In this view structure marks out boundaries, just as a fence defines where one person's garden ends and their neighbour's begins. As decision makers, our boundaries are marked by rules, procedures and protocols that tell us what we can and cannot do.[52]

The 'garden fence' image of structure depicts us as working within boundaries. Supposing, however, we imagine structure as improvisational jazz.[53] Jazz players see their musical compositions (structures) not as restraints but as free-hand sketches, a base from which they can explore their own ideas. The distinction is important because if we change our image of structure, instead of seeing people as working within boundaries, we see a subtly different possibility, that is, people as forever *testing* boundaries. Jazz players test boundaries in order to see what they can get away with. The same happens in decision making.

Moreover, when we test the boundaries, even the most apparently rigid rules can prove surprisingly flexible. This is because rules do not interpret or apply themselves. The very exercise of judgement implies discretion, and when we exercise discretion we basically discover what we can get away with.

In theory the Nazi rulers of occupied countries were in an extremely powerful position. Yet despite the omnipresent shadow of the gallows, the firing squad and the gas chamber, the Nazis discovered that things did not always go quite their way. The local administrators on whom the Nazis depended to execute their directives proved as lithe as eels. Whereas outright sabotage such as blowing up railway tracks would have provoked reprisals, the Resistance pushed the boundaries as far as they dared. Directives were reformulated, elaborated and diluted. Railway engines would mysteriously end up in the wrong place, wagons would be delayed and so on to the Nazis exasperation.[54,55] Thus was the harsh edge of tyranny blunted.

Boundaries can flex in curious ways. Appearances might suggest that prison warders are much more powerful than inmates. In practice, the relationship between the two parties is often finely balanced. Inmates exert a measure of control because they know that warders who are forever placing prisoners on report are likely to be seen as harsh and officious and may even be perceived as being unequal to the job.

Even the most heavily regulated environments can prove unexpectedly flexible. On Sunday 3 March 1974, a DC-10 operated by Turkish Airlines left Orly Airport at 12.30 pm bound for London. The plane was built by one of the best-run aerospace contractors in America. In addition, every aspect of the plane's design and construction had been approved by the Federal Aviation Administration. Unknown to the 346 souls on board, however, that particular DC-10 'had a lie in it'.[56] Ten minutes after take-off 'the lie' caused the plane to crash into the Forest of Ermenonville, killing everyone on board.

According to McDonnell-Douglas, the company that built the plane and sold it to Turkish Airlines, the disaster was caused by an 'illiterate' baggage handler failing to close a cargo door properly. A *Sunday Times* investigation discovered, however, that although the handler, Mahmoud Mahamoudi, spoke no English, he had carried out his duties properly. Mahmoud Mahamoudi was not to know that the design of the DC-10's locking mechanism on its cargo doors was flawed in that they appeared locked when they were not.

As the *Sunday Times* investigation team delved further into the circumstances surrounding the crash they discovered that there had been a dress rehearsal for the Paris disaster two years earlier. In 1972 a cargo door blew off another DC-10 sending a coffin plunging two miles to earth and leaving a flight attendant struggling to remain inside the plane. When the door blew off, the sudden change in air pressure caused the cabin floor to collapse, severing vital cables. The crew, who had more experience of flying DC-10s than Turkish Airlines would have two years later, managed to land the plane safely. Even so, the incident clearly showed that the DC-10 required modifications to its cargo doors and vulnerable cabin floor.

According to the paperwork issued by McDonnell-Douglas, the requisite modifications had been carried out to the plane that crashed near Paris. In fact, no such modifications had been made. Moreover, the paperwork relating to a DC-10 supplied to the now-defunct Laker Airways proved to be similarly misleading.

It is unclear precisely how the paperwork was produced. What is certain is that the Airworthiness Directives that would have compelled the requisite modifications were withdrawn following a 'gentleman's agreement' between the president of McDonnell-Douglas and the chief of staff of the regional Federal Aviation Authority, whereby McDonnell-Douglas undertook to fix the 'goddam plane'.[56] In fact, all that happened was some 'beefing up' of the electric wiring on the door followed by service bulletins recommending more changes to the door-locking mechanism. The bulletins were issued among scores of others without any indication that these were life or death matters.

In other words, the disaster happened because the chief of McDonnell-Douglas negotiated around the rules to see if he could get away with keeping the fleet airborne. In turn, the person responsible for applying the rules, the regional aviation chief, had become so identified with the industry that he was willing to stretch a point to the extent of allowing DC-10s to continue in service with potentially lethal design faults.

A more recent example of how boundaries are tested to the very limits concerns the so-called pensions mis-selling scandal. In the late 1980s and early 1990s the UK financial services industry wrongly advised almost 2 million people to buy a personal pension. Although the government intervened and forced the industry to make restitution, it will be at least 2002 before the last cases are dealt with. The final cost is estimated at over £11 billion.

The causes of the pensions mis-selling scandal are complex. Not least of these was a failure to ensure that commission-hungry sales' staff were properly trained to give advice, and a failure to monitor sales. Yet the government must bear some responsibility because of the manner in which the rules were framed. The government ought to have anticipated that the financial services industry would push their freedom of action to see what they could get away with.

Yet no matter what we do to clarify and tighten the rules, ambiguity always lurks. We can see this best if we imagine ambiguity as 'empty space'.[53] Empty space gives us the freedom to add our own ideas. Railtrack's signalling rules may be clear, but that it is not the same as saying the various railway companies apply them in an identical fashion. A supermarket may operate a clear and inflexible rule that requires any frozen foods that become partially thawed to be discarded. Consider a box containing cartons of fish fingers that has been left unrefrigerated for two hours. The cold-store supervisor feels a few of the cartons and decides that they are 'all right' because the packets feel cold even though the contents are beginning to soften.

The question is, what are people actually doing when they exercise discretion? Why should a cold-store supervisor take such risks? What appears as the exercise of discretion may in fact be employees replaying the organisational values and culture in a different key.

Organisations are capable of blackmail. Moreover, organisational blackmail is always an inside job. On the one hand, standards are set and the rules are clear. The corporate lawyer knows it is not in the client's best interests to pursue litigation and that the firm always acts in the client's best interests. The university lecturer knows that the essay is not worth the paper it is written on and that the university insists upon standards being maintained. The sales representative for the gas company knows that your central heating system is old but it will do a bit longer and that the company does not recommend unnecessary work as a matter of policy.

Yet organisations put on pressure, often without saying precisely what they want. They steer employees where they don't want to go, but in a way that's so powerful they have to give in. The pressure comes from what they don't say.

Chapter 4

Ghosts and shadows: reflections on information and decision making

'. . . if you understand. I hope you don't!' (Wilfred Owen, *Collected Letters*)

Consider the following entry in the Fine Roll of 1204–5:

> The wife of Hugh de Neville gives the lord King 200 chickens that she may lie with her husband for one night. Thomas de Sanford stands surety for 100 chickens, and her husband, Hugh for 100.

Historians have long puzzled over this item. Is it an example of King John's tyranny or were the recording clerks the worst for drink?[57]

This chapter focuses upon the role of information in decision making. In theory, information leads us closer to reality. Yet as the data pertaining to King John's chickens shows, information can create problems. More specifically, the purpose of this chapter is to show how information can actually lead us *away* from reality.

'What we seek is but a shadow,' says the proverb. To understand why information can lead us away from reality we need to step back a little and ask ourselves what constitutes information.

If we want to explain what the human body is like we might supply an anatomical sketch or a painting of a nude. Each representation is basically a system of notation for describing reality that defines differently what are to be taken as the basic facts.[37]

In other words, different representations focus upon different facts to the exclusion of others. A map of the London Underground reveals how the various stations are connected but excludes the labyrinth of escalators and tunnels that may unexpectedly delay us if we rely upon the map alone to plot journey times.

Returning to the nude and the anatomical sketch, it is not a question of asking which representation is the more correct. Each basically tells reality in a different way. It follows, therefore, that there may be a number of possible 'correct' views of reality though each may be differently encoded. Few documents cut a greater contrast than an estate agent's particulars of a property and the surveyor's report. The contrast arises because the former is constructed around the potential selling points of the house such as the beamed ceilings, open fireplaces and mullioned windows, whereas the latter is constructed around the potential liabilities such as dry rot, unstable chimneys and rising damp. Both forms of notation are accurate (estate agents are forbidden in law to issue misleading particulars) yet each gives a completely different impression of reality.

The same principle applies to the information we use for decision making. Our charts, graphs, statistics, progress reports and other forms of decision support are representations. They too are forms of notation that depict reality in a particular way. For example, we can represent the organisation by drawing a chart showing post titles, salary grades and reporting relationships. The information tells us something about the organisation but it is not the living, breathing organisation. The organisation chart tells us nothing about the informal leaders, the reporting relationships that have broken down, the cliques and cabals and so forth.

Green Light Spells Danger

It was suggested in Chapter 3 that we can only know one thing through the image of another. Again, the same principle applies to our management information. Our charts, graphs, progress reports and other forms of information basically stand surrogate for something *else*.

Part of our problem as decision makers is that we can easily end up taking our information literally and become lulled into a false sense of security as a result. A traffic light at green means that we have a right of way at a junction. It does **not** mean that the road is clear. Yet how often do we proceed unthinkingly simply because the light is 'at green'?

We might choose a particular abattoir because it has a high official hygiene score. Yet all such ratings may be measuring are factors like the number of wash rooms. While a high score suggests that the preconditions for safe food handling exist, the information does not mean that actual day-to-day working practices are safe. Likewise, short hospital waiting lists suggest efficiency.

Yet a short waiting list can mean that GPs have given up referring patients for treatment which they know they will never receive. Or the GPs may be taking the time and the trouble to treat patients themselves. Alternatively, short waiting lists may mean that hospitals are rushing patients through the system, discharging them faster than is clinically wise.

What matters is not what our information reveals, but what it conceals.

An 'X' in a summary sheet may denote that a particular project is 'on time'. While the summary enables us to grasp the broader picture, the danger is that we glance at it and immediately conclude that all is well. Yet does that 'X' really mean that every element of the project is running exactly according to schedule, every sub-contractor has done exactly what they were supposed to do, that every last detail of the project is in place with no 'ifs' or 'buts'?

Do You Understand?

The quotation at the beginning of this chapter is from a letter written by Wilfred Owen to his sister Mary Owen. The letter is dated 8 May 1917. The address is Casualty Clearing station. Owen tells his sister that it was not the recent bombardment that shook him up:

But it was living so long by poor old Cock Robin (as we used to call 2/Lt. Gaukroger), who lay not only near by, but in various places around and about, if you understand. I hope you don't![58]

It was the words, 'I hope you don't' that first attracted me to the quotation. Owen recognised that:

Knowing is not the same as understanding.

More precisely, Owen understood that it is one thing to be aware of the facts of a situation, that is, living amid the remains of a comrade who has been blown to pieces. It is another to understand what that experience actually means.

As decision makers our colourless managerial language ensures that we know more than we understand. Consider the following statement: 'There is sufficient data currently available to support the upgrading of the occupant crash protection standards in commercial aircraft.'[13] Whatever this statement means, it is a hardly calculated to convey a sense of urgency and galvanise us into action. Donat Desmond now says the same thing using different language. Mr Desmond was a passenger travelling with his wife on a British Midland 737 to Belfast in January 1989. The plane was just outside East Midlands Airport, over the village of Kegworth, when smoke began to enter the cockpit followed by a series of loud bangs. Realising that an engine was on fire, the crew promptly shut it down and prepared to land with only one engine when the co-pilot shouted 'Jesus, there's a motorway.!'

In fact the crew had shut down the wrong engine leaving the failing one to power the plane. Forty-seven people were killed in the ensuing crash. In addition, all but five of the survivors suffered serious injuries as the floor and seats of the plane deformed on impact. Even with the help of passing motorists, it took over eight hours to rescue survivors in the cold and dark of a winter night. Here is the managerial language of 'structural integrity of seats', and 'crashworthiness,' and 'survivable accident' rewritten by Mr Desmond:

> My seat had . . . broken through the floor and partly descended into the luggage hold. The row of seats in front of me . . . had concertinaed on impact and were pinning my legs down. . . . I had nearly severed my left arm off the seat in front of me . . . both ankles and my back were also broken . . . . I remember a man in front of me dying as his lungs filled with blood caused I imagine by his smashed ribs piercing his chest cavity. Maria, my wife, died when she broke her neck off the seat in front of her, thankfully she died instantly. . . . A young man I know only as Graham . . . tried to keep five of us conscious and alive during the following hours we drifted in and out of consciousness. I felt so sorry for him, as I watched him give his everything to keep us alive. Sadly two of us five died. But I admired him as I watched him trying to bale out that vast pool of human suffering with his small thimble.[13]

Desmond's emotional account enables us to understand the reality of an air crash and the need to improve safety standards in a way that no amount of factual or statistical data can enable.

*The danger is we **think** we understand.*

Although Coca-Cola and Pepsi have long been commercial foes it is a war within limits. Those limits were revealed in 1999 when Coca-Cola's cans were found to have been contaminated. Pepsi publicly supported their arch-rival, emphasising that Coca-Cola had done all the right things and even offering to help. Pepsi's attempts to preserve Coca-Cola's credibility may have been motivated by the knowledge that when Perrier discovered traces of benzene in its bottles, sales of mineral water as a whole slumped. Pepsi may also have been moved by a sense of mutual vulnerability in that six years earlier, a syringe was found in one of Pepsi's cans, costing the company $35 million in sales.[3]

In contrast, the McDonald's libel case ranks as one of the biggest failures of understanding in business history. The case is discussed in more detail in Chapter 5. All we need be aware of now is that McDonald's issued a writ for libel against two unemployed environmental activists called Helen Steel and John Morris. McDonald's failed to understand that Steel and Morris were only the tip of the iceberg, the outward manifestation of a formidable and implacable force of trade unionists, environmental pressure groups, sympathetic and highly capable lawyers, potential expert witnesses and former employees of McDonald's. Even more dangerous, it was a counter-culture that McDonald's little understood. Whereas the Cola wars were fought between business school graduates with similar mindsets and values, McDonald's decision to sue for libel brought them into confrontation with aliens. McDonald's knew their opponents' e-mail address, 'www.MeatStinks.com'. They doubtless read leaflets setting out the concerns of separatist women's groups who deplore the violence done to female animals. Yet still they could not understand why they were so unloved. That failure of understanding meant they were fighting the case with one hand tied behind their back.

Painting God

Recall, information can be seen as a form of notation that tells reality in a particular way. There is a twist to the tale, however. So far it has been assumed that information reflects reality. In fact:

Information changes reality.[37,49]

In Chapter 3 I asked you to choose a title for your auto-biography. Now I ask you to imagine the task of telling your life story. You might need to consider the following questions:

• What were the important events in your life?
• Who were the important people in your life?
• How important has love been to you?

Answering such questions forces you to decide what aspects of your life will be highlighted in the story, who were the central characters and who was destined to play a bit part. Indeed, you may need to refine your thinking and decide:

• What was the most important event?
• Who was the most important person?
• Is it more important to you to love or be loved?

By turning the spotlight in a particular direction, by amplifying issues, polarising and so on, the work gains shape and coherence. The point is, you make the work but the work also makes you, that is, you end up *creating* yourself.

It is like the small boy painting a picture of God. 'Ah,' says an adult, 'but we don't know what God looks like.' 'You soon will,' replies the child. Our information is like the child's picture of God, that is, reality exists as we make it.

When we think of the 1960s we probably think of the Mini motor car and the mini skirt, Marilyn Monroe, the Beatles, the Rolling Stones, the Paris riots and the Apollo moon landings. Yet these images are not the 1960s but images invoked in the construction of memory. They have been used to *make* history.

Likewise, when we process information we change it. One Thursday lunchtime I was passing through the London Underground. A young man who looked as if he had been sleeping rough approached an escalator with what looked like a home-rolled cigarette in his hand contrary to the 'no smoking' rule. A uniformed member of staff stepped out of a kiosk, stopped the young man and asked to see his ticket. The young man had no ticket and was led away.

What have we just witnessed here? The young man was probably homeless and looking for somewhere warm to sit for a while. How he came to be homeless is a story in itself as is the experience of being homeless. Yet once the incident is recorded in the statistics it becomes something *else*. For example, it might be recorded under the heading of 'passengers travelling without a valid ticket' and/or under the heading number of infringements of safety regulations. In other words, the story of homelessness gets lost in the statistics. Instead it is retold as a story of minor lawlessness.

The people who compile information must exercise discretion as to how data is recorded and categorised. Such discretion implies scope for creativity. For example, school league tables are by no means an infallible guide to excellence. A high pass rate in examinations may conceal numbers of children debarred from entering in the first place for fear of depressing the score. Truancy rates may be improved by booking trips to football matches and other questionable absences as 'educational visits'.

In a management context it is also important to remember that the further up the organisation information travels, the more processing and refinement it undergoes. The greater the amount of processing and refinement, the more removed from reality the data becomes. By the time it reaches the decision maker's desk it may not be an abstraction so much as a contortion.

Creating Confusion

Historians estimate that if the dead of the First World War returned to life, marching four abreast it would take them three and a half days to pass the Cenotaph.[59] What does this statistic mean?

Surely the only meaning is the meaning we attach to it. Winston Churchill found statistics about sunken merchant shipping far more menacing than dealing with the prospect of imminent invasion.[60] Whereas an invasion has shape, form and trajectory, and a very clear meaning, what did X tonnage sunk in week 14 imply?

Our management information presents us with a similar problem. Our computer printout indicates that X units of stock were sold in week 14. Yet what do we know? Likewise, our statistics tell us that AIDS has already killed 11 million in Africa and another 22 million are living with HIV/AIDS. In Zambia a 15-year-old has a 60% chance of dying of AIDS. AIDS has left Africa with 8 million orphans, a figure that is expected to rise to 13 million by end-2000.[61,62] Yet what does this information mean?

One of the frustrations of decision making is that our information frequently tells us everything except what we need to know. For example, a health service manager said:

> What I can't answer is, 'Is Mrs Jones in the second bed from the left getting the same quality of treatment that she was two years ago?' I can't answer that – and I need to know.[63]

The manager here attributes uncertainty to lack of information. There is another possibility, however, that is:

More information = more uncertainty.

Far from removing uncertainty, information may actually create it. More specifically, whenever a problem arises we experience uncertainty and call for information, 'get me the file on such and such'. When the file fails to satisfy, we typically demand more information. The more information we have, the more complicated the problem seems, thus deepening our sense of uncertainty.[27,64] Consider just one potential measure of quality of hospital treatment:

> You . . . were worried about the variation in the length of time spent in pre-op. Well, it all depends, for example, on whether there's a new SHO [senior house officer], and on training time – and that sort of information is missing [from the system . . . .] You asked in your last question was there too much information or too little. I'd say too little.[63]

Again, the manager insists that the problem is too little information. The business school cliché states that decision makers operate in an increasingly complex environment. It may be more accurate to say our information technology enables us to create an increasingly complex environment – one where we risk losing sight of the wood for the trees. Indeed, why do we need to know about the length of time in 'pre-op' in the first place?

Ghosts and Shadows

To develop our understanding of what information can conceal, we need to take another step back and ask what counts as information. 'Give me facts,' said Dickens' fictional Mr Gradgrind. 'Facts alone are wanted'.[65] Gradgrind would doubtless be impressed by our modern day decision-support facilities that enable us to gather and process prodigious quantities of factual data. The problem with our decision-support systems is that facts alone are wanted to the exclusion of other ways of knowing.

For instance, by Act III in the play *The Roses of Eyam* the implications of persuading the villagers to remain in the sealed-off village (see page 36) are becoming clear; fifty-six dead in nineteen days. The two rectors meet on the stage: *'Their meeting is not a naturalistic one that can be defined in terms of time and place. It is a meeting of their private terrors and thoughts.'* (italics in original).[26] (15). Note what happens here. Not a word is spoken yet there is a powerful exchange of perspectives. Moreover, the mortality statistics comprise only part of the sensemaking process. The rectors' private terrors reflect the mounting tensions and sheer suffering that have flowed from their decision. Now they understand what they have done.

The point is, factual analysis is a mode of representation that tells reality in a particular way. If it seems more accurate than other ways of knowing it may only be because we have become so used to speaking its particular form of code that it seems real. We get so used to seeing the line drawing of the London Underground that we imagine the stations as existing along straight lines.

Likewise, the language of the decision sciences with its references to 'testing the sensitivity of assumptions', 'identifying the main uncertainty drivers', 'anticipating risks and their interactions'[66] is basically a system of notation that represents risk as something that can be managed and controlled. It can lull us into a false sense of security because we become so used to it that we start to see risk as something that can be managed and controlled.

To see what we may be missing consider how the merchant bankers of old conducted risk assessment:

> One talks about everything except the matters one really would like to talk about – such as getting a million-pound credit. The conversation is about farming, roses, horses politics, families. . . . The guest . . . doesn't know that all the time he is being carefully scrutinised – his manners, his clothes, his speech, his sense (or lack) of humor, his attitude and personality. The general impression will decide whether he's going to be backed by a million pounds and whether any security will be demanded. This is the merchant banker's assessment – a mixture of experience and flair, analysis and instinct . . . . Merchant banking is not a concrete science but an abstract art, and during lunch the practitioners of this art seem to work at their best. By the time the butler has served the traditional fruit cake and fine old port, there is usually unaniminity in the minds of partners about the risk – and about the client.[67]

The author was writing in the mid-1960s when a million-pound credit was a very significant sum. What is interesting is that the decision rests upon a holistic view of risk of which factual analysis is but one part. The rest comprises *feelings*, *intuition* and a sense of *context*.[64]

In other words, factual analysis is by no means the only way of knowing. A business plan can be made to look convincing. Social contact enables the senses to get to work. Amid all the small talk the merchant bankers of old were 'sniffing' the client, feeling for the metaphorical joins and fault lines in both the people and their proposals, quietly deciding whether the whole thing feels right and trying to gauge the wider implications of agreeing or not agreeing to a loan for the bank.

New Labour learned this lesson in 1999 when their statistics told them that there was little electoral mileage in pensions. Armed with this information they decided to increase the state pension by a miserly 75p a week. The ensuing uproar shows what can happen when decision makers rely solely upon machine-processed data. That is, the facts and figures gave no impression of social and emotional significance of pensions. New Labour misjudged the electorate because their statistics obscured the millions of voters who are not pensioners but for whom the state pension functions as a barometer of social justice.

Conversely, a pivotal factor in encouraging Sir Richard Branson to launch Virgin Cola was that he noticed that Coca-Cola had launched a 'new improved' version of Coke. Branson interpreted this information as a sign of insecurity. He saw it as a chink in the armour, an indication that the formidable Coca-Cola company was not as invulnerable as it seemed. No spreadsheet analysis, however powerful, could have yielded such insight.[68]

Indeed, even hallucinations can show us reality. We began with the war poet Wilfred Owen. Let us end with him. During the First World War, Harold Owen (brother of Wilfred Owen), served in the navy. One sultry afternoon Harold Owen's ship was lying off Victoria:

> I had gone down to my cabin thinking to write some letters. I drew aside the door curtain and stepped inside and to my amazement I saw Wilfred sitting in my chair.

He asks Wilfred how he got there, but Wilfred is silent:

> He was in uniform and I remember thinking how out of place the khaki looked amongst my cabin furnishings. With this thought I

must have turned my eyes away from him; when I looked back my cabin chair was empty . . .

. . . I felt an overpowering sense of emptiness and absolute loss.

. . . I wondered if I had been dreaming but looking down I saw that I was still standing. Suddenly I felt terribly tired and moving to my bunk I lay down; instantly I went into a deep oblivious sleep. When I woke up I knew with absolute certainty that Wilfred was dead.[69]

In this case, a telegram was superfluous. Wilfred Owen was indeed dead.

Chapter 5

Tricks of mind

On Thursday 23 February 1995 the Directors of Barings Bank hosted a lunch for City magnates. The conversation was animated, focusing upon Barings' new venture in Mexico. The directors had good reason to be optimistic. For the last three years Barings had been enjoying a bubble of profit due mainly to the activities of Nick Leeson, their star trader in Singapore. Leeson's success had convinced Barings' directors that the time was ripe for expansion, hence the references to Mexico. 'They had no idea,' said a guest afterwards, 'no idea.'

Barings' directors had no idea that the bank, one of the oldest and most distinguished institutions in the City of London, had only hours to live. As Barings' directors chatted to their guests, staff from the finance office were struggling to make sense of the accounts in Singapore. No matter how they framed their calculations, Barings appeared to have paid out nearly £100 million more than it had received from its customers. Moreover, trading in Singapore was rising when it was supposed to be falling. The luncheon guests had barely dispersed when a new problem emerged. Nick Leeson, Barings' star trader in Singapore was missing. Staff began looking through the computer printout on Leeson's abandoned desk in the hope of finding answers to their questions. As they leafed through the papers, curiosity gave way to alarm. The printout contained details of thousands of financial contracts based on Nikkei and Japanese government bonds of which they had never heard. Worse than that, each contract depended upon the market rising to be in profit. Yet the market had long been falling, and was set to continue falling. As Leeson's colleagues began to analyse the positions, they realised that not only was Barings losing money, but the contracts were so volatile that the losses were escalating by the second:

> It made no sense . . . . Every single contract they could identify was losing money . . . . Using Barings' precious capital, Leeson had taken the largest losing bet in history. It [Barings] could have lost more than £200 million already, but the frightening thing was that Leeson had pushed it into a bottomless hole. Barings . . . . did not have much capital. The Nikkei was falling and Barings' bill was growing even bigger. The Baring Foundation's shares had a balance sheet value of £308 million and it had a further £101 million in loan capital. If Leeson's losses ate through this Barings was finished.[70]

Leeson's final losses exceeded £800 million, that is, twice Barings' capital. On Monday morning Barings was formally declared insolvent – finished in other words. Although the rumours about the level of Barings' exposures had been circulating in the financial markets of the Far East for nearly a month, Barings' directors were astounded by the bank's sudden and utter collapse. 'It was the last thing we expected,' said Barings' chairman, Peter Baring.[71]

What shocked Barings' directors most was the gap between what they had understood and believed to be true and the reality.

> The account(s) showed a shocking disparity between what they thought Leeson had been doing and the truth.... The daily reports they received from him had been a complete fiction.... Several of those in his office had met daily and discussed the profits and supposedly tiny risks of Leeson's trading. But all this had been a fantasy.[70]

How could it have happened?

One of the problems of decision making is that in order to make sense of anything, we must simplify. In order to simpifly we take mental shortcuts that enable us to scythe through detail and grasp the essentials.

The danger, however, is that we can *over*simplify and shut out portions of reality as a result. This is what happened to Barings. That is, the signs of malfeasance were there from the start but Barings failed to make correct sense of them. Psychologists have identified specific mental short cuts that can distort our perceptions of reality. Let me now explain how these short cuts operate and how they can undermine our judgement.[72,73]

DÉJÀ VU?

One way of simplifying problems is to categorise them. For example, although there are many different forms of sore throat, almost every case will respond to the same treatment. Categorising problems can be very efficient because it saves us from reinventing solutions. The danger, however, is that:

*We see only the similarities between past and present and **not** the differences.*

Psychologists call this particular bias the representativeness heuristic. What it means is that one case is judged by its similarity or representativeness to other cases. For instance, a doctor can examine a patient's throat and decide that the inflammation looks similar to previous cases of throat infection. The danger, however, is that the doctor misses information pointing to a more serious condition.

Barings succumbed to this form of bias. One danger sign that Barings misinterpreted was that Leeson's trading was not only profitable, it was also apparently risk free. In investment banking, higher profits almost invariably signal higher risk.

As Barings understood it, Leeson's profits derived from arbitrage. If apples cost 10p in London and 11p in Liverpool, the arbitrageur buys a quantity of apples in London and then sells them in Liverpool. In theory, arbitrage involves minimal risk because it does not involve predicting whether prices will rise or fall. Arbitrage merely involves exploiting price differentials that already exist, like shooting fish in a barrel, as the saying goes.[70]

The notion of a lone star shooting fish in a barrel made sense to Barings because it had happened before. In the early 1980s, Barings acquired a small stockbroking firm led by a man called Christopher Heath. Under Heath's leadership, the venture prospered to such an extent that within a few years it was generating most of Barings' profits. The bonanza eventually diminished, however, as competitors awoke to the opportunities and seized a share of the market. Peter Baring, Barings' chairman at the time of the bank's collapse, said:

> We had experienced, on a number of occasions specific operations which were relatively low risk and relatively high profitability; the most pronounced example of this was the Japanese warrant trading business. . . . We had a number of businesses of that order of magnitude . . . [that] were low risk and high profitability. What none of us believed was that this business would last. The basic instinct . . . that there is something about this business that defied gravity is something which we shared; but it was in terms of its durability . . . . In our experience, these businesses could last for a period but then they would go. That would happen to us again and again.[71]

In other words, Barings saw history repeating itself. They failed to see crucial differences between past and present. First, the opportunities of the mid-1980s no longer existed. Second, whereas Heath was a highly talented, experienced and knowledgeable stockbroker, Leeson was an office clerk. Third, other investment houses had tried and failed to make money in arbitrage. To be more precise, Barings' competitors had discovered that, in practice, arbitrage is by no means risk free. By the time I transport my oranges from London to Liverpool, the price in Liverpool could have fallen, leaving me with a loss. The same principle applies to the financial markets. The price differentials between markets that appear on computer screens are wafer-thin to begin with, and apt to change in the seconds it takes to execute a contract. Even more significantly, Leeson's own colleagues had made the same discovery and abandoned arbitrage as too risky. How Leeson could be making a million pounds a day out of it was a mystery to them.

Why Bad Publicity is Better Than None

Another form of shortcut is known as the *frequency* bias. Briefly, the mind tends to recall events that occur frequently and/or recently. The reason why advertisers spend millions of pounds bombarding us with 'new improved Sudso' and slogans informing us that 'Washo washes whiter' is that experiments have shown that we are more likely to buy a particular product if we can recall it easily.

Likewise, one reason why popular music charts featuring 'all-time greats' and the like contain a disproportionate number of recent 'hits' is because people can remember them more easily. This also explains why bad publicity is better than no publicity at all. Purchasing managers may end up placing contracts with suppliers who are being sued by other firms because they remember them! Likewise, performance appraisals covering a one-year period may be biased towards the preceding three months, that is, the period most easily recalled.

Another manifestation of such bias is that we may be more ready to believe people whom we see frequently than those we seldom see. We can do someone an injustice as a result or fail to investigate a potential disciplinary matter properly because we are so close to the person accused that we refuse to believe they are capable of misconduct.

Weigh Anchor

It was suggested in Chapter 2 that it can be useful to see things as existing in a constant state of becoming. One reason why we may miss the subtler movements is a phenomenon known as *anchoring* adjustment.

The mind develops estimates by starting from an initial anchor based upon whatever information is provided. That initial anchoring point then forms the basis for subsequent adjustments as new information is received.

Anchoring bias means we think we are exercising independent judgement and responding objectively to new information when in fact our decisions are heavily but unconsciously influenced by what has gone before. A commission-hungry estate agent may persuade a client to lower the price of their house in order to achieve a fast sale. In theory, lowering the price should make no difference to the valuation carried out by the purchaser's surveyor. Indeed many surveyors believe that they can estimate the value of a property to a high degree of accuracy. Yet experiments suggest that surveyors are influenced by the suggested selling price. If a house is priced at, say, £150 000 the surveyor may value it at £145 000 – deducting £5000 in the general interests of good order and discipline. If the same house is priced at £140 000, however, the surveyor's valuation may well be £135 000. In other words, lowering the price of a property can lead to a substantial loss. Moreover, the surveyor's artificially depressed valuation then appears to confirm the estate agent's judgement which then serves as ammunition to dissuade the seller from reinstating the old price.

Likewise, what is a safe speed to drive a car on a motorway? When the speed limit was reduced to 55 mph in America, speeds of 70 mph appeared reckless – something only drunken teenagers would attempt yet it was and still is the UK national limit. Anchoring effects can also prejudice salary negotiations because the candidate's existing salary forms the base reference point for any rise. It is too bad if the candidate is underpaid to begin with!

Anchoring adjustment may also explain why first impressions are important. If our first encounter with someone is negative it may require a lot of effort to persuade us to change their initial valuation.

Anchoring adjustment can lead us to underestimate other people because we tend to see them as they once were rather than for what they have become. For example, the Americans were blind to the growing strength and tactical sophistication of their opponents in Vietnam.

'It Could Be You'

Another way in which we can oversimplify reality is when we become hypnotised by our more dazzling information – a phenomenon known to psychologists as the vividness effect.[74] Vividness can undermine our judgement by making things appear more probable than they actually are. If we see two or three people wearing orange coats in a crowd, we might erroneously conclude that orange is fashionable. The judgement is wrong because it ignores the hundreds of people wearing coats in drab colours. Our perceptions are distorted because the very vividness of the colour makes it seem more frequent than it really is. If you are the buyer for a major clothing company and stock up on orange on the strength of your observations, it is a fairly fundamental mistake! Vividness effects also explain why estate agents hoist red 'sold' signs. 'Sold' signs make agents seem successful because they detract attention from all unsold properties languishing on their books.

If our information is sufficiently vivid and compelling it can cause us to ignore our relatively dull statistical data. Risk and danger enter if the statistical data contradicts the bright promises implicit in our more vivid information. Statistically we have we have more chance of being murdered than of winning a 'jackpot' prize in the National Lottery. Yet how often do we think about the miserable odds when we part with our money?

More importantly, what induces us to part with our money? Advertising slogans such as 'It could be you' exert a powerful effect because they make success seem close. Similarly, the old-style 'pools' coupons asked entrants to tick whether, in the event of winning, they would prefer no publicity. The aim of the question is not to seek out competitors' preferences but to make success seem just round the corner.

Barings' management also succumbed to a form of vividness effect. That is, they became so mesmerised by Leeson's apparently escalating profits that they failed to undertake any rigorous analysis of his activities. Unknown to Barings, Leeson was selling financial contracts known as options. An option gives another party the right, but not the obligation, to buy or sell a given quantity at some date in the future in return for payment of a premium – for example, to buy 1000 apples at 10p each in 9 months' time. Options trading is highly risky because if the price of apples rises, the loss may far outstrip the premium received. Leeson was forbidden to expose Barings to such danger, though he was allowed to trade on behalf of Barings' customers. Leeson covered his tracks by suggesting that he was acting for a 'Customer X', an individual apparently determined to corner the market.

Leeson's options depended upon the Nikkei index remaining

virtually stable. On 17 January 1995 an earthquake struck Japan, prompting a wave of selling. The index fell sharply and continued falling. Leeson's options lost millions of pounds, forcing him to double and redouble his bets in a desperate effort to force the index up. Since the premium received also increased dramatically, Leeson's apparent profits soared.

To Barings' management this was a glorious opportunity. Barings realised that Leeson's apparent profits were extraordinary. However, instead of seeing that Leeson's success was too good to be true, Barings erroneously concluded that it was too good to last. Peter Baring again:

> When I finally saw the January 1995 figures, which I saw a number of days before the crisis broke, those figures seemed to me alarming in ... that I believed this could not last.[71]

Believing that the bubble of profit must burst soon, Barings made a catastrophic error of judgement. That is, they resolved to make hay while the sun shone. Barings then became so preoccupied with raising the huge amounts of collateral required to support Leeson's trading that no one stopped to ask exactly how the money was being used. Every day Leeson faxed his requirements to London. Latterly, Barings were remitting sums in excess of £30 million virtually upon demand. Leeson recounts. 'My funding requests were becoming ridiculous.... As each day went on, and my requests continued to be met, the explanation dawned upon me: they wanted to believe it was all true'.[75]

Barings ultimately paid out over £700 million to support trading which it did not know existed.

'Wow! Grab it!'

Barings' management also succumbed to what psychologists call the 'Wow! Grab it! Too good to lose' syndrome. As the term suggests, if an opportunity seems too good to lose we may seize it without considering the risks involved.[16]

If an opportunity seems to good to be true it probably is.

It may seem trite to mention this cliché but it encapsulates the risks of acting upon impulse. The 'railway mania' of Victorian times saw speculators falling over themselves to buy shares without fully considering the implications of investing in infrastructural projects. Despite the lessons of 'railway mania' investors in Eurotunnel bought shares on the promise of ease of construction, fantastic profits plus the general idea that the pie was so big, there would be plenty to go round whatever happened, 'Wow! Grab it!' Once construction started, however, delays and huge cost overruns destroyed the optimistic projections. More importantly, it is questionable whether the projected return on investment was ever sufficient for the risks involved. Besides, building a tunnel is only the beginning. No less risky is the need to make a commercial success of it.

The collapse of some potentially promising Internet trading companies may owe something to 'Wow! Grab it!' sentiments. More specifically, the eagerness of such companies to sell their goods has not always been matched by managed attention to creating a solid administrative and financial foundation for success. Like the biblical seed scattered upon stony ground, such companies shoot up rapidly only to discover that success is unsustainable.

'Wow! Grab it!' sentiments can undermine decision makers' judgement in other ways. Many of Britain's universities over-extended themselves by indulging in a 'Wow! Grab it!' spree when the government offered incentives to increase undergraduate recruitment. Likewise, the unprecedented boom in the UK housing market in the late 1980s held out enormous promise. People stretched their finances in order to pay inflated prices secure in the knowledge that property never loses its value. Surveyors, technicians and bricklayers abandoned secure jobs in local government as the private sector cried out for staff and rewarded those who responded to the call accordingly. Law firms expanded their conveyancing departments to cope with burgeoning and lucrative workloads. Eventually, however, rising prices forced first-time buyers out of the market thus creating a chain of collapse. Redundancies and repossessions followed as 'boom' turned to 'bust'.

Vividness effects may have motivated some ill-advised mergers and acquisitions. The investment bank known as Goldman Sachs had a very clear rationale for its prospective flotation. Flotation, Goldman's said, was a strategic imperative which would enable the firm to operate more flexibly and create acquisitions currency. The *Financial Times* influential Lex column in 1998 had another word for it, that is, 'greed'.[76] While Goldman's partners and employees stood to gain payouts of up to $65 million, the firm was in danger of losing its collegiate culture that had previously enabled it to recruit the most talented people and to outshine firms with far greater resources. $65 million? 'Wow! Grab it!'

'Too Soon Deject and Too Soon Elate'

In the words of the poet Alexander Pope in *The Rape of the Lock*, we frail humans ever blind to fate, 'too soon deject and too soon elate'. Both elation and depression can undermine our judgement. Elation is synonymous with overconfidence. Overconfidence is dangerous because it results in a cavalier attitude towards risk.

The risks of misjudgement are heightened in stressful conditions and where a solution suddenly emerges after a long and arduous search. Specifically, we may succumb to myopic vision seeing only the advantages of a solution and not the risks.[16] People who are stressed because they are on the rebound from a previous relationship are vulnerable to the effects of elated choice if a new suitor suddenly appears on the horizon.

Dejection can be just as harmful as elation but for the opposite reason. That is, if a vision or an image is sufficiently dire we may overestimate the danger and forgo an opportunity.

As human beings we are not only prone to elation and despair, we sometimes get angry. Although anger can be psychologically liberating, ultimately it is usually counterproductive. This is because:

Anger blinds us to our interests.[77]

When we are angry the natural impulse is to strike back at the other party or break off a relationship. Such destructive behaviour may afford us momentary psychological satisfaction, but it rarely enables us to achieve our objective. We can tear up the contract, we can walk out of the discussion, we tell the other party just what we think of them, but then what?

Ending the Pain

Fatigue does not help either. When the search for a solution is long and arduous the temptation is to make a decision, *any* decision just to end the pain of uncertainty.[16] We may buy a hat just to get out of the shop. We may light upon a house, or a car, that we would otherwise have rejected just to end the uncertainty. It becomes a case of 'hang the expense' and 'to hell with the consequences'.

Returning to the issue of simplification, the striking feature of the Barings debacle was management's utter conviction of the reality of Leeson's profits. Research by psychologists suggests that what makes mental simplification dangerous is that it occurs unconciously. In other words, we believe that we are seeing reality when, in fact, the reality we perceive is an invention.

Chapter 6

The essential lie: exploring the myth-making process

A quieter day in Robert Kennedy's campaign trail involved a visit to a day nursery.... Most of the children were from broken homes. Two little girls ... came up and put their heads against his waist and he put his hands on their heads. And suddenly it was hard to watch, because he had become in that moment the father they did not know.[78]

In May 1964 the city of Aberdeen was overtaken by an outbreak of typhoid fever. Within the space of a few days, over 400 people succumbed to an illness that had previously been relegated to history. The cause of the outbreak was traced to a tin of corned beef. The meat had been cooked in tins in a processing plant in Argentina. At the end of the cooking process the tins were cooled in the river. They were then held in storage for two weeks as a precaution on the assumption that any that had punctured at the seam because of the intense heat of cooking would reveal themselves by exploding.

In fact, this assumption proved wrong. The tin that was

responsible for the outbreak of typhoid fever developed a minute hole and survived the quarantine period. Moreover, the water supply in which the tins were cooled had become contaminated by the town's sewage. The existence of a minute hole allowed contaminated water to make contact with the beef.

One of the mysteries of the case was that the tin contained six pounds of corned beef – sufficient for about fifty to sixty servings. Yet over 400 people became infected albeit with varying degrees of intensity.

The contaminated tin finished up in a grocer's store in Aberdeen. There it was divided into two. One half was kept on the counter ready to serve customers. The remainder was displayed in an unrefrigerated south-facing window to stand in the May sunshine before being sold. In addition, the knives used to cut the corned beef were then used, uncleaned, to cut other cooked meats contaminating these in the process. Another factor in the spread of infection was that staff were not trained to wash their hands after each serving – nor were there washing facilities available.[79]

The Aberdeen typhoid case makes grim reading not least because, as the report notes, the hygiene practices in the shop that sold the corned beef were the norm in Britain. Yet the report also notes that health experts had long warned of the dangers prevailing in the UK's food stores and restaurants. So why was their advice ignored?

Our scientific models depict the decision maker as calmly and logically analysing all the facts then choosing the best course of action. Such models are perhaps best understood as describing what rarely happens in decision making.

The decision-making process is more accurately seen as the rise and fall of a myth. A myth represents the dominant viewpoint about what should be done.[80] During the 1980s the dominant viewpoint in the Church of England was that it should invest exclusively and aggressively in the property market, even if it meant borrowing money to embark upon speculative developments ahead of planning permission.[81] More recently, when an outbreak of foot and mouth disease overtook the UK in early 2001 the dominant view was that animals in contact with the disease should be slaughtered.

A myth is a simplified view of reality that manages to gain credence. Some myths are completely wrong but most are partly true.

*Since nearly all myths are partly true, logically, all myths are partly **untrue**.*

It is the part that is untrue that matters because once a myth gains credence, decision makers commit themselves to policies on the strength of it. Officially smallpox has been eradicated. Does that mean we can assume that the disease is utterly extinct? The polio virus that killed thousands of people until a vaccine was introduced in the 1950s is officially extinct in France. Yet suspected strains of the virus were recently found in a Strasbourg sewer.[82] The Phillips report into the BSE crisis has endorsed the suggestion that BSE started spontaneously in a cow. This is now the received viewpoint. Yet some scientists believe that BSE originated in sheep infected with scrapie.[83] The response to foot and mouth disease is based upon measures that were last applied almost 40 years ago. Does it really do any good to splash car wheels with disinfectant? Is it really neccessary to slaughter thousands of animals?

Building on Mud

The world is shot with myths competing for dominance, for example, the controversy surrounding the safety of mobile phones and genetically modified crops. The myth-making process usually starts with a crisis.

*Crisis means danger **and** opportunity.*

Crises erupt when something happens that shows an old myth is no longer working, hence the allusion to danger. The existence of a crisis also creates an opportunity for competing myths to gain credence, that is, new ideas about what should be done.

A myth can be seen as a kind of theory. Unlike scientific theories, however, a myth cannot be tested before we adopt it as policy.

We can only test a myth by acting upon it.

The only way to find out whether comprehensive education would deliver the promised benefits was to set up a system of comprehensive schools. A senior barrister discussing the possibility of relocating his chambers said:

> We are toying with the idea of moving out to somewhere like a small industrial park outside town ... where you haven't got the problems with parking, you're in between the two major centres where you do most of your work ... a perfect location but, on the other hand, you haven't got the drop-in ability – in other words, there's no solicitor who is going to come in to you after court for a

cup of coffee, to say hello . . . . That, we feel, is going to lose us a lot of business.[84]

We can imagine all the arguments here about what should be done with some members of chambers in favour of moving and others who are against the idea. The only way to find out whether moving would cost a lot of businesss is to try it and see!

That being so, you might think that decision makers would proceed extremely cautiously when implementing their ideas, always mindful of the doubts and half-expecting to fail. Yet experience suggests that it is frequently the opposite that happens. That is, decisions begin in a spirit of confidence. Many of the system-built housing projects of the 1960s were a technical and social disaster. Some of the tower blocks that were built were never even commissioned because the structural joins failed. Those that were inhabited proved prone to condensation and other problems that made them unpleasant and expensive to live in – to say nothing of the social alienation, crime and vandalism produced by these 'streets in the sky'. Yet none of this was predictable from the extravagant claims made by politicians or the professional bodies of architects and surveyors who underwrote the new technology or the local authorities who rushed through the planning consents.

We will return to the issue of confidence in Chapter 9. Suffice be it here to note that such enthusiasm makes a lot more sense when we consider the pressure on politicians to relieve the acute post-war housing shortage, the fees paid to architects and surveyors, and the lucrative incentives for local authorities to achieve housing targets.

Dressed to Kill

Vested interests play a critical role in the making of a myth. Their first task is to seize the decision premises by getting their definition of reality adopted. The second is to control the alternatives that are considered. The third is to control information about the alternatives.[48]

In order to achieve those objectives, vested interests lose no time in documenting their ideas. Documents have a curiously hypnotic effect upon the decision process. Once pieces of paper are put before people, decisions begin to take shape.

Paper does more than that, however. The decision-making process comprises two levels of reality. The first level is the surface meaning. The second concerns the symbolic underworld, which represents the hidden reality, the hidden meaning that lurks beneath the surface. Although gossip can involve the malicious spread of information, its real function rests in defining social boundaries.[85] Secrecy serves a similar purpose. Frequently the actual content of a secret is trivial. What makes secrecy special is that it offers the possibility of a second world.[86]

The most mundane act can be vested with hidden meaning. We write Christmas cards to people whom we never see from one year to the next and may never see again – why? The hidden meaning may be that we remember recipients for two minutes so that we can *forget* them for another year. When crowds wept over the death of Diana, Princess of Wales, were they mourning her or something in their own lives?

Life may be suffering. Life may be nasty and brutish, even on a good day. One consolation is that when we are dead we will look better than we ever did when we were alive. The undertakers will see to that. Whereas for most of us death is an unusual and terrifying experience, undertakers deal with it every day. Moreover, they can ill afford to have their work disrupted by distraught onlookers. Undertakers solve this problem by making everything associated with death seem as life-like and normal as possible. For instance, the corpse is made up and left to appear as if asleep. If death has occurred at home the bed is made and the room left neat and tidy.[87]

Paperwork is vested with hidden meaning. Ostensibly business plans, cost/benefit analyses, feasibility studies and the like are compiled to help us to make decisions. In reality, documentation is to decision makers like embalming is to undertakers, that is, it serves to dress up a decision that is already *made*.

Paperwork is more important for what it signifies than what it actually says. The setting out of objectives, evidence that plans are underscored by a clear rationale, elaborate analysis and explication denote intellectual rigour, objectivity, and, above all, due diligence. In other words, the real purpose of paperwork is to confer an air of respectability upon the decision process.[88,89]

An important theme of this book is that rationality is not a guide but an achievement. When we write our policy papers, our rationale for a cross-border merger, what we are in effect doing is disguising the emotional impulses that are driving the decision, the unconcious fears, jealousy and so forth by making everything *appear* rational.

The plans for Manchester's extended tramway system suggest that the proposed network will carry 45 million passengers a year. A child might look at that figure and say 'how do they know?'

Manchester's decision makers can study maps. They can calculate how many people live in the areas to be served by the new network. They can analyse socio-economic data and use the analysis to model commuting patterns. Ultimately, however, they can only *guess* how many people will actually use the new network. It may be an educated guess but it is still a guess. Moreover, it is a guess concerning developments that lie far out into the future.

Just as the embalmed corpse takes on a life-like appearance, projections that are reasoned and well researched can seem like statements of fact. Just as psychotherapy offers present comfort for our fears of the past, planning does this for our fears about the future. Like soothing a frightened child, planning takes all the doubts, all the uncertainties that lie ahead and smooths them away.[37] The result can be a sense of certainty where none exists.

Waving the Magic Wand

Experts play an important role in the making of a myth. They contribute to the air of certainty by using their mystique to *legitimate* plans. Peter Rawlins, former chief executive of the London Stock Exchange, said the same thing using different language:

> There was this curious belief that I found all over the City, this lemming-like belief by people who generally don't know what they are doing, that as long as you appoint a household name ... to oversee it for you and they tell you it's OK then it's OK.[89]

The power of expertise rests in the belief that the expert is serving our interests and not their own.[90] Yet experts have their living to earn and their axes to grind. The so-called safe drinking limits for women are 33% lower than those for men. Is that a clinical truth or a reflection of sexist bias? Likewise, whose interests are served when an overbooked barrister persuades a client to plead guilty?

Experts are careful to maintain the appearance of impartiality. Beneath the surface, however, they are alert for the subtle cues hinting at what is required. For instance, outside experts are frequently asked to criticise proposals. Critical scrutiny acts as a legitimating device. Yet no one really welcomes criticism – whatever surface appearances might suggest. Experts know that if they are too critical, 'giving us grief' as the saying goes, they will not be asked back. Yet they must be seen to play the part. Experts walk this tightrope by confining their criticism to areas where the risk of damage is minimal.[48]

Moreover, expert reports may be subject to quiet negotiation. In order to maintain goodwill, flexibility is shown. A recommendation is toned down because it would be onerous to implement, a potentially embarrasssing item is omitted from a report on the understanding that it will be dealt with. Ethical codes are pushed to their limits. The problem of confidentiality is solved by the twinkle of an eye, the pointed silence, and the significant look.

Ostensibly outside expertise keeps the decision process honest. The hidden reality is that experts are part of the conspiracy. If they say 'it's OK' it's OK.

Writing the Hymn Sheet

The point is, it is only partly 'OK'. The myth-making process is about negotiating the *official* definition of reality. It is about writing the hymn sheet for everyone to sing to.

In the early 1970s a favourite interview question asked of prospective law students was how they would defend making the wearing of seat belts compulsory. Today it seems strange to recall the controversy that car seat belts provoked when they were first introduced. You may say, 'Ah, but that was before the benefits were recognised'. True, but what do we mean by *recognised*?

Politicians in Africa are refusing to recognise AIDS as an illness. They cling to the myth that AIDS reflects poverty and/or immoral behaviour in order to avoid an overwhelming demand for expensive drugs. Nearer to home, some dentists are challenging the myth of the six-monthly 'check-up' and 'scale and polish' arguing they merely waste resources. Will their views ever be officially recognised? Will mobile phones and genetically modified crops eventually be recognised as dangerous as blue asbestos?

There are no absolutes in defining risk.

Until 1996, the dominant viewpoint among health experts was that there was no risk to human health from BSE. That was not the same as saying beef was completely safe to eat. Rather the dominant viewpoint was that the risk of BSE jumping the species barrier to harm humans was so small that beef could be officially declared safe to eat.[91]

Ultimately, what we call an acceptable level of risk is something that is negotiated. Negotiation takes time. Consequently, the dominant viewpoint frequently lags behind reality. Some doctors, alarmed by patients reporting tingling sensations, stopped prescribing the drug thalidomide long before it was officially banned. When the first cases of AIDS began to be reported in America, homosexual males who frequented so-called bath houses where they might have sexual encounters with upwards of fifty partners in the space of a weekend assumed that if the bath houses were unsafe, someone in authority would have acted. By the time the danger was officially recognised the disease had spread far and wide.[50]

Another reason negotiation takes time is that it frequently involves consultation. In theory, consultation informs decision making. In reality, it too is mainly important for what it signifies. Ritual means a prescribed way of doing things. In decision making, consultation is part of the prescribed way of doing things. This is because consultation signifies involvement. Conversely, failure to consult, however perfunctorily, can rob a decision of legitimacy even though it would have made no difference to the outcome.

The problem is that the world does not stop revolving while decision makers consult with interested parties. This was one of the lessons learned from the BSE fiasco:

> The production of written documents by officials and by advisory committees frequently entailed a process of wide consultation and drafting refinement. This was a 'Rolls-Royce' system, but one which tended to result in lengthy delays. Consultees would be tempted to suggest drafting improvements, which would then result in a further round of consultation. These were often not changes of sufficient substance to justify the delay they caused.

For example:

> It took *two-and-half years* for . . . advice on the dissection of bovine eyeballs to be passed on to schools and up to *three years* to issue simple occupational warnings and basic advice to some of the high risk trades [emphasis added].[91]

Singing From the Hymn Sheet

Ritual can speed up the decision-making process because since everyone knows what to expect, there is no need to renegotiate the psychological contract every time the parties meet. The adage 'my word is my bond' dispenses with the need for written contracts. The ritualistic hammering of the gavel, 'going, going, gone', signifies the end of the auction – everyone understands what is happening.

The danger, however, is that ritual can become a substitute for communication:

'Have you been riding today, Mr Greville?' asked the Queen. 'No Madam, I have not,' replied Mr Greville. 'It was a very fine day,' continued the Queen. 'Yes, Madam, a very fine day,' said Mr Greville. 'It was rather cold though,' said the Queen. 'It *was* rather cold, Madam,' said Mr Greville. 'Your sister, Lady Frances Egerton, rides, I think, doesn't she?' said the Queen. 'She does ride sometimes, Madam,' said Mr Greville. There was a pause, after which Mr Greville ventured to take the lead, though he did not venture to change the subject. 'Has Your Majesty been riding today?' asked Mr Greville. 'Oh yes, a very long ride,' answered the Queen ... 'Has Your Majesty got a nice horse?' said Mr Greville. 'Oh, a very nice horse,' said the Queen. It was over. Her Majesty gave a smile and an inclination of the head, Mr Greville a profound bow, and the next conversation began.[92]

In this exchange between Queen Victoria and her courtier, Mr Greville, the ritual is observed. Significantly, by the end of it no one is any wiser. The same problem can occur in decision making. What may appear to be a discussion about a problem may be decision makers merely reciting a setpiece, taking up predictable positions whenever a conflict arises. It was suggested in Chapter 2 that conflict facilitates communication because it enables an exchange of perspectives. In contrast, ritual blocks communication. The danger is that decision makers *think* they are communicating. They think they are responding to issues and challenges, when in fact like Queen Victoria and her courtier, Mr Greville, by the end of the discussion, no one is any wiser.

The Essential Lie

All myths are contradicted by reality to some extent. Yet while a myth remains unchallenged it provides an interpretation of reality upon which decision makers act.

Who dares challenge a myth supported by powerful vested interests? Myths are ultimately perpetuated by what is called the 'essential lie' whereby the parties involved refrain from saying what they really think or believe for fear of bringing down the whole edifice. Indeeed, how many of us would retain our jobs and our marriages if we really spoke our minds?

The essential lie sustains a myth because it means denying reality. Until recently, BSE was officially confined to the UK. Yet there have been cases of BSE in countries that were officially free from the disease, though not according to official sources.

The essential lie is often told in silence.

Recall, the myth-making process is about negotiating reality. Sometimes the negotiations are tacit rather than explicit. The burghers of Manchester are proud of the Bridgewater concert hall.

So they should be after all the money invested in it. The only weakness in the design of the building is the acoustics. You might say this amounts to a fairly fundamental flaw in a concert hall. The myth of a superb facility is maintained because no one mentions the acoustics.

Christina Rossetti's hymn about fishermen begins 'When lamps are lighted in the town, the boats sail out to sea'. In some ports, little has changed since those words were written over 100 years ago. In particular, the method of unloading the boats is primitive. Heavy cartons of fish are hauled off the boats and then dragged into the auction hall. You might think there are easier and more efficient ways of accomplishing the task. The most resilient myths are those that have become so 'taken for granted' that no one even thinks of challenging them. Such myths are basically *non*-decisions.[93,94] Non-decisions may be more important than decisions because:

Supreme power is invisible.

The most potent form of power is that which is rarely made obvious but which rests in all the unspoken presumptions about what should be done. Non-decisions are the sleeeping dogs of power. Their existence only becomes obvious when they are challenged. The primitive technology used to unload the fishing boats helps to keep fishing as a male preserve. The exposé of Liverpool's Alder Hey hospital's practice of retaining the organs of dead children and foetuses without parents' knowledge destroyed the myth about involving parents in decisions as it showed whose interests came first.

The Suspicion of Witchcraft

Recall, myths are theories that cannot be tested in advance. Myths lose credence as the ripening of events exposes weaknesses and as other myths compete for dominance. The Church of England suffered a crippling £800 million loss when the property market collapsed.[81] Was the raising of entry standards in the nursing profession a good idea? A director of nursing services said:

> Nurses have lost credibility because they have left the bedside.... Our nurses are not being trained to give basic nursing care. They're trained to be mini doctors. I want basic nursing care .... I want toilet care – that's what I want. We are building nurses now who think that bedpans and cups of tea are not nurses' jobs.... You hear it from doctors all the time that you can't get nurses to give basic care nowadays.... We've pushed up the entry requirements far too high so that a lot of girls who'd make very good nurses can't gain entry. Girls with two A-levels are a very good thing for the profession – so long as they'll change beds.[63]

Part of the value of a myth is that it prevents decision makers from overreacting to reality by changing direction every time something happens that contradicts the myth. Consequently, in order for a competing myth to gain credence it is frequently neccessary to denigrate the old one. When the diesel traction engine arrived, steam was suddenly found wanting:

> British Railways were losing money – public money it was emphasised – and gradually the opinion began to harden that it was all the fault of steam. It was dirty, it was antiquated, and then came a new ploy – the sociologists began to exclaim that it was undignified for a man to shovel coal all day to earn his living. In many areas in Britain

the railways had been slow to recover from the effects of the war. In certain parts of the London commuter zones the local tank engines were in poor shape. Morale was low. Services had to be cancelled because of crew absenteeism. 'It was all the fault of steam!'[95]

More recently, the BSE crisis revealed that since many abattoirs were working at the margins of financial viability, local authorities tended to be lenient in enforcing hygiene regulations. In order to justify establishing a central government inspectorate, officials painted the following picture of the results of local authority control:

Slaughter hall floor heavily soiled with blood, gut contents and other debris – no attempt to clean up between carcases. Car cleaning brush heavily contaminated with blood and fat being used to wash carcases. Knives and utensils not being sterilised. Offal rack and carcase rails encrusted with dirt. Missing window panes in roof – birds, flies and vermin entering. Another slaughterhouse report: Filthy equipment and surfaces congealed and dry blood on offal racks. Effluent discharging across floor under dressed carcases – risk of contamination. Slaughtermen at cattle sticking point not sterilising knife. No sterilisers to wash basins in pig slaughter hall. No fly screening on open windows.[91]

Failing leaders frequently suffer the indignity of degradation. Teams of inspectors descend upon poorly performing schools to seek out evidence of poor management – an essential precursor to the head teacher's subsequent removal.

One day in Chiawa, Zambia, a tractor carrying farm workers overturned and nine people were killed. Although the driver of the tractor was subsequently found to have been extremely drunk, there was no question that the accident was caused by witchcraft.

This incident coming on top of a series of other mishaps convinced the chief that there was too much evil in the village. A witchfinder was duly hired to carry out cleansing duties.[96]

Beneath the veneer of rationality our approach to decision making is driven by primitive fear and superstition. We too invoke sorcery in order to explain mischance. The difference is that instead of blaming angry gods, storms and thunder we refer to 'economic trends' and 'difficult trading conditions'. Likewise, few people would admit to basing a decision on astrology yet we see no contradiction in acting upon what analysts predict. When a myth fails, it may seem to decision makers that there is 'too much evil' in the organisation. They too hire witchfinders to carry out cleansing duties. The only difference is that modern witchfinders are called auditors, inspectors or external consultants. For all their seeming scientific objectivity, the real purpose of organisational restructuring exercises may be to drive out evil influences – once and for all!

We should not underestimate the fear that people may experience when a myth fails. Philip Zeigler's fictional but graphic account of the Black Death in a medieval village suggests how peasants coped with the terrifying effects of bubonic plague that shattered their faith in God and the Church:

> Impotent, resentful, panic stricken: the villagers were in a mood to revenge themselves on any target that came within their range. Poor Mad Meg provided an easy victim. Someone had met her by night conversing suspiciously with her diabolic cat. Someone else had seen her lurking near the well – armed with poison without a doubt. A crowd of villagers worked themselves into a drunken frenzy on beer looted from the house of the ale-brewer and marched indig-

nantly towards her house. Mad Meg heard them coming and slipped away into the woods. Probably she would have escaped their clumsy pursuit if one of the peasants had not seized hold of her cat and, brandishing it by the tail, smashed its head against the rock. in hysterical defence of the only creature that had shown her any love, Meg ran out from her hiding place among the trees. The villagers attacked her with sticks and stones and battered her to death in the clearing outside her miserable hovel.[97]

Naming and punishing witches helps to restore social stability. The sanitised modern name for witches is scapegoat. When a myth fails, naming scapegoats helps to restore stability because by shouldering the blame, scapegoats deflect attention from other people's performance thus enabling them to walk away from the mess. Significantly, employees often refer to organisational investigations as witch hunts.

Interestingly, just as suspicions of withcraft reach their zenith during times of social instability, failing organisations are characterised by everyone blaming everyone else, that is, naming witches and frequent restructures that are basicically repeated attempts to be rid of evildoers.

'Then Came the Cat'

A crisis occurs when a myth can no longer even partly account for reality. Some myths tumble like lightning-struck castles, brought down by a single cataclysmic event. The explosion at Chernobyl destroyed the myth that nuclear power is safe. The discovery in 1996 that BSE had jumped the species barrier to infect a cat prompted a public outcry because it destroyed the myth that BSE could not under any circumstances be transmitted to humans.[91] The sudden collapse of Marks & Spencer's share price destroyed the myth that the so-called 'M&S way' was meeting customers' needs.

Some myths sink slowly like a house built on a swamp. The UK's social security framework sinks further and further every year, overtaken by changes in society. Many universities cling to the myth that they are research-led while drawing more and more of their income from teaching.

Part of the value of a crisis is that because old myths are clearly inadequate, people become more receptive to proponents of a new myth. The problem is, that in the time it takes to develop a new myth the organisation may be beyond help.

'An Intensity Beyond Belief'

Sorcery, the world of secrecy – some of the ideas expressed in this chapter may seem far-fetched. Yet symbols can be more important than substance. In September 1940 Winston Churchill toured a badly bombed area of London:

> It was a harrowing sight, with ARP and other officials digging out from the ruins injured people and bodies. From one forlorn group alongside the remains of their homes an old woman shouted, 'When are we going to bomb Berlin, Winnie?' Instinctively – without time for thought – Winston swung round, waving his fist . . . and growled with menacing emphasis, 'You leave that to me!' Morale rose immediately; everyone was satisfied and reassured.
>
> Afterwards I pondered the incident . . . . What could a Prime Minister at that time and in such desperate conditions say that was not

pathetically inadequate or downright dangerous? 'When are we going to bomb Berlin?' 'As soon as we are able to' ... 'In a year or two when we have built up a striking force' ... 'Not just yet – you must be patient' ... Almost anything – except what he did say – would have been wrong.[98]

When organisations face threats from mergers and takeovers they willingly pay huge fees to firms like Goldman Sachs to assist them. Ostensibly, Goldman's add value by contributing rigorous analysis. Yet what firms are really buying is the emotional reassurance that comes from Goldman's reputation.[99] For all their sophistication, they are like the little girls that clung to Robert Kennedy.

Returning to the practices of undertakers, the point is:

If symbols can convert something as final as death into life, what is their power?

On Sunday 7 May 2000 the Vienna Philharmonic orchestra took up positions in the quarry of the former concentration camp at Mauthausen to play Beethoven's Ninth Symphony. Around 10 000 people, including survivors of the camp, heard the concert, a performance:

Charged with an intensity beyond belief. How could it not be, with Beethoven's epic journey from darkness to freedom echoing around this, the final resting place for those who lost all hope, all joy, all freedom?[100]

Yet it was controversial, not least because of the orchestra's past association with the Nazis and also the rise of Jorg Haider's right-wing Freedom Party and its association with xenophobic policies.

In addition, there were those who argued that the camp should be left as a shrine – forever silent:

> Silence did finally come. Right at the end, instead of the applause, 10 000 people holding candles many of them weeping stood in complete stillness for a minute or more.[100]

Chapter 7

High tides and green grass: the illusion of control

'No man so much in danger as he who dreadeth none.' (Proverb)

In Act III of Tom Stoppard's play *Rosencrantz and Guildenstern Are Dead*, Player says to Rosencrantz, 'Life is a gamble, at terrible odds – if it was a bet you wouldn't take it.' Actually, you just might, *provided* you can deal the cards. Psychologists call it the illusion of control. Imagine choosing a lottery ticket. Which option would you prefer?

(a) To accept a ticket from the shopkeeper (you can assume the shopkeeper is honest), or

(b) To choose the ticket for yourself.

Intellectually it makes no difference who chooses the ticket because the probabilities of winning a prize are identical in each case. Emotionally, it is a different story. When the moment of decision arrives most people prefer to choose their own ticket. In other words, as human beings we tend to believe that we can control events that are actually entirely due to chance. Research by psychologists indicates that gamblers often fall silent for a few seconds before throwing the dice then shaking softly if needing a low number on the dice, and vigorously when needing a high number – as if they can command fate by sheer concentration and will.[101]

The illusion of control is potentially dangerous because it rests upon overconfidence. Almost all decisions involve risk. Overconfidence can lead us to take bigger risks than the situation warrants – even to the point of recklessness. This chapter explains how the illusion of control arises and how it can affect our behaviour as decision makers.

Illusion

The illusion of control is heightened when we either have or believe we have some control over chance events. Imagine playing a fruit machine. You need three cherries to win. You pull the handle, the reels whirl, the colours spin, one cherry clinks into place, clink, clink, so does another and then chunk – a lemon. The experience is both exciting and frustrating, so near and yet so far. The same goes for lottery scratch cards that yield two out of the three requisite numbers. In each case, the natural impulse is to try again.

That is exactly how we are meant to react. Fruit machines and lottery scratch cards are engineered to yield a high proportion of 'near-misses' in order to encourage us to continue playing. For if we kept on losing we would conclude that the odds are stacked against us (as indeed they are) and give up. The experience of a 'near-miss' has the opposite effect. 'Near-misses' impart a powerful surge of optimism because the mind *re*presents them as 'near-wins'.[102]

Our ability to transform losses into 'near-wins' is dangerous because we lose sight of the objective probabilities. Instead we become overconfident, and more willing to stake time, money and effort in the mistaken belief that success is close.

Feeling in control encourages risk taking.

Studies of betting on games of dice suggest that players tend to feel more confident and bet more money when they throw the dice themselves than when other players throw it.[103] Fruit machines incorporate 'nudge' and 'hold' buttons to create an illusion of control. Specifically, 'nudge' and 'hold' buttons imply that winning involves an element of skill. As such they provide an invitation to players to pit their wits against chance.

Internet share trading has created a new form of risk. Until recently if you were a private investor, buying and selling shares was a slow and uncertain business. Private investors were obliged to instruct a broker who would then deal either at a stipulated price or not at all, or deal 'at best'. The investor then had to wait for the broker to communicate the results. Ostensibly Internet trading reduces risk because it means that private investors can track prices on their computer screens and 'lock in' at a definite price thus reducing uncertainty. While this is true, investment psychologists are now worried that the resultant sense of control is encouraging investors to trade too frequently. Frequent dealing is risky partly because the transaction costs can outweigh the gains, but more particularly because investors are in danger of losing sight of the sum total of gains and losses.

'Feel Lucky, Punk?'

If we believe we can control chance events, how much more dangerous does that belief become when the game really does involve skill *and* luck – as indeed most decisions do?

Illusions are dangerous precisely because they are believable. The mirror in the funfair reflects us as either ridiculously fat or ridiculously thin. The image is so extreme that we know it is not us. In contrast, an illusion is like a mirror in a clothes store. Whereas the mirror in the funfair *distorts* the facts, the mirror in the clothes store is invidious because it *accommodates* them.[103] It *re*presents us as more elegant than we really are. The person reflected in the glass is not ourselves but an illusion. We believe in the illusion because it is plausible, and because it takes us and *re*presents us as we want to see ourselves.

As human beings we look in the 'mirror' and see an image of ourselves that is stronger, more intelligent and more capable than we really are.

The illusion of control whispers we can spin straw into gold.

The illusion of control explains why people buy pubs that have already bankrupted a succession of owners. That is, they make the decision on the assumption that they have the unique ability to succeed where others have failed. Usually all that happens is that the loss-making pub claims another victim.

Likewise, in the words of *1066 And All That* King Ethelred was habitually unready and finally taken completely unawares by his own death[104] because his unrealistic optimism made external threats seem less ominous than they actually were. Hitler confidently suggested that invading Russia would be like kicking open the door of an empty room. 'Precisely,' muttered his generals, 'you never know what you might find inside.' Significantly, Goebbels cancelled a plan to produce a map of the campaign. The terrain was so vast that Goebbels thought it might worry the German people.

More recently the British government may have succumbed to the psychology of 'near-miss' when it decided to spend £80 million reworking the SA-80 rifle. The rifle became standard British army issue in the mid-1980s. On paper and under test conditions the rifle performs well. The sight is good and the shape easy to handle. In the field, however, it can be 'fiddly' and unreliable especially in heat and dust. Soldiers are said to distrust it. The SAS declined to use it. The Paras preferred to take older, heavier guns to Kosovo. In August 2000 a secret report leaked to the *Daily Telegraph* newspaper revealed that the SA-80 had failed in battle. At a critical moment the safety catches jammed, leaving troops unable to defend themselves. The argument for reworking the gun relates to its paper strengths. Yet as the *Daily Telegraph* argued in its editorial, it is a case of 'so near and yet so far': 'Soldiers do not use the weapon in laboratory conditions. They have to fight in muddy Balkan trenches, or dusty Gulf deserts or sweaty equatorial jungles. It must work and work first time.'[105]

Moreover, hope invariably triumphs over experience. Every day many of us write out our 'to-do' list with every intention of getting things done. Yet the list is almost invariably an overestimate of what we can realistically hope to achieve as telephone calls, interruptions by colleagues and other minor setbacks eat into our time. Yet next day we make up another list that is just as hopelessly overoptimistic[103] – we just never learn.

Lightning Strikes

Although we take comfort in the adage that lightning never strikes twice in the same place, there is no reason why it should not. In October 2000 a train hit a broken rail and crashed near Hatfield killing four people. In February 2001, a Land Rover and trailer careered off the M62 motorway near Selby and plunged down an embankment onto a railway where it was struck by a train that then derailed and was then hit by a goods train travelling in the opposite direction. Ten people were killed in the accident – a toll that might have been much higher but for the fact that there were only 100 or so passengers on the train. Incredibly it was the same engine that was involved in the Hatfield crash. The lesson is:

Chance has no memory.

Psychologists call it 'gambler's fallacy'. The fallacy is to assume that the reels, the dice, the roulette wheels and other artifacts of chance possess a memory. Gambler's fallacy can lead us to become over- or underconfident. One factor that encourages us to go on playing fruit machines is the intuitive belief that because a particular machine has not paid out for a long time, it must yield soon. Alternatively, we may miss the chance of scooping a 'jackpot' prize if we assume that because a machine has just paid out a large amount, there will be no more large wins for a while.

Gambler's fallacy does not always apply, because we can become superstitious of something and believe that it is permanently dogged by bad luck. Green cars are hard to sell because many people believe that green is unlucky. Gambler's fallacy is worth knowing about, however, because it can lead to an illusion of control. When Concorde crashed in flames near Paris in July 2000, travel operators worried that passengers would refuse to fly in the ageing machines. Yet in the immediate aftermath of the accident, the reverse happened. Many passengers decided that, statistically, Concorde had drawn its share of bad luck and was therefore probably safer than other makes of aircraft. The fallacy was exposed when the media discovered Concorde's long-standing history of tyre problems, including a near-catastrophic incident in 1979 when it returned to the airport with fuel pouring from its wing after debris from a burst tyre had ruptured it.[106]

Companies specialising in so-called 'penny shares' make a living by exploiting a form of 'gambler's fallacy'. Penny shares are shares that have lost so much value in the stock market that they are worth literally pennies. The fallacy is to assume that having reached near rock bottom the only way the shares can move is up. In fact, 'penny shares' frequently sink into oblivion.

Illusion Piles Upon Illusion

When success involves a combination of luck and skill it can be difficult to determine whether the outcome was due to skill or to luck. In the board game of 'Monopoly', players can improve their chances of winning by deploying strategy. Yet they may also be helped by a lucky throw of the dice, or the bad luck of another player.

What is certain is that, as human beings, we seldom suffer agonies of doubt. Almost invariably we attribute success to our abilities and failure to bad luck. When a group of psychologists in America analysed a large sample of company reports they discovered that poor results were always blamed on factors beyond senior management's control, such as commodity prices and currency fluctuations.[107] To cite just one UK case at random, when Carlsberg's shares fell by nearly 7% in 1998 the decline was blamed on falling beer consumption in Denmark and Germany, competition from low-priced brands in the rapidly expanding Chinese market and an upsurge in cross-border sales and differences in excise duties.[108] Obviously a company will try to put the best possible public relations 'spin' on its performance. The danger arises when we start to believe that all our failures are due to factors beyond our control and all our successes represent personal triumphs against the odds. The point is, as human beings we have an innate capacity to nurture such beliefs.

Conversely we tend to see our competitors' success as due to luck rather than superior skill. Our competitors succeeded because they were in the right place at the right time, or because of who they knew rather than what they knew. Likewise, how often do we hear football spectators claim that their team was well ahead when the other side scored five or six 'lucky' goals!

Moreover, such is our innate belief in ourselves that we tend to minimise the contributions made by others to our success. We may pay lip service to sentiments like 'team effort' and all that, but secretly we believe that but for us, it would never have happened. For instance, in 1923 two Canadians, Barting and Macleod, won the Nobel Prize for the discovery of insulin. Barting claimed that Macleod had been more of a hindrance than a help while Macleod omitted Barting's name from all the speeches describing the research leading up to the discovery.[103]

Moreover, when things fall apart it is never our fault. This may seem like a sweeping statement. Yet have you ever met anyone who thinks they were responsible for the problems and failures of their organisation? A disgruntled estate agent commenting on the performance of a conveyancing solicitor said:

> Whenever you telephone about anything she's always waiting for someone else to do something. It's never her that's holding things up. *She's* always on the ball.

It is a small step from automatically blaming other people for our errors and omissions to actually believing that we are always efficient. Risk and danger enter in because the gap between how we see ourselves and how the rest of the world sees us widens. We can end up living in a world of fantasy, oblivious to the faults and weaknesses of our operations until something dramatic happens to force us to recognise reality – like being struck off or sued for negligence.

We saw in Chapter 5 how Barings bank collapsed because they became oblivious to reality. One question that has not yet been answered is why Barings found it so easy to believe that Leeson's apparently phenomenal profits meant that history was repeating itself. Barings may ultimately have collapsed because they succumbed to an illusion of control. More specifically, they concluded that Leeson's apparently phenomenal profits vindicated their strategy of achieving early entry into emerging markets. In other words, as Barings saw it, they had been right all along. Moreover, Leeson's apparent success confirmed what Barings wanted to believe, that is, that a small merchant bank could outwit the largest and most powerful investment houses. Leeson's apparently escalating profits fuelled the illusion of control.

Nothing Succeeds Like Success?

Although the proverb suggests that nothing succeeds like success, success can be dangerous. More specifically, research suggests that early wins in games of chance tend to make players believe that their success is due to some unique skill. It is a small step to believing that we can control the game.

Control raises the stakes.

To be more precise, once we believe we control the game we are prepared to raise the stakes. This explains why cardsharps invariably allow their victims to win the first few games. The experience of winning makes victims feel overconfident and encourages them to raise the stakes.

The Next clothing company succumbed to the pitfalls of early success. Next saw a market for stylish clothing for a slightly older group of women neglected by fashion chains. The venture soon prospered. However, the experience of an early win led Next to conclude that its success reflected not a fleeting dominance of a neglected market but, '... a universal management genius applicable to a wide range of retail activities. It went on a spree of acquisition and diversification and came close to nemesis as a result.'[109]

Fine Tuning the Odds

There is only one thing more dangerous than success and that is repeated success.

Repeated success is especially dangerous because it breeds complacency. Complacency is the enemy of safety.

The point was dramatically and tragically demonstrated on 28 January 1986 when the spaceship Challenger exploded seconds after it was launched, killing all seven crew plus a teacher, Christine McAuliffe. There have been disasters involving far larger loss of life but few quite as public. A horrified audience of television viewers saw the rocket lift off and then disintegrate in an orange ball of flame.

The immediate cause of the disaster was a ring seal that failed to close because of the extreme cold. NASA had been warned by the manufacturers of the rocket not to attempt a launch if the ambient temperature was below 53°F. Yet on 28 January, the ambient temperature around Challenger was 28°F, that is, 15°F lower than any previous shuttle launch.

NASA's engineers knew that the ring seals had occasionally been eroded by the hot gases. The manufacturers had tried to solve the problem by fitting an additional ring seal into each joint to compensate if the first ring failed to close. A post-flight examination revealed that a secondary ring seal had been damaged, possibly because of the low ambient launch temperature, and did not close up for two minutes. Such erosion came to be accepted as a 'normal' occurrence. It was as if NASA's managers thought 'We can lower our standards a bit because we got away with it last time'.[110]

On 28 January 1986 NASA had the experience of twenty-four successful launches working against them. That is, repeated success had changed NASA's attitude towards risk:

> When the shuttle flights continued to depart and return success-fully, the criterion for a launch – convince me that I should send Challenger – was dropped. Underestimating the dynamic nature of

reliability, managers inserted a new criterion – convince me that I shouldn't send Challenger.[110]

It would never have happened during the Apollo space programme. NASA, however, had long since dropped the exacting and thorough procedures that distinguished the Apollo launches. The former were seen as highly risky whereas NASA had come to regard the shuttles as routine events involving operational technology. NASA's chief engineer Milton Silveria said:

> In the early days of the space program we were so damned uncertain of what we were doing that we always got everybody's opinion. We would ask for continual reviews, continual scrutiny . . . to look at this thing and make sure we were doing it right. As we started to fly the shuttle again and again, I think the system developed false confidence in itself.[110]

A clear sign of complacency is when we start to believe that we have 'done enough'. NASA's engineers decided that there was nothing more they needed to do, as regards that particular launch, to enhance the probability of success. Likewise, once hygiene and fire safety certificates have been issued, how many restaurant and nightclub owners walk around their premises studying what more can done to improve safety?

If anything, the opposite tends to happen. Once a successful operation is established, the temptation is to cut corners. Just as NASA got away with launching rockets with potentially lethal ring seals, the restaurant gets away with using out-of-date food, and the nightclub owner with packing one or two more people into the disco. Once corners start to be cut, the temptation is always to go on cutting, 'because we got away with it last time'. So, the food gets a little more out of date, a few more people are packed into the disco. Metaphorically speaking, every time the ship returns safely to harbour the Plimsoll line gets painted a little higher. Consequently the risks become greater as the margin of safety gets smaller. What makes such slippage all the more dangerous is that it tends to occur gradually, almost imperceptibly.

Another source of danger is that slippage becomes seen as eliminating unnecessary effort. The householder decides that it is a waste of money having the chimney swept every twelve months. The gas engineer concludes that the regulations on ventilation are overly fussy and rigid.

Times change – so do probabilities.

Relatedly, while we can assess risk we cannot assume that the probabilities associated with a particular risk will remain constant. Organisations exist in a constant state of flux and transformation. As people, systems, equipment, procedures and so forth change, so do probabilities. Moreover, not only does such change also tend to occur gradually, almost imperceptibly, but the effects are not always immediately predictable.

Such changes can push risky practices to dangerous extremes. The restaurant changes one of its suppliers. The new supplier works to a much lower margin of safety on its 'use-by' dates. That new factor then combines with questionable hygiene practices in the restaurant itself. The householder starts burning a different, more sooty, grade of coal. That factor then interacts with the inadequately swept chimney.

The dynamic nature of risk was tragically highlighted on 6 March 1987 when the ferry known as the *Herald of Free Enterprise* capsized. Pictures of the wrecked vessel lying on its side clearly showed that the ship had sailed with its bow doors open. The subsequent investigation revealed that the ship had previously set sail in this unsafe condition. However, on 6 March a change in routine turned risk into disaster. The ship had been designed for the Dover–Calais route. It was transferred to the Dover–Zeebrugge crossing in order to release another ship for maintenance work to be carried out. The design of Zeebrugge harbour is different from Calais. Consequently, the task of loading and unloading the ship took much longer than usual with the result that the *Herald* began running late. Moreover, tidal conditions meant that the loading ramp would not reach the upper loading deck without the ship ingesting many tons of seawater ballast to keep the bow down. The night was dark and bitterly cold when the *Herald* finally drew away from the quay at 18:05. On board were approximately 459 passengers, 80 crew, 81 cars and 47 freight vehicles. At 18:20 the *Herald* passed the inner breakwater. Three or four minutes later, as the vessel passed the outer mole leaving the lights of Zeebrugge behind, it began to speed up. The bow was lower in the water than usual because of the ballast. That factor plus the increasing speed caused the *Herald* to begin shipping water. Passengers heard a call go out for the ship's carpenter – a coded message signifying a dire emergency. It was too late. Almost immediately the ship began listing. Its stability destroyed, the *Herald* capsized within three minutes. The ship struck a sandbank as it went down otherwise the loss of life would have been even greater. As it was, 192 people (154 passengers and 38 crew) were killed in the ensuing turmoil.[111]

In short, fine tuning the odds – until something breaks.

Water Seeping

Imagine water seeping through a wall. Complacency has the same effect upon organisations. Just as water corrodes the steel in concrete blocks, complacency affects everything – working practices, training, even attitudes. Until 1987, the London Underground had a good safety record. For over 100 years trains had rattled through its tunnels carrying millions of passengers in almost complete safety. Events on the night of 18 November 1987 showed, however, that:

A good safety record does not mean safe.

'Like a Child's Sparkler'

The story is as follows. On 18 November 1987 at about 19:29, a financial consultant, Philip Squire, commuting home to north-west London, alighted onto the platform at King's Cross underground station. As he was travelling up the escalator from the Picadilly Line towards the main booking hall, he noticed what appeared to be a smouldering cigarette butt in the treads of the escalator.

As Mr Squire bent down to take a closer look, he realised that the smoke was coming from between the escalator steps:

I looked through the gap and saw a ball of white sparks, like a child's sparkler. Smoke started to come out and pour down like dry ice. The sparks were intense but there was no heat.[39]

Mr Squire jumped over the sparks, ran up the escalator and reported the fire at the ticket office.

As required by the London Underground rulebook, the relief

station inspector went to investigate. Simultaneously, a policeman on duty in the booking hall decided to summon assistance. As his radio did not work underground he had to travel to the surface to make the call.

Meanwhile another passenger had raised the alarm at the ticket office. The employee on duty in the ticket office said 'There didn't seem to be any more smoke than when I previously looked out. I didn't think it was very serious, so I didn't leave the booking office.'[112]

By now the relief station inspector had located the fire. Fires on escalators happened frequently and he was not unduly alarmed. The inspector saw the water fog controls but did not think to operate these. Instead, he brought a carbon dioxide fire exting-uisher but discovered he was unable to use it.

'A Fire the Size of a Cardboard Box'

At 19:39, 10 minutes after the alarm was raised, the police officers on duty in the ticket hall decided to evacuate the area. The ticket clerks were instructed to stop selling tickets. An emergency call went out instructing trains not to stop at King's Cross.

Three minutes later, at 19:42, the fire brigade arrived and went to assess the fire, now 'about the size of a large cardboard box but with flames licking up the handrail'.[112]

As the fire brigade were carrying out their inspection, two trains stopped and let out passengers. The passengers made their way up escalators and passages close to the fire before surging into the crowd in the booking hall.

'Make Pumps 4-Persons Reported'

The fire crew returned to the booking hall. Station Officer Townsley then ordered one of the crew, Temporary Leading Fireman Flanagan, to send the message, '**Make pumps 4-persons reported**'[112] thereby confirming the seriousness of the fire and the need for ambulances. It was now 19:44.

Temporary Leading Fireman Flanagan started walking to the surface to send the message. By now the heat was becoming intense. People began screaming and thick black smoke engulfed the booking hall. Temporary Leading Fireman Flanagan ordered his crew to lead out the public and run for their lives.[112] Simultaneously Station Officer Colin Townsley shouted reassuringly, 'It's all right, love, it's all right' as he went to rescue a woman whose hair and coat were on fire:

> And then it happened. A massive fireball, generating temperatures of 1,200°C and more than six megawatts of energy exploded upwards consuming nearly four tonnes of material and incinerating thirty-one people in seconds.[39]

The digital clock at the head of the Piccadilly Line escalator was stopped by the heat of the flashover. It was 19:45. Station Officer Colin Townsley was among those killed in the disaster.

Whereas the Challenger disaster was partly a reflection of NASA's swashbuckling 'can do' culture, the King's Cross disaster suggests that the more prosaic organisations may be the most dangerous of all. This is because success is not always accompanied by drum rolls and flashing lights. Any organisation that runs day in, day out is an example of repeated success. What makes such organisations dangerous is that their good safety record makes them *seem* safe.

Although London Underground had a good safety record there had been numerous fires in previous years including alarming reports of passengers being led to safety from smoke-filled tunnels. Despite such incidents there was a long-standing policy of allowing passengers to smoke on the Underground generally and on wooden escalators in particular. The flashover happened because the flames were borne upwards by the air from the moving escalator and then touched the non-flame-retardant paint of the wall. The official Inquiry concluded that the disaster was caused by deep-seated complacency. Specifically:

> A belief that fires were inevitable, coupled with a belief that any fire on a wooden escalator, and there had been many, would never develop in a way which would harm passengers. . . . That approach was seriously flawed for it failed to recognise the unpredictability of fire, that most unpredictable of all hazards. Moreover, it ignored the danger of smoke, which is almost certainly more deadly than fire.[112]

The King's Cross fire also shows how a small, potentially containable incident can rapidly spiral out of control. It was, as the cliché goes, 'an accident waiting to happen' except that:

*Accidents do not happen, they are **caused**.*

One reason why small events like the fire at King's Cross can spiral out of control is that the incident places a strain on the broader organisational arrangements, a strain that the organisation is unfitted to bear. It is at that point, the omissions start to tell. Staff at King's Cross were ineffectual because they had received no training in firefighting and evacuation procedures. The station inspector failed to use emergency equipment. The ticket office clerk was ineffectual because he saw his duties as confined to the ticket office. No one alerted the staff of the Bureau de Change or shops adjacent to the booking hall to the danger. The disaster also revealed that the system for communications was seriously inadequate. Trains from the Northern Line continued discharging passengers as late as 19:48, 3 minutes after the flashover had occurred.

High Tides and Green Grass – in the Desert

The illusion of control is exalted when reality is suspended. Amusement arcades combine darkness, flashing bulbs, strobe lighting, loud music and the sound of coins falling into metal trays with a satisfying clatter, to create another world.[113] The experience of living in another world encourages playing because the significance of money, risk and loss is distorted.

Our offices and boardrooms can create a similar effect. The thickness of the walls and carpets create feelings of solidity, comfort, safety, even superiority.[114] Once inside those rooms, although we feel we are part of the organisation we may be so far removed from reality that we are as good as in an amusement arcade. For instance, Shell's pleasant head office in London's Finsbury Square gives no clue to the 100-foot waves and winds of 100 mph battering its oil rigs far out in the North Sea.

The danger is that we can end up living in a world that is unreal. When the media gatecrashed the christening ceremony of prime minister Blair's son Leo, Downing Street cancelled the photocall of the Blairs on holiday. A correspondent to *The Times* newspaper retorted that if Mr Blair believed that such deprivation constituted punishment he was indeed out of touch with public opinion.

Once reality is removed from the equation, anything seems possible. The generals of the First World War worked in the comfort of their chateau, many miles from the front line. They conquered the terrain by running pencils over their maps. This also explains why ideas conceived on holiday seldom survive more than half a hour back in the organisation. Likewise, the energy and optimism generated by 'away-days' soon dies in the cold light of Monday morning.

The ultimate illusion of control is known as 'bunker mentality'. The term was coined after Hitler's behaviour as the Allied armies advanced upon Berlin. He retreated into a concrete bunker deep beneath the Chancellery, seldom emerging into the bomb-blasted city. Hitler became hopelessly detached from reality, manoeuvring armies that no longer existed, and directing an air force that had long since been obliterated. A more recent example of bunker mentality is Nigeria's former ruler General Abacha. As the price of Nigeria's oil fell and debts mounted, industry was reduced to a third of its working capacity. Schools and hospitals ceased to function and even the university stopped ordering books. General Abacha reacted by retreating to his heavily guarded presidential compound and staying there until he died, a cut-off ruler in a cut-off country.[115]

Milder forms of bunker mentality are seen in headteachers who give up teaching and retreat to their offices; the managers who desert the shopfloor, the building site and the hospital ward immersing themselves in paperwork. They may arrive at seven in the morning and remain in their bunkers until seven at night but their grip on reality is an illusion. They might as well be on another planet for all the use they are.

A bunker mentality is the last refuge of a decision maker confronted by overwhelming odds. The school is out of control. The market for the goods has almost vanished. The hospital is overwhelmed. Moreover, leaders are by no means always to blame for the situations in which they find themselves. In such circumstances there may be little that anyone can do. The point is, once we retreat into our bunkers we are not there to do anything.

Chapter 8

Tales of the unexpected: exploring the paradox of consequences

'He's honest. You've just got to watch him'.
(Groucho Marx referring to Chico Marx)

Common sense may seem like a virtue in decision making but it can be a liability. This chapter explores some of the paradoxes of decision making and explains why common sense can produce some unexpected results.

The Tudor flagship *Mary Rose* was the most formidable vessel of the day. In July 1545 the ship set sail from Portsmouth Harbour watched from the shore by King Henry VIII and his courtiers. We can only imagine the onlookers' horror as the sea gushed into the open gunports as the vessel made a sharp turn and then tipped over and sank, drowning almost every one of the 500 men on board.

Ironically this powerful warship met its end not in the midst of battle but in the calm waters of the Solent. Although the precise cause of the disaster remains unclear, the ship had undergone a series of refits during its 35 years of service. One such refit was undertaken shortly before its final voyage. Bracers and riders had been added to her hull and the main deck beams replaced. The stern of the ship may have been changed – a major undertaking – and new gun ports added close to the waterline. Although the *Mary Rose* looked familiar, the ship that set sail from Portsmouth Harbour on that fateful day was profoundly different from the original.

The refitted ship was untested and its crew had no experience of managing it. *Mary Rose* was also carrying the extra weight of 300 soldiers dressed in armour. Perhaps the crew were so used to turning the ship without closing the gun ports that they forgot about the new ones lower down.[116] All that was needed was a sudden gust of wind to cause the ship to dip below the waterline.

Polio was once the scourge of poverty. In the 1950's, however, it mysteriously appeared among the children of the American middle classes. The cause of the outbreak was eventually traced to housing developments. Huge areas of scrubland adjacent to parks had recently been released for residential building. The new estates were highly desirable – on the edge of parkland with deer cantering in the distance. Deer are carriers of polio.[117]

The lesson in both cases is that decisions that seem like a 'good thing' can become a 'bad thing'. Measures intended to strengthen *Mary Rose* created a fatal weakness. The construction of seemingly idyllic housing estates unleashed a lethal disease.

'Kickback': The Paradox of Consistency

Many of our ideas of what is good in decision making reflect 'more is better' logic. The assumption is that if A causes B, and B is good, then the more A we apply, the better things will become.[123] To a point, this may be true. The question is, 'and then what?' In nature, nothing goes on getting better indefinitely otherwise trees and plants would grow to infinity. In nature, trees and plants regress to the mean.[118] In decision making, the consequences of consistency can be much more dramatic. Like driving a car too fast in too low a gear, there may be a sudden 'kickback'.

The medieval Cistercian monasteries were highly efficient organisations. They may even have invented some of the techniques of modern management including job descriptions, standardised procedures, and specified work processes. Initially, monastic efficiency was a means to an end, that is, to maximise the time for prayer. Eventually, however, the Cistercians' good husbandry generated considerable material wealth. They engaged in finance and business, became active as pawnbrokers, and were extremely successful merchants dealing with wine, wool, iron, copper and salt, using their own ships to transport goods and profiting from 'tax breaks' granted by the worldly rulers. In short, the order became wealthy because it renounced wealth but, as a result, lost its ascetic credibility.[119]

Nietzsche has observed that madness is the exception in individuals but the rule in groups.[120] Effective groups are characterised by cooperation, goodwill and unity of purpose. Yet when it comes to decision making, a cohesive group can become a liability. Psychologists have identified a phenomenon known as 'groupthink' whereby group members stop engaging in rigorous questioning and analysis in order to preserve the pleasant atmosphere. 'Groupthink' is dangerous because it means that reality testing ceases as meetings descend into 'tea and biscuits' chats. When reality testing ceases, a sense of perfect unity descends upon the group. Perfect unity exists because there are no dissenting voices. Since there are no dissenting voices, the group feels invulnerable. Few things are more conducive to risk taking than the conviction that one cannot fail.[120]

'Groupthink' may explain Neville Chamberlain's questionable policy of appeasement. Chamberlain drew most of his support from an inner circle of ministers. This inner circle watched as Hitler's troops invaded one territory after another, reassuring themselves that whatever happened, Britain would have the last word. American naval commanders may also have succumbed to 'groupthink' when they scornfully dismissed a warning that a dawn patrol launched from Japanese aircraft carriers could achieve complete surprise at Pearl Harbor. They assumed that Japan would never dare to precipitate war against a much larger country. Yet the American blockade was fast depriving Japan of cotton, oil and other vital supplies. The diminished mental rigour that affects groups afflicted by 'groupthink' may explain why the naval commanders never imagined that such deprivation might drive Japan to drastic measures. Captain J. B. Earle, the local chief of staff, said 'We considered this point, but somehow or other, we always felt that *"it couldn't happen here"* . . . we didn't believe that the Japanese would take that chance'.[120] Besides, even if Japan did attack, the group assumed that approaching hostile aircraft would be detected and destroyed. Yet this assumption was never tested, despite the doubts of junior naval commanders who were not members of the decision-making group.

Problems, Problems

In theory, the purpose of decision making is to solve problems – once and for all. In practice, in trying to solve problems we frequently end up making matters worse.

Today's problem was yesterday's solution.[121]

Our problem/solution mentality conditions us to believe that we can solve problems just like we can take an aspirin for a headache. Rarely is it so simple. When we intervene in a problem, we risk upsetting the dynamic stability of the situation. More specifically, when we try to impose order *upon* chaos, we risking disturbing the order that exists *within* chaos.[37,122] Imagine a chimpanzees' tea-party. The spectacle appears chaotic as the chimps tip their cups upside down, spill their orange juice and scatter food all over the place. Yet in the midst of all the mess and confusion, the chimps do actually eat their tea, albeit after a fashion. Now imagine a keeper trying to force the chimps to eat their tea nicely. The result would be pandemonium. The point is, intervention adds to chaos whereas if the chimps are left to their own devices the problem of eating actually solves itself. This may be one reason why some business process re-engineering programmes have failed. By trying to reassert control such initiatives end up destroying the self-organisation and responsible autonomy that already exists.

According to the proverb, prevention is better than cure. Yet our anxious efforts to prevent something from happening can create the very situation we were trying to avoid. Imagine two people trying desperately trying to steady an already steady boat.

By tugging frantically at the sails, they end up capsizing the vessel.[122,123] In other words:

A becomes B by avoiding B.

Molière's miser in his play *L'Avare* loses his money by trying to preserve it. The medieval craft guilds were so opposed to the idea of mass production that the owners of the new factories did not even try to negotiate new working practices with them. Instead, they set up business in the new towns that were beyond the power of the guilds.[124] The increasingly anachronistic guilds gradually perished. Yet it was not mass production that destroyed the guilds, but the guilds' implacable determination to avoid any association with mass production.

More recently, we have seen how police efforts to avoid drugs-related violence can actually create it. Although police raids and arrests are intended to curb violence by removing potentially dangerous criminals from the streets, they upset the balance of power in gangland. Suspicions are raised, vengeance is demanded. The resultant tensions and uncertainties are then resolved through shootings and other forms of violence.

*The solution **is** the problem.*

The adage 'operation successful: patient dead' should remind us that the cure can be worse than the disease.[29] Tram lines were ripped out of cities because they were impeding the movement of cars. More recently, bus lanes have been created on some motorways in order to ease congestion. The result is one lane standing virtually empty and two lanes blocked solid with traffic. Likewise, safety devices can actually create danger. The joke in the shipping industry is radar-assisted collision. Autopilots make planes so easy to fly that the problem now is keeping aircrews awake. Train drivers miss red lights because they hear so many safety bells and buzzers in their cabs they cancel them almost automatically.

Some magazine publishers have tried to boost sales by offering gifts on the covers. The solution has become a problem in that publishers end up selling the gift rather than the magazine. Moreover, since the gifts tend to be worth more than the magazine, they can actually harm sales as regular readers desert them in search of more tempting gifts. Publishers have not only discovered that it is an expensive idea but that they end up expending more time and effort on the gifts than on the magazine itself.[125] Thus do organisations become blown off-course.

Inspections are a solution to the problem of questionable standards in schools. Failing schools are instructed to have teachers plan lessons to account for every five minutes. The solution only makes the problem worse by creating stress and destroying all spontaneity and responsiveness.

Although e-mail makes communication easier, it also creates a problem of communication. Communication is, above all, a social exchange involving more than the transmission of words. When people e-mail one another, the opportunity to oil the social wheels more fully is lost. E-mailing deprives us of the information swaps, the whispered exchanges and other essential components of the sense-making process. So too are the non-verbal aspects of the exchange as there is no opportunity to observe and experience the signals, the gestures, the mood, the signs of enthusiasm or hesitation that may say more than the words themselves. The risk is a loss of meaning, a quiet disintegration of relationships that can have far-reaching consequences. Moreover, the very ease of e-mail can create a problem in that it increases the likelihood of people despatching ill-considered and intemperate messages. From July 2000, Safeway's new chief executive, Carlos Criado-Perez, embarked upon implementing a strategy aimed at turning the supermarket chain from an 'also ran' into the UK's fastest-growing grocery chain. The first phase of the cure was the launching of a price war of unprecedented proportions on selected goods in order to get more people into the stores. The operation has been successful in that Safeway now has a million new customers. Whether the patient will survive the treatment over the longer term is another question. Critics have described it as a suicide mission first, because it assumes that shoppers lured into the stores by huge discounts on some goods will pay Safeway's relatively expensive prices for the rest of their shopping. Second, it depends upon new customers continuing to shop at Safeway once the bargains cease.[126]

The Hunter Becomes The Hunted

It was suggested in Chapter 3 that the manner in which we conceptualise a problem determines how we try to solve it. Yet it can be the other way round, that is, instead of decision makers seeking solutions to problems:

The solution determines the problem.

The world is shot with solutions looking for problems to attach themselves to. Decisions can become blown off-course because once a solution finds a problem to attach itself to, the solution changes the problem. A client once invited an architect to lunch.

The client asked the architect what he would like to eat and drink. After the architect had chosen, the client then said, 'No, no, try this, that and the other instead.' When the architect began to look frustrated, the client said, 'this is exactly what you do to me'.

Budgets are a solution to the problem of control. Economists call budget depletion a non-informative loss, that is, by itself it tells the decision maker nothing other than that the budget has been spent. It follows, therefore, that to stop a line of activity solely because the budget is depleted is incorrect because the allocation may have been inadequate in the first place. Yet how often do administrators and financial controllers force us to do precisely that? We worry about decisions that go awry. Yet how much greater are the losses from worthy projects that never see the light of day for no good reason other than there is no more money in the budget?

Winner's Curse

Few things are achieved without will and determination. Yet we can become so absorbed in the pursuit of an ambition that it becomes an obsession. Obsessions are dangerous, not least because they rob us of all sense of proportion. When that happens, it becomes a case of 'must have'.

> *You can have anything you want provided you are prepared to pay too much for it.*

'Must have' sentiments can lead us to cripple ourselves by paying too much for whatever it is that we 'must have'.

The auction for the UK's third-generation mobile phone licences may turn out to be a case in point. The *Financial Times* called it the most expensive poker game in history, a gamble of heroic proportions as companies desperate for additional spectrum bid billions of pounds for the ability to provide broadband services. Yet they were bidding without knowing what the services will look like, or how many people will be prepared to pay a premium for them. In effect, they are buying an option that may never come into the money.[127]

As the bidding for the licences rose, analysts began to mutter 'winner's curse'. Winner's curse occurs because the winning bidder forgets to consider the implications of having a bid higher than that of other bidders. That is, by definition the winner of an auction is bound to pay more for an item than it is worth. As it happened, analysts forecast that the winning contenders might end up paying as much as £3 billion or even £6 billion for the privilege. In fact, the auction raised over £20 billion, the real winner being the government. Moreover, the gavel had only just fallen when the first uncertainty emerged. The government said that it might restrict the use of mobile phones by children on grounds of potential danger to health – an announcement that the government found it convenient to postpone until after the auction – winner's curse indeed.

The Tale of the Boilerman

Decisions are usually a means to an end. What can happen, however, is that the pursuit of an objective becomes an end in itself with deleterious consequences. A local government department decided to close the building over the Christmas holiday period in order to save heating costs. The director was determined that it would happen – or else. After a frantic effort to make the necessary arrangements, and to everyone's surprise, the closure was effected. When staff returned to work early in the New Year they noticed that the building felt pleasantly warm. Of course, in the rush to finalise the arrangements no one remembered to instruct the boilerman to turn off the heating!

Bureaucracy can become an end in itself. One morning as I drove past the small animal hospital of the University of Liverpool, I noticed two veterinary nurses walking a dog – presumably a patient of the hospital. It was a glorious summer's morning, the sun was shining, the trees were resplendent in green, the nurses looked happy, even the dog looked happy. Shortly afterwards I attended a committee meeting. As the discussion droned on I was struck by how remote it seemed from the actual activities of the university – including the two nurses walking the dog. It was as if the real university was going one way and the decision processes another – rather like two parties boring a tunnel destined to miss one another in the middle.

The phenomenon is by no means peculiar to the University of Liverpool. Any moderately complex bureaucracy can become diverted from its mission by the very systems, procedures and cadres of expertise that were intended to propel it along the path to success. Research and development staff are not employed to design exciting and innovative products as such but commercially useful ones. The trouble is, commercially useful products are not always the most exciting. The new Toyota MR2 sports car is exciting, innovative and true to the notion of a sports car which means it has virtually no boot space. Although the new model may reach its sales targets, how many more cars might Toyota have sold if the designers had sacrificed some technical purity for practicality?

Interestingly, the original MR2 launched in the mid-1980s had hardly any boot space either and was subsequently redesigned to make it more practical.

The Icarus Paradox

Until January 1999, Marks & Spencer was the epitome of success. The company prided itself upon the M&S way of doing things, that is, high-quality goods, an exemplary exchange policy. Yet on 2 January 1999 the unthinkable happened. Marks & Spencer issued a profits warning. Shortly afterwards, the share price tumbled. The 'M&S way', that is, no changing rooms, no credit card facilities other than Marks & Spencer's own, no goods on offer other than Marks & Spencer's own brand, was no longer working.

Marks & Spencer had shared the fate of the fabled Icarus of Greek mythology. Icarus was equipped with wax wings that enabled him to soar above the common lot. Icarus flew higher and higher and eventually got so close to the sun that his wings melted and he fell to his death in the Aegean Sea.[128]

What makes us successful can also destroy us.

Just as the power of his wings enabled Icarus to behave with an abandon that eventually destroyed him, the things that make people and organisations successful can precipitate their downfall. Attention to detail becomes obsession with minutiae. Innovation becomes gratuitous invention. Planned careful growth becomes unbridled expansion.

In short, the forces for success become pushed to dangerous extremes. Marks & Spencer's chief executive, Sir Richard Greenbury, had worked his way up from the shopfloor. He knew the business inside out. The proverb teaches that a good horse requires the master's eye. For a long time, Marks & Spencer benefited from Greenbury's eye. No detail was too small for his attention even to the extent of approving the colours, price, and quality of every new range of jumpers, socks, shirts and so forth.

Eventually, however, attention to detail translated into autocracy and closed-door management. The result was to discourage creativity and innovation, 'Merchandising departments became demoralised when they tried to do new things. It was a long process .... They started ... thinking, "We're the biggest retailer in the UK so we must be doing it right"'.[129] Likewise, a former personnel officer found working for Marks & Spencer a frustrating experience: 'You were just handed a package and told to get on with it.' Inside the package was the 'M&S way,' the tried and tested formula.

Interestingly the road to ruin is frequently strewn with flowers. This is because initial efforts to extend success usually work. The trouble is, success then confirms our feeling about what works thus binding us with even greater certainty to the tried and tested approach. In organisations, previously successful systems, routines, and programmes then become set in stone. The formula for success is implemented automatically and, above all, *unquestioningly*. In short, 'continuity triumphs'.[128]

A Runaway Bull

Project Taurus exemplifies how common sense can produce bizarre results.[89,130] Taurus was an IT venture sponsored by the London Stock Exchange. It was intended to pave the way for speeding up share transactions by removing paper from the system. The securities industry spent £400 million in preparation for Taurus and the London Stock Exchange £80 million on development costs. Taurus was staffed by a powerful team of experts, led by one of the best project directors in the country. Every detail of the design and construction was approved by the securities industry. Yet in the end it was all for nothing. On 11 March 1993, after three years of intensive effort, the project was cancelled.

Taurus was cancelled because it became so large and so complicated that it could not be built within an acceptable timescale or budget. Significantly, no one *decided* that Taurus should be large or complicated. Indeed, the original Taurus design known as Taurus 1 could have been built within six months using tried and tested technology. So what went wrong?

To a point, consultation with interested parties results in better decision making. This is because consultation usually means decisions are better informed, and because involving others in the process helps to create commitment. Yet as the London Stock Exchange discovered to its cost, it is possible to have too much of a good thing.

Taurus was a textbook example of consultation. The Stock Exchange made every effort to ensure that the securities industry had a proper say in what the system would look like. The securities industry is very diverse, however, and everyone wanted something different. The former chief executive of the Stock Exchange, Peter Rawlins, describes what happened:

> There were at least thirty committees connected with Taurus. . . .
> Most of them had nothing to do with the Exchange but they all
> seemed to have a bearing on it. They were springing up all over the

City.... The committee of London clearing bankers had a committee on Taurus, so did the registrars, so did Snoops and Jones. You add them up and everybody was giving input to Taurus.

The Stock Exchange had allowed two months for the Taurus design to be finalised. Two years later, the securities industry was still arguing over it. Hopes ran high every time the technical team presented a new proposal, 'Oh that's very interesting. We quite like that,' said the committee. Then as the implications dawned, 'Good Lord! Oh no.'

The Tragedy of the Commons

The problem with Taurus was that while part of the securities industry stood to gain from abolishing the old paper-driven system, other sectors of the industry made their living from it. Eventually, the Bank of England intervened to mediate between conflicting factions. The bank suggested that Taurus should be built without seriously harming existing business interests.

Ironically, the very principle that enabled an agreement to be reached ultimately destroyed Taurus. More specifically, Taurus exemplifies 'the tragedy of the commons'. The commons were areas of land offering free grazing rights. Such freedom made it logical for every peasant to graze as many cattle as possible on the land. This seemingly beneficial policy led inexorably to disaster because it locked individuals into a system that compelled them to increase their herds, 'Without limits – in a world that is limited.... Freedom in a commons brings ruin to all'.[131]

The Bank of England's suggestion of building the system around existing business interests locked every sector of the securities industry into pursuing its own interests. The result was collective ruin:

> There were multiple meetings at multiple levels with different constituencies who would have to interface with Taurus and were constantly impacting upon its structure and design: 'We are the custodian community and we would need this sort of information and we would input in this way.' So they, the technical team were constantly saying, 'OK, well we will have to recode and redo to cope with that.' Then the software manufacturers would say, 'Ah, but then you have to make this change and you have to make that change and you have to interface these things that are now from different suppliers.' So the complexity just grew and grew. [A member of the Taurus monitoring group.]

Once the securities industry saw what Taurus might look like they began demanding changes, even down to such details as the number of characters per line or the number of lines in an address box. Consequently the requirements never stood still. The result was chaotic as one programmer recalls, 'More records came in, some went out, things on record changed, the description of what that record was used for might grow. That process happened too many times. . . . It used to drive us crazy.'

'It Was a Crucial Decision, It Was the Wrong One'

The one thing that the securities industry did agree on was the timescale. Eighteen months was the maximum they would tolerate. It was an ambitious deadline to say the least. In order to meet it the technical team decided to buy a software package known as Vista to supply part of the functionality. Vista is a good package. A rule of thumb in software engineering suggests, however, that if the requisite alterations are likely to exceed 20%, it is better to build from scratch.[132] A member of the Taurus monitoring group said:

> I have been building systems for twenty-five years and you get a feel.... I was dead against buying American software and changing it because I believed that it would need to be changed far too much. All these off-the-shelf packages are fine if you just tinker round the edges. If you have to re-engineer them to anything more than 20% ... you always have to travel.

'It was a crucial decision,' said a member of the technical team, 'it was the wrong one.'

Indeed, it soon became apparent that the task of re-engineering Vista was more complex than anticipated. Another problem was the constantly changing requirements. A member of the technical team said:

> Like all these things, they have a product that does a certain task. It has some similarities but when you examined it in any level of detail, it wasn't really there. Probing it more and more, we realised how way off-beam this was going to be.... We said, 'what is Vista going to do out of this totality of an outline design we think we might have got?' .... We talked to Vista about various things and: 'Well, we can't do that. We don't handle it. Anyway it doesn't work very well....'

Building Taurus became synonymous with re-engineering Vista. Ultimately, the solution became the problem. 'It was like one of those toys you bash with a hammer,' said a member of the technical team. 'You bash down one peg down, another flies up at you. Bash that peg down again, another one flies up.'

The estimated cost of re-engineering Vista was £4 million. By the time the project was cancelled in March 1993, the Stock Exchange had spent over £14 million and the task was still far from complete.

Brilliant and Daft

The story of Taurus shows what can happen when a decision becomes an end in itself. By mid-1991 it had become clear that the task of re-engineering Vista was going to be much more difficult than had been envisaged. Moreover, when the Taurus design was finally agreed, certain parts of the system were marked 'to be decided later'. In mid-1991, the government changed the goalposts by insisting upon elaborate security arrangements. In addition, the Stock Exchange had assumed that legalities would be straightforward involving only 'five or six pages of mechanics'. Yet Taurus proposed to dispense with paper. In law, paper is important because it is the means whereby possession is evidenced. As the complexities of dividends, rights issues, Scots law, nominee accounts and 'entitlement' as distinct from 'ownership' unfolded, the 'five or six pages of mechanics' evolved into 200 pages of almost unfathomable clauses and sub-clauses. 'This is what really scuppered us,' said a member of the technical team. 'We thought we could deliver on those regulations, but I don't think anyone really understood them.'

It was at that point in mid-1991 that Taurus should have been stopped. It is a matter of record that Taurus was not stopped. Instead, as the timetable slipped further and further, the technical team began working long hours in an effort to deliver the project.

For their part, the Taurus monitoring group demanded more information from the technical team in an effort to tighten their grip on the project. A member of the monitoring group recounts:

> You'd say, 'How many of these issues have you resolved?' And they would say, 'We have resolved all of them'.
>
> And there was another page that was risks: 'What risks are you running?' There was a long list of risks ... Every meeting they'd come with this chart and that chart and they would say, 'We have resolved all these issues, and now we have got another set of issues ...'
>
> So there was lots of progress from where you were at the last meeting. However, when you sat back and said, 'Are we any closer to the end?'
>
> 'We-ll, not really.'
>
> And that was really what was happening .... You knew people were working hard and they were getting work completed and putting it behind them and then they discovered there was a whole set of other things.

The real problem was that the project had evolved further and further away from its original simple conception because of all the people who had interfered with it.

As 1991 shaded into 1992, the pressure to deliver Taurus intensified. The Taurus monitoring group told the technical team:

> Now you *have* to meet the next date. 'Why?' Because this is an issue of credibility. People out there are spending money preparing their systems for Taurus in anticipation of those dates. [Member of the Taurus monitoring group.]

Notice what is happening here. Attention has become riveted to meeting the next deadline. Such was the sheer determination to finish no one stopped to ask whether it could be finished. A member of the Taurus monitoring group said:

> In every project there will always be people who say 'I wouldn't have done it that way' or 'I would have done it differently' or even 'we shouldn't be doing this at all.' We saw that it was going to be difficult to deliver Taurus, but our focus was on getting it done.

By late 1992, almost three years after construction had commenced and with no sign of Taurus emerging, the chief executive was growing impatient. He decided to take a closer look at the project. Consultants Arthur Andersen were briefed to investigate two questions, namely:

(1) Is Taurus compatible with the general trading infrastructure? and

(2) Are you confident you can operate Taurus when it is handed over to you?'

Andersen's report was devastating:

(1) 'There is no operating system. There is no centre. It is not designed let alone built.'

(2) 'Are we going to be able to operate it? Well, here is a list of fifteen things we have reservations about.'

Although the technical team had openly and deliberately started building the outer parts of the system first in order to maintain the commitment of the securities' industry the significance of that decision only became clear to the chief executive as he read Andersen's report. Taurus was a distributed system of 500 computers communicating with each other. In order to do that, the system required a unified architecture. Now the chief executive realised there was nothing in the middle. It was like trying to build a house by digging the foundations last.[132] No one in the City had realised what was happening because the technical team had employed a highly sophisticated simulation harness to test the system, 'Very sexy,' he said, 'I had rocket scientists working for me.'

Time had also caught up with the project. A member of the monitoring group said 'There was the emerging knowledge that much of the code that had been written wasn't usable. It had been built up over time, changed, built, changed, built, changed – much of it to do with the changing legal framework and security algorithms.'

Andersen's report also revealed how one sub-optimal decision can force another. As planned, Taurus would have been built round the Stock Exchange's Talisman system in place since 1979, 'Disaster!' said the chief executive, 'It was the right decision at the time. It was taken because they thought they would try and get the whole thing done in seven months.'

The decision to build Taurus around Talisman was inspired by the ambitious timescales. One sub-optimal decision then forced another, one that was as logical as it was absurd:

> Let's do it quick and cheerful . . . so, on line system. On line? The boys had been spending three years buggering about with it to make it a batch system so that it was compatible with 1970s technology. It's brilliant! And daft!

The result is a 'paradox of consequences' whereby the powerful team of technical experts assembled by the Stock Exchange to build Taurus ends up devoting its ingenuity to turn a 'state of the art' system into one that is obsolete, hence brilliant *and* daft. Andersen's report revealed that Taurus would require another two years and another £90 million to finish. Meanwhile the securities industry would need to stand down their entire teams while the Stock Exchange completed the central architecture. Moreover, once the architecture was finished there was no guarantee that existing work carried out in preparation for Taurus would be usable. A member of the monitoring group said:

> I think anybody listening to that would have to say, 'Well, maybe that's £120 million and four years.' There isn't another £90 million worth of benefit in the project. There probably never was anyway. Now that's pretty straightforward: that decision makes itself.

On 11 March 1993, the 360 members of the technical team who had worked so hard to deliver the Taurus were summoned to an 'off-site' meeting and declared redundant. Simultaneously, the chief executive resigned. Nothing was salvaged from the project. 'That's the sadness that's left,' said a member of the technical team afterwards. 'We did so much that was good. Then it got wiped out in a day.'

Everyone became so absorbed in finishing Taurus, 'Let's get the bloody thing done and behind us,' that a vicious circle ensued characterised by the diligent bashing down of pegs. Research suggests that when organisations begin to fail their first response is to tighten their routines and monitoring procedures. The same happened to Taurus. As the difficulties intensified the decision makers' frame of vision narrowed. A member of the monitoring group said:

It's easy to look back and say, 'Why didn't you see it all the time?' Well, most disasters look obvious in hindsight. When you are in the middle of it and your objective is to get to the end you take each issue and you try to deal with it, and then another issue and you try to deal with it, and another issue and you try to deal with it. . . . It is only when the issues accumulate that you finally say, 'When is this going to end?'

Chance Has Got Nothing To Do With It

Finally, an important theme of this book is that we cannot predict the future. It is always the unexpected that happens. That is not the same, however, as saying that the unexpected always happens by chance. The unexpected can happen simply because common-sense styles of thinking blind us to less obvious possibilities.

Common sense might suggest that regiments who experience high casualty levels are most vulnerable to collapse. Yet in the First World War, it was the worst knocked-about regiments that retained their fighting spirit the longest.[133] Common sense might suggest that rape victims who escape serious physical injury are relatively fortunate. Yet might they suffer more mental anguish than victims who are visibly injured?

Common sense thinking conditions us to see cause and effect. Indeed, sometimes the relationship is straightforward. For example, a direct link exists between poor sanitation and diseases like typhus and cholera. It is not what common sense reveals that matters, however, but what it conceals. In the First World War ostensibly the German High Command surrendered because the morale of the troops had collapsed. Or was it because the High Command looked like surrendering that morale collapsed?[133]

The ultimate function of prophesy is not to predict the future but to create it.

At the end of the Second World War fortune tellers did a roaring trade in the ruins of Berlin, most of it from women desperate to know whether their partners would return. The allure of fortune tellers is that they offer certainty even though their predictions are subsequently contradicted by events.

What is interesting is that some predictions are uncannily accurate. Fortune tellers know that the mere suggestion that something is *going* to happen can make it happen. Tell someone who is terminally ill that they have six months to live and that may be exactly how long they survive.[123] If a horoscope tells someone to expect a disappointment, they may very well behave in a manner calculated to guarantee failure.

The purpose of this chapter has been to suggest that common sense can produce unexpected results particularly when taken to extremes. What may appear as helplessness in the face of disaster may be what decision makers have created for themselves. The same applies to prediction. We can cause something to happen that would not have happened but for the fact that we predicted it was *going* to happen. During the petrol crisis of 2000 the merest hint of an impending fuel shortage sent motorists dashing to the pumps to top up their tanks, thereby creating the very shortage that had been forecast. Every trade has its tricks. Fortune telling may be no exception.

Chapter 9

Riding a tiger: escalation in decision making

He who rides a tiger can never dismount. (Chinese proverb)

In 1990 a small group of environmental activists took to the streets of the London Borough of Hackney. The purpose of their mission was to undermine the carefully crafted public image of the hamburger chain known as McDonald's by distributing leaflets entitled *What's Wrong With McDonald's*. According to McDonald's the so-called 'factsheet':

> Alleged that . . . McDonald's causes evictions of small farmers in the Third World, destroys rain forests, lies about its use of recycled paper, misleads the public about the nutritional value of their food, sells food high in sugar and salt to encourage an addiction to it, uses gimmicks to cover up that the food is of low quality, targets most of their advertising at children, are responsible for the inhumane treatment of animals, sells hamburgers liable to cause food poisoning, [and] pay bad wages.[134]

McDonald's demanded an apology from those involved. All but two of the activists duly complied. The two who decided to resist were Helen Steel and Tom Morris. McDonald's then issued a writ for libel against Steel and Morris alleging that it had been 'Greatly damaged in its trading reputation' and 'brought into public scandal, odium and contempt' by the '"fact sheet"', the contents of which the corporation 'vigorously denied'.[134]

Seven years later, on 19 June 1997, after the longest libel trial in legal history including 313 days of evidence and submissions, 40 000 pages of documents and witness statements, the court delivered its verdict. The defendants, Helen Steel and David Morris, were fined £60 000 for libel. However, the court found against McDonald's for 'exploiting children', 'cruelty to animals', deceiving customers about the nutritional qualities of their food, and paying 'low wages'.[134] Three days later, on 21 June, a 'McLibel Victory Day of Action' saw no fewer than 400 000 of the offending leaflets distributed outside 500 of McDonald's 750 UK restaurants, and solidarity protests in other countries.

If McDonald's had ignored the leaflets, the damage to their reputation would have been relatively slight. By reacting to the provocation, however, McDonald's took a marginalised protest and made it relevant. In trying to protect its reputation, McDonald's precipitated a public relations disaster.

Would McDonald's have pursued Steel and Morris if they could have foreseen the outcome? Would United Artists have commissioned the film *Heaven's Gate* if they had known that the decision would put them out of business? Would investors have been quite so eager to acquire shares in Eurotunnel if they had known what lay ahead?

The Chinese proverb 'He who rides a tiger can never dismount' warns us that once we become involved in a course of action, there may be no turning back. This chapter explains how we can become entangled in an escalatory spiral and end up pouring time, money and emotional energy into a lost cause.

Mounting a Tiger

A feature of many escalation scenarios is that they start small. That is, they begin as limited commitments involving few resources and minimal risk. McDonald's did not begin by instructing teams of libel lawyers and issuing writs; they merely sought an apology. Likewise, Roger (a pseudonym), the owner of a unisex hair-dressing salon, decided to engage a part-time assistant. There was only one applicant for the job, an 18-year-old female. Roger invited her to work for a day 'to see how we got on'. Roger was un-impressed as the applicant was clearly ill-equipped to work on women's hair and barely competent as a barber. Reservations notwithstanding, he decided to employ her. Roger said:

> With gents' hairdressing [the customers] don't give a sod ... any-thing thereabouts will do ... I did think [that] so long as she gets through the volume at a cheap enough price, we might come up with a reasonable turnover of people to cover the wages, holiday pay and so on.

After the first day, Roger's doubts deepened. The employee was slow and appeared to lack confidence. Roger said 'I thought, I'm not too sure. Well, as long as she is only doing the guys [men] it will do until Christmas.'

Shortly before Christmas another part-time employee left. Roger's new employee then pleaded with Roger to convert her post to full-time working. 'She made for the job,' said Roger, 'Please give me a few more days then I have got a full-time job. I am employed.'

Roger had his doubts but agreed to the request, 'It was the convenience of her ...' he said, '[Besides] there are so many poor people in this job, you just think you are not going to get anything better.'

Building a clientele normally takes a year, though a good stylist may accomplish it in 6 months. Roger's new employee, however, never exceeded 50% working capacity. 'I kept giving it a week and then another week,' said Roger. Moreover, as time went on, Roger regularly saw his new employee turning potential clients away:

Say she had an appointment at mid-day and somebody walked in the door at quarter to [twelve] and said 'Could I have my hair cut?', She'd say, 'We-ll, I have got someone coming in shortly.' Then the [mid-day appointment] would come in at ten past [twelve], so she'd spent the last 25 minutes doing nothing.

Roger had several talks with his employee about her continuing failure to build a clientele but got nowhere:

I said 'We are not doing enough people ...' We actually looked at the hours worked and for the eight hour day she was working four hours. She said, 'Well I can't drag them [customers] off the streets can I?' I said, 'No, but when they do come in you could leap up a bit and be a bit more excited ... give them a card with your name on it and say you look forward to seeing them again. She said 'Oh, I don't agree with all that.'

This was in July. In September the employee requested a month's holiday. Roger decided to sack her but changed his mind because it seemed unfair. Roger said 'Every penny she had was vital towards this holiday. So it was *that*, with all the inconvenience.'

Finally, one year later in November Roger told his employee she must find another job, 'That's it,' he said. 'You've had long enough now.' The employee, however, pleaded with Roger to change his mind. She said 'Can't I stay awhile, till Christmas? I will try and do a few more people. I am just building up.' Roger agreed to keep her until Christmas, 'And that's it,' he said. As Christmas approached, however, Roger changed his mind, 'On Christmas Eve you can't just give somebody their wage ... and say, "Happy Christmas and we won't see you again"'.

The two finally parted company on the first week of January. Meanwhile, the business had suffered. Roger said 'It was just very, very convenient to have her there in support even though she wasn't actually doing anything.... I was letting myself down, letting the business down, letting the clientele down.'

It is easy to say that Roger should have sacked the employee when it became apparent that she was failing. The point is, having offered her employment, Roger felt obliged to persist until he could well and truly justify her dismissal. Roger said:

> She was supposed to start at nine, but she called off at the super-market for a bottle of water so it was always five past nine before she arrived. Then, because of all this water, she was always going to the loo [toilet]. So I wasn't only losing money on her work, it was costing me a fortune because she used so much bloody water. She went to the toilet so often you could deduce when she left from my water bills ... And the amount of toilet paper she used ... Instead of saying 'What is all this about?' you let it go till you are actually noticing toilet paper.[135]

Roger's mistake was to invite the employee to work for a day. Although in theory the invitation did not commit Roger to anything, in practice it proved to be the thin end of a wedge as it gave the candidate a 'foot in the door'. Roger would have been better advised to have kept his distance by administering what is known as a trade test with a promise to notify the candidate later.

Hidden Depths

Although strictly speaking nothing is inevitable, escalation scenarios are characterised by an air of inevitability. This is because when a venture fails to turn out as expected, we may well discover that our only hope of turning matters around is to go on committing resources.

Karen was a successful business owner. When Bob (both pseudonyms), her husband, was made redundant the couple decided to open another shop selling high-class baby clothes. They used Rob's redundancy money to convert a spare room in Karen's existing premises and to buy stock. The town supports a number of speciality shops though two similar businesses have failed. Before reading any further, pause for a moment and consider whether the venture is a good idea. What do you see as the risks involved?

The shop opened in November in time to catch the Christmas trade. When the coupled locked up on Christmas Eve, however, hardly an item of baby clothes had been sold. Two months then passed with still hardly a sale. 'You have to give these things time,' Karen told Bob, 'people don't know we're here.' The remainder of Bob's redundancy money was then spent on advertising. The campaign failed. 'We spent loads of money,' said Karen, 'It didn't bring one customer.'

March arrived and agents began calling for orders for spring and summer clothes. Karen ordered a shipment of goods on credit as the couple were unable to pay cash. Under the terms of the credit agreement, Karen and Bob were obliged to pay £500 a fortnight to the clothing company.

Bob became increasingly fractious and depressed at the continuing failure of the venture. In May, six months after opening the shop, Bob eloped leaving Karen to cope with two businesses and two small children. Karen was unable to maintain a reliable service. Consequently, her existing business suffered as customers drifted away, diminishing her income and the means of paying her creditors.

Two months later Bob returned and the couple were reconciled. Shortly afterwards, a notice appeared in the shop window announcing a 'closing down' sale. The plan was to sell off the stock at cost price and close down the business by the end of the month. July came and went, however, and still no one bought. Months passed while the couple waited for customers. Meanwhile they struggled to meet the repayments on their non-returnable stock. Karen said:

> We're robbing Peter to pay Paul. What I'm making, working all week, is going to pay bills. We're in debt. We spent so much on that shop and all it's done is to drag this one [Karen's business] down .... They [the agents] could take it back and sell but we'd still owe them money. It's what they could do to us.

Four months later the couple were in a desperate plight. Still hardly an item had been sold. Moreover, by now the rent and payments to the clothing company were in arrears. It could only be a matter of time before the creditors acted. 'So,' said Karen, 'I don't know what's going to happen.'

Karen and Bob's mistake was to order a shipment of goods on credit. Again it's easy to say 'I would never have done that'. Although with hindsight the couple should have cut their losses in March, caught up in the pressures of the moment it seemed that their only hope of giving the decision a chance to work was to commit more resources to the venture, thus compounding the risk.

Finally, one weekend, the couple quarrelled. The decisive moment was when Karen said:

> We're staying open, paying rent, rates, electricity, taking a couple of quid a day . . . just to see the agents get their money. It's their fault we're in this mess . . . for sending us all this stock.

Notice what happens here. We saw in Chapter 2 that all meaning and understanding comes from looking backwards. When we look back we can choose to see what we want to see. When Karen looks back she sees quite clearly who is to blame! According to Karen their present misfortunes have been visited upon them by the agents who supplied the goods on credit. Blaming the agents may be irrational but it serves three important purposes. First, it is a form of ego-defensiveness in that it means that Karen and Bob avoid taking responsibility for their present predicament. Second, shifting the blame allows the couple to avoid destructive recriminations and concentrate upon dealing with the impending crisis. The third purpose served by this irrational outburst is that the subsequent decision to close down the shop and to break the contract by sending the clothes back becomes surrounded by an air of moral rectitude. Why should they stay open paying rent, rates and so forth just to see the agents get their money?

Returning to the subject of escalation, the lesson of Karen and Bob's story is that what may seem like a limited commitment involving minimal risk can have far-reaching consequences. The problem is, the possible consequences only start to emerge when the decision fails to turn out as expected. McDonald's may have assumed that since Steel and Morris were not entitled to legal aid, they would change their minds about offering an apology once they received a letter from McDonald's lawyers requiring them to prove every one of their accusations against the company.

Steel and Morris had other ideas, however. After receiving the McDonald's letter, Morris spent twenty days on the telephone in an effort to produce the requisite evidence:

> They [Steel and Morris] had three weeks.... The task was enormous. Not only did they have to find ex-employees and people with first-hand experience of working in the corporation and persuade them to give evidence on their behalf, they had to find experts in every area from nutrition to diet, disease, employment, the rain forests, animal welfare, even advertising techniques and child psychology.... The response was tremendous ... in three weeks they had collected sixty-five witness statements from a dozen countries.... The bundle they exchanged with McDonald's solicitors on the day of the deadline was the basis of the case against the corporation.... 'It was a mountain to climb, but people climb mountains,' said Morris.[134]

The McDonald's legal team were apparently visibly surprised that they could get the signed statements together on time. 'Instead of being a legal walkover, as the corporation might have expected, it was becoming clear that there would be a full fight. We began to be taken seriously,' said Morris.[134]

When the United States first intervened in Vietnam the decision makers had no intention of becoming involved in a full-scale war. Once American soldiers began to get killed, however, it became necessary to deploy more troops in order to justify becoming involved in the first place.

Promises, Promises

Alternatively, some escalation scenarios begin with bright promises. We saw in Chapter 5 how vividness effects can induce myopic vision and blind us to the risks involved in a particular course of action. United Artists were ecstatic when they contracted Michael Cimino to produce the film *Heaven's Gate*. Cimino's previous film, *The Deer Hunter*, had been a huge box-office success and *Heaven's Gate* promised to repeat history. Believing that they could not fail with Cimino in charge, United Artists agreed to all his conditions including complete artistic freedom and control over the making of the film and other onerous terms. The decision was a disaster because Cimino locked the film away while it was being made. It was only when the project was well over budget and behind schedule that United Artists realised that *Heaven's Gate* was unwatchable.[136]

In order to get off the drawing board a venture must command support. In order to do this, it must promise much. Although all projections are guesses, what can happen is that intelligent guesses degenerate into outlandish optimism. Estimates of costs are pared down, timescales are shortened, projected revenues rise until the venture makes economic sense. For example, when planners say that Manchester's new tram line extension will carry 45 million passengers a year, what they really mean it *had better* carry that number of passengers if the project is to be financially viable.

The trouble is that we can easily lose sight of the amount of tinkering. Consequently, our plans and prognostications can become increasingly detached from reality without realising it. Moreover, when reality begins to contradict our hopeful forecasts, we may end up revising our projections so that they become even more optimistic in order to maintain a semblance of rationality. World trade fairs have an unhappy history. Only a minority have broken even, far less made a profit. When the Canadian government began planning 'Expo 86' in 1980, the estimated cost was $80 million. A crucial factor in the equation was the projected number of visitors, that is, 12.5 million. This figure assumed that 'local residents will exhibit a very high propensity to attend the event on a repeated basis.'[137] By 1984 the estimated cost had risen to over $140 million, prompting the Canadian government to announce that any losses would be compensated for by increased sales of lottery tickets. No mention was made of how those sales would be achieved. Moreover, in order to balance the books, attendance estimates were boosted to 28 million, that is, almost every man, woman and child in Canada.[137] Likewise, when the Millennium Dome failed to live up to expectations the projected number of visitors was revised from 12 million to 8 million. In fact, the actual number of visitors in 2000 was about 6.5 million, that is, significantly below the initial estimate – far less 12 million.

What is interesting about such revisions is that although they are usually complete fiction, everyone subscribes to the fantasy. In short, we believe because we *want* to believe.

All is Human

We want to believe because once we become identified with a decision our personal credibility is at stake. History is rich in examples of bloody deeds done by decision makers convinced that what they were doing was right. Protestants knew it was right to burn Catholics at the stake. Catholics were equally certain that it was right to burn Protestants. Indeed most of us would rather be seen to be right than wrong and sometimes we will go to any lengths to prove it.

One reason why the mass murderer Peter Sutcliffe, known as the Yorkshire Ripper, eluded detection for as long as he did was that the hunt for him became tinged with vanity. 'It's between him and me,' declared George Oldfield, the assistant chief constable in charge of the case. Oldfield worked fourteen hours a day, seven days a week on the case but Sutcliffe eluded him. Indeed, Oldfield's obsession may have caused him to miss important clues as to the killer's identity. His attitude certainly did not help because it devalued the rest of the police force. In contrast, when Oldfield was eventually removed from the case, his successor stressed that 'The odds [of an arrest] are on a plain copper making a routine enquiry'. As we shall see later in this chapter, that is exactly how Sutcliffe was caught.[138]

It is not every councillor who, like the Bastard in *King John*, will say to their hierarchical superior:

But if thou be feart to hear the worst,
Then let the worst unheard fall on your head.

As decision makers we are inherently reluctant to hear the worst. When Thomas Telford was a young and unknown engineer, the parish council commissioned him to investigate a leak from the vestry roof. Telford reported that the problem was serious. The church was badly built and the whole of the north side-wall was showing signs of movement, hence the dripping water. The parish council refused to listen. Indignantly, they informed Telford that they were not in the business of providing work for him and his engineering friends. In that case, retorted Telford, he advised the council to move into the churchyard for he could not guarantee the safety of the building. Shortly after refusing to hear the worst, the worst fell about the parish councillors' heads as they ended up running for their lives when the building suddenly collapsed.[139]

As human beings, we have an astonishing capacity to believe that things are better than they really are or even to see things that are not there at all if it suits us. When cheap textile imports began to corner the UK market in the early 1960s the millowners ignored the writing on the wall, 'no cause for alarm' they said. More recently, the UK banks were initially reluctant to believe that companies like First Direct posed any threat to their business. McDonald's executives may have believed that Steel and Morris would eventually give up the unequal contest despite mounting evidence suggesting otherwise.

Recall, we believe because we want to believe. One way we have of sustaining self-serving beliefs is to see and hear what we want to see and hear. As decision makers we have an almost uncanny ability to seize upon information that supports our hopes while downplaying or even ignoring potentially disquieting information. Moreover, since we tried to process information unconsciously we may not realise that we are actually convincing ourselves that it is worth persisting with a failing course of action because things are actually not that bad after all, and besides, everything will come right in the end. Like players working a slot machine, we feed in another coin and pull the handle confident that the next coin will surely 'do the trick'. When that fails we feed in another and then another in the absolute certainty that success is close.[140]

Our capacity for self-deception can exert itself in subtle ways. Research by psychologists suggests that managers bias their performance appraisals in favour of employees whom they were personally responsible for selecting.[141] It is as if they unconsciously say to themselves, 'I chose the person so they must be good'.

Incidentally, such bias may work in reverse. That is, if we are unhappy about a decision we may look for evidence of failure to prove to ourselves and to other people that we were right.[140] All is indeed human.

Keeping up Appearances

Even when failure becomes well and truly apparent we may feel driven to persist in order to keep up appearances. It would have been unthinkable to have closed the Millennium Dome before the end of 2000 even though it was obvious months earlier that expectations would not be met. Relatedly, by early autumn 1999 it was clear that hotel bookings for the millennium celebrations were far fewer than expected. Some hotel chains halved their exorbitant prices. Others, however, preferred to see empty rooms rather than incur the ignominy of bowing to the market.

Peter Sutcliffe's murderous career was also facilitated by West Yorkshire police's refusal to admit to a possible mistake. More specifically, the police published extracts from letters apparently written by the killer and a tape recording apparently of his voice. The letters and tape were given enormous publicity. Samples of the handwriting were posted on advertising hoardings. Extracts from the tape were played out at football matches and on radio and television. Yet still the killer remained at large.

The author of the letters claimed seven victims. Shortly after the letter was received, however, the police discovered the body of Yvonne Pearson hidden under a settee on a patch of waste ground. Pearson had been reported missing two months earlier in January 1978. Most of Sutcliffe's previous victims were prostitutes and Pearson had been due to appear in court to answer charges of soliciting. Moreover, Pearson had suffered massive head injuries similar to those inflicted on other women whose deaths had been linked to Sutcliffe. The discovery of Pearson's body strongly suggested that the letters and tapes were hoaxes. That is, the author made no reference to an eighth victim because he was unaware of the existence of Pearson's body.

Besides, the intense publicity campaign ought to have led rapidly to the killer's arrest. Despite those doubts the police continued to insist that letters and tapes were genuine. Sutcliffe subsequently killed another six women and seriously injured another two. Significantly when the press demanded that Scotland Yard be called in, West Yorkshire police allegedly replied 'Why should we? They haven't caught their own Ripper yet'.[138]

Then, in January 1981 two uniformed police officers ('plain cop-pers') on vice patrol in Sheffield's red light district noticed that the number plates on a parked car appeared to be false. When they approached the car they discovered that it contained a prostitute and a man. The officers then questioned the man about the num-ber plates and ascertained that they were indeed false. The man (Sutcliffe) then asked if he could urinate behind a bush before accompanying the police officers to the station. Having handed Sutcliffe over, the officers thought no more of the incident. The following evening, however, one of them, Sergeant Bob Ring, came back on duty. He learned that Sutcliffe was still being questioned:

Acting on a hunch he returned to the scene of the arrest. In a pile of leaves near the spot where Sutcliffe had apparently urinated, Bob Ring found a ball-pein hammer and a knife.

Confronted with this evidence ... Peter Sutcliffe began to tell a different story. An horrific, unbelievable story.[138]

Hell Hath No Fury

Desire for revenge is powerfully conducive to escalation. Revenge is sweet because it restores our self-esteem.[142] Since self-esteem is worth more than money, no price may be too high to pay if it enables us to achieve restoration. Desire for revenge explains why people sometimes pay ridiculous prices at auctions. Outbidding a rival may be ruinously expensive but feels worth while because success restores the individual's self-esteem. More importantly, what happens when the leaders of armies and mega-corporations feel slighted? Did General Montgomery propel the British army to disaster at Arnhem out of a sense of pique having been denied overall command? Does desire for revenge explain some of the potentially suicidal price wars between supermarkets, airlines and newspapers? Interestingly shortly after Camelot's contract to run the National Lottery was renewed, the losing contender Sir Richard Branson, announced that he was setting up a team to investigate the possibility of establishing a lottery in competition with Camelot. If Branson's idea succeeded that would be revenge indeed.

Money Sunk and Lost

The shareholders of the former Manchester Sheffield and Lincolnshire (MSL) railway company described their unprofitable investment decision as 'money, sunk and lost'. Any hopes they may have had of a recovery when the MSL was subsequently merged to form part of the Great Central railway were dashed as the Great Central turned out to be an even worse loss maker, prompting shareholders to dub their investment 'gone completely'.

Investors in the beleaguered MSL would have been wise to sell their shares while they were still worth something instead of watching their investment dwindle away. 'I don't understand it,' said a stockbroker, 'clients sell their good shares and hang on to the rubbish.'

The broker may have been thinking of Jim, a private investor who bought shares in a company called Spring Ram. Jim said 'I thought I'd play dangerously. I decided to take a risk and it looked like a good one.'

Jim bought 1400 shares at £1.45p each, making an investment of just over £2000. Three days later, however, Spring Ram's share price plummeted to 80p. The following week it rose to £1.20.

Within days, however, the company issued a profits warning and the share price plummeted to 48p. Jim's original investment of £2030 was now worth only £672 – 'money sunk and lost'.

The crash revealed that Spring Ram's apparent success owed something to its accountancy procedures. For instance, sales were recorded when customers placed orders and not when they actually took delivery of goods. Depreciation charges had been modest. Development costs had been treated as assets. 'How anyone can make a profit out of kitchen furniture in the middle of a recession when no one's buying houses is beyond me,' said Jim. 'But that's with hindsight.'

When asked why he had kept the shares Jim replied, 'What – at 48p when I paid 145p! If it [the company] sinks without trace so be it.' Spring Ram did eventually sink and Jim's investment was 'gone completely'.

Intellectually, past investments, be they time money or other resources, are irrelevant to decisions concerning the future. The economically correct decision is to take whatever course of action promises the best return on investment. Jim should have cut his losses and invested the remaining monies elsewhere. Emotionally, it is a different story. Jim's emotional attachment to his original £2000 prevents him from acknowledging the situation for what it has become, that is, £672 left to invest.

As human beings we hate loss. The pain of losing a £20 note measures higher on the emotional Richter scale than the pleasure of finding the same amount. Indeed, the pain of loss can drive us to recklessness. Experiments by psychologists show that faced with a choice between accepting a definite loss and the possibility of incurring a much greater loss later on, we tend to become *risk seeking.* Imagine a day at the races. You took £100 betting money with you. You have lost £95 on unsuccessful bets leaving you with just £5. The last race is about to be run. Which option would you prefer?

(a) Bet on the 3 to 1 favourite, or
(b) Bet on a 20 to 1 'long shot'.

Most people would take the highly risky decision of betting on a 'long shot' in a last-ditch effort to recoup their losses. In other words we throw away the chance of emerging with something, preferring all or nothing, usually to end up with nothing. (Incidentally, experiments suggest the phenomenon works in reverse. That is, faced with a choice between a certain gain and a possible bigger gain, we tend to choose the smaller but certain gain.[143,144]

Our innate unwillingness to accept a definite loss can contribute to escalation. Roger's reluctance to incur the inconvenience involved in sacking his unsatisfactory assistant meant ultimately incurring a much greater loss. If Karen and Bob had cut their losses instead of ordering goods on credit, the damage to their livelihood would have been substantially less. Officials' unwillingness to slaughter a few thousand cattle as a precaution when BSE was first diagnosed in the UK led to the destruction of millions of healthy cattle later on. A chief executive once said of a failing employee:

> He's the worst director we've ever had. We know that. But if we get rid of him, it'll be at least eighteen months before we fill the post, if we manage to fill it. Even then, there's no guarantee that we will get anyone better. He's all we've got, so we may as well make the best of him.[145]

Notice what happens here. What appears as managerial prag-
matism basically amounts to a refusal to accept a definite loss. By
persisting with the appointment the organisation concerned
eventually incurred the much greater loss of a failing department
plus the problem of replacing the director in any case.

The deeper our involvement, the more difficult it becomes to
accept a loss. The design of the piers of the first Tay Bridge
assumed a rock base. It was only after construction commenced,
however, that the builders discovered that the borings had been
misleading and that the riverbed comprised a mixture of sand and
gravel. At that point, all work should have stopped while the
bridge was re-designed. Yet one can imagine the pressures on the
engineer Sir Thomas Bouch. Having spent years persuading the
burghers of Dundee to sponsor the venture, stopping work would
undermine confidence and revive opposition to the scheme, to
say nothing of the costs involved in standing down teams of contractors and sub-contractors. Instead of accepting the loss, Bouch
tinkered with the design. On the night of 28 December 1879, just
over a year after the bridge had been opened, Dundee was swept
by a hurricane. At about twenty minutes past seven, a train crossed
onto the bridge heading for Dundee. Observers from nearby houses
watching the progress of the train saw two or three great flashes of
light and then, nothing. The moon rose to reveal that the central
section of the bridge known as the High Girders were gone. So
too was the train and 75 men, women and children. The subsequent inquiry revealed that the force of the wind combined with
the weight and speed of the train had proved too much for the
flimsy construction.[146]

A more recent non-tragic example of escalation and risk-seeking behaviour concerns Covent Garden's last-minute decision to cancel Ligeti's *Le Grand Macabre*. It became obvious weeks before the theatre was due to reopen that late-running building works would eat into the time allowed for mastering the new equipment, the most technically complex ever built for the theatre. Management's refusal to accept a definite loss by cancelling the performance sooner rather than later only resulted in a deeper loss as the sudden cancellation damaged their carefully crafted image of new-found efficiency.[147]

We can end up deepening our losses in other ways thanks to our emotional attachment to our investments. Research by psychologists suggests that the more we pay for a theatre ticket, the more likely we are to endure a bad performance.[148] We see it as getting our money's worth yet what it actually means is that not only do we lose the price of a ticket, we make matters worse by wasting an evening as well! Likewise, research by psychologists suggests that the amount of money invested in star players tempts football managers to play them regardless of their actual performance.[149] Thus do we compound our losses.

The experience of loss can undermine our judgement in other ways. It was not the fact that King John lost France that led to Magna Carta and a subsequent fatal surfeit of peaches and cider; John's mistake was to exhaust the exchequer and the patience of his barons by spending ten years trying to regain the lost territory.

A more modern example of the dangers of pursuing a lost cause concerns Patrick (a pseudonym), a high street solicitor. Patrick was disappointed when a trade union that had instructed him in a lot of personal injuries work switched to a larger firm. Patrick was determined to win the work back.

Pursuit of the unattainable is at the expense of the possible.[123]

The adage if at first you don't succeed try, try again can be counterproductive. In his pursuit of the unattainable, Patrick ignored opportunities to expand the practice in other directions. He even closed down a thriving branch office because he saw it as peripheral to his main purpose. Consequently, by the time Patrick finally recognised that the door of trade union work was closed forever, he discovered that competitors had grown in the intervening period and were making substantial inroads into criminal legal aid work – the mainstay of his practice.

The March of Folly

Any decision involving investment, whether to remain on hold on the telephone or continue with an infrastructural project, can lead to escalation. Generally, the longer we persist, the more difficult it becomes to withdraw. This is because the longer we persist, the more we have invested. The more we have invested, the greater the emotional pressure.

Finance also enters the equation. Some projects become almost as expensive to abandon as they are to complete. Chicago's sewer system (derided by journalists as 'money down the drain') owes its existence to the sheer cost of ripping out works, filling in holes, paying off contractors and so forth. Although it was politically expedient to keep the Millennium Dome open, when the costs were considered, there was little to be gained by premature closure.

Indeed, we can reach a point where we have invested so much

in something that persistence becomes the only option. An engineer recounts how his organisation ended up buying a software package simply because they had spent so much money assessing it. Yet they began by merely asking to see the documentation:

> 'You wanna see some documents. Right! You gotta pay some money.' There was this enormous fee, £1 million, just to see the damn documentation. Then it was down payments for this, down payments for that.

The budget for the film *Heaven's Gate* was $7.5 million. After a series of contractual problems with the producer Cimino, United Artists considered cancelling the project but were dissuaded from doing so because of the $5 million irretrievably spent. By the time the cost had risen to $10 million, United Artists realised that the final cost of making the film might exceed £40 million and consume the company. United Artists persisted because it seemed that their only hope of recouping their investment was to finish the project.[136] In 1964 the newly elected Labour government decided against abandoning Concorde because of a penalty clause in the contract that required them to pay France's development costs.

'If we had known how much it was going to cost we would never have started,' said Sir Alistair Morton, the former chairman of Eurotunnel. Most prone to escalation are the so-called 'long-haul' projects that require huge investment and yield no revenues until the work is finished.[150] Long-haul projects are potentially fraught because:

Time = risk.

Time changes the nature of risk.[118] When Concorde was designed oil was cheap. By the time the plane entered commercial service that assumption no longer applied. In the late 1960s the Philips record company embarked upon an ambitious venture to record the complete Monteverdi madrigals. By the time the project was finished over four years later, musical tastes had changed leaving Philips with an eight-disc set aimed at a market that had virtually vanished.

More recently, some contractors working on London's Jubilee Line project submitted tenders based on the lowest possible price in order to win the work. They subsequently claimed additional payments for unforeseen extra work, pushing up costs by over £100 million. In addition, a tunnel being built at Heathrow using the same novel technology collapsed, causing a six-month delay. Then, as the deadline for completion approached electricians began holding the project managers to ransom by threatening industrial action.[149] The point is, none of this was predictable from futuristic images of steel and glass displayed in the architect's plans.

Tomorrow and Tomorrow

Economists might argue that economic forces eventually curb bad decisions. Indeed, the Millennium Dome eventually closed. Roger eventually sacked his recalcitrant assistant. Karen and Bob eventually quitted the premises.

The trouble is, by the time market forces act, the damage is done.[152] Looking round her once-thriving business Karen said:

Those floor tiles cost £800 and we'll never get the money back. Same with all the light fittings. . . . It's a relief sending the stuff back but its also very sad. I have been running my own business for six years and now I've got nothing to show for it.

Some escalation scenarios are fairly trivial. Others have more far-reaching and even tragic consequences. One thing they have in common is that the ultimate cost of throwing good money after bad is what might have been.

Chapter 10

'An ace of success': knocking at the door of fate

'What puts me off is not the chances of war but the certainties of commonsense.'[153]

All decisions have unintended consequences. Sometimes, however, the results are the complete opposite of what was intended. How does it happen? Moreover, although failure may take us by surprise, in retrospect it frequently seems to have been inevitable. Strictly speaking, if something is unexpected it can hardly be inevitable. How can this apparent contradiction be explained?

This chapter tries to answer these questions by telling the story of the Dardanelles expedition, one of the great 'if only's' of history. The expedition promised a swift end to the First World War at minimal risk. Moreover, it came within an 'ace of success'[154] but was abandoned in favour of the disastrous Gallipoli campaign. It is not giving the game away to say that the venture was undermined by many of the factors already identified in this book. What is new is that the story enables us to see how emotional forces and the subtly shifting tides of organisation can combine and interact to produce disaster.

The chapter is structured in two parts. Part one tells the story. Part two considers what went wrong and what we can learn from the mistakes of those long-dead decision makers.

THE EVENTS UNFOLD

'Are there not other alternatives to sending our armies to chew barbed wire in Flanders?'

The story begins on Christmas Day 1914. The Secretary to the War Council (the body responsible for directing the war), Lieutenant-Colonel Sir Maurice Hankey, is seated at his desk. Hankey is writing a long memorandum on the conduct of the war. He has a lot to think about. When the war began in August 1914 it was said that it would be over by now. The scale of the casualties has been shocking: the result, stalemate. Surely the situation could not continue through 1915? Hankey's colleagues on the War Council were coming to the same conclusion. 'Are there not other alternatives to sending our armies to chew barbed wire in Flanders?' wrote Winston Churchill.[155] Likewise David Lloyd George emphasised in a memorandum on 30 December 1914 that.

> A clear and definite victory ... alone will satisfy the public that tangible results are being achieved by the great sacrifices they are making, and decide neutrals that it is at last safe for them to throw in their lot with us.

Hankey concluded that Germany could be most effectively struck through her ally Turkey. Turkey, however, is protected by a narrow sea passage 41 miles long, known as the Dardanelles. The Dardanelles were guarded by forts built into the steep cliffs of the Gallipoli peninsula, supplemented by mobile field guns known as howitzers. Moreover, the sea was riddled with mines. At least 150000 troops would be required to capture the peninsula. Even then, it would be a dangerous undertaking. Besides, the High Command was implacably opposed to any move that might weaken the Western Front. 'Until the impossibility of breaking through on this side was proved, there could be no question of making an attempt elsewhere'.[156]

'This war had brought many surprises'

In January 1915 a crisis erupted as Russia tottered. If Russia collapsed, Germany could concentrate its entire force against the British. At the very least, a demonstration was required in the Dardanelles in order to support Russia. This dire emergency prompted Churchill to revisit an idea he had once dismissed as impossible:

> Like most other people I had held the opinion that the days of forcing the Dardanelles were over; .... But this war had brought many surprises. We had seen fortresses reputed ... to be impregnable collapsing after a few days' attack.[155]

As First Lord of the Admiralty Churchill had maintained a fleet of twelve pre-Dreadnought battleships in readiness for active service. Might they now come in useful? At 1.28 pm on 3 January 1915 Churchill telegraphed the area naval commander Vice Admiral Carden:

Do you consider the forcing of the Dardanelles by ships alone a practicable operation? It is assumed older battleships ... would be used. Importance of results would justify severe loss. Let me know your views.[155]

Two days later the admiral replied, '... I do not consider Dardanelles can be rushed. They might be forced by extended operations with a large number of ships'.[155] Churchill replied 'Your view is agreed by high authorities here....' and instructed the admiral to prepare a plan.

'Worth trying'

Carden's plan reached the War Office on 12 January. The admirals discussed it first. None criticised the idea. The War Council met the next day. The meeting was about to end with nothing resolved except to await the results of the next offensive in France. Hankey describes what happened next:

> The War Council had been sitting all day. The blinds had been drawn to shut out the winter evening. The air was heavy ... the table ... dishevelled .... At this point events took a dramatic turn, for Churchill revealed his well kept secret of a naval attack on the Dardanelles! The idea caught on at once. The whole atmosphere changed. Fatigue was forgotten.[158]

After months of loss and futility, here, it seemed, was the master stroke:

> The Royal Navy was in a position to destroy Turkey at a single blow, to relieve Russia, to provide the bait with which to force each Balkan state to turn against the Central Powers, and by rapid exploitation of victory on the southern flank to bring the whole war to an end....

All this could be done by battleships that were too old to be of use
. . . elsewhere.[159]

The minutes of the meeting record that:

'LLOYD GEORGE liked the plan.
LORD KITCHENER thought it was worth trying. We could leave off
the bombardment if it did not prove effective.'[156]

Accordingly the Admiralty were instructed to: '*Prepare for a naval
expedition in February to bombard and take the Gallipoli peninsula, with Constantinople as its objective*' (italics in original).[156]

An 'obstinate and ominous' silence

During the next fortnight, however, Admiral John Fisher (also a
member of the War Council) began to have doubts about relying
upon ships alone. Fisher argued that a naval attack would only
waste men and materials, 'I make no objection . . . if accompanied
by military co-operation,' he wrote to Churchill on 28 January
1915.[155]

Prime minister Herbert Asquith persuaded Fisher to withdraw
his opposition to the plan. Consequently when the War Council
next met on 28 January, few people were aware of Fisher's reservations. Instead, Churchill told the War Council that preparations for
the attack were underway. 'He asked if the War Council attached
importance to this operation, which undoubtedly involved some
risks?'[160] Fisher replied that he had understood the matter would
not be raised that day. The prime minister was well aware of his
views. Asquith replied, 'In view of the steps which had been taken,
the question could not well be left in abeyance.'

The War Council was still enthusiastic about the idea:

LORD KITCHENER considered the naval attack to be vitally important. If successful, its effect would be equivalent of that of a successful campaign fought with new armies. One merit of the scheme was
that, if satisfactory progress was not made, the attack could be
broken off.[160]

Arthur Balfour then listed the possible results: the Turkish army
cut in two, control of Constantinople, access to Russian wheat,
restoration of Russian exchanges, the opening of a passage to the
Danube, 'It was difficult to imagine a more helpful operation,' he
said. 'The Turks would be paralysed with fear when they heard the
forts were being destroyed one by one,' said another minister.[160]
Throughout the meeting, however, Fisher maintained an 'obstinate
and ominous' silence wrote Asquith to Venetia Stanley.[161]

'We cannot trust to this . . . .'

Fisher soon broke his silence. Although Captain Richmond, a senior
admiral, dismissed him in his diary as 'old & worn-out & nervous',
his continued lobbying made an impression. On 10 February
Hankey told the prime minister, 'Every naval officer . . . believes
that the Navy cannot take the Dardanelles without troops.
[Churchill] still professes to believe that they can do it with ships,
but . . . we cannot trust to this.'

Hankey suggested that naval operations be supported by a substantial military force. 'I [am] coming to the same opinion,' the
prime minister wrote to Venetia Stanley. Surely it ought to be possible to 'scrape together' troops without harming the Western
Front.[161]

On 16 February an expedition unrelated to the Western Front was cancelled. The War Council met informally and decided to transport the surplus troops (75 000 including the 29th Division) to a location near the Dardanelles.[156] Three days later, on 19 February, the naval bombardment began. 'It is an absolutely novel experiment,' wrote the prime minister, 'I am curious & rather anxious to see how it develops'.[161]

Later that day, Kitchener told the War Council that the 29th Division could not be released after all as it might be needed in France. Consternation ensued. According to the Secretary's notes:

... MR CHURCHILL said that no one could foretell the results of success in a country like Turkey. He did not ask for troops to be sent to the Dardanelles, but only that they should be within hail. It might give us a tremendous opportunity.[160]

Lloyd George agreed with Churchill, 'We ought to send more than three divisions. It was worthwhile to take some risks in order to achieve a decisive operation, which might win the war' he said.[160] Kitchener was adamant, however. Afterwards Asquith wrote:

The chance of forcing the Dardanelles ... presents such a unique opportunity that we ought to hazard a lot elsewhere rather than forgo it. If K [Kitchener] can be convinced, well & good: but to discard his advice & overrule his judgement on a military question is to take a great responsibility. So I am rather anxious ...[161]

'Now absolutely committed'

When the War Council reconvened on 24 February, bad weather had temporarily halted the attack. Churchill suggested that events might yet move rapidly. 'Moreover,' he said, 'we were now absolutely committed to seeing through the attack on the Dardanelles'.[158] Lloyd George asked if Churchill was now contemplating a military attack. Churchill refuted the suggestion but stressed, 'He could, however, conceive a case where the Navy almost succeeded, but where military force would just make the difference between failure and success.'[160]

Lloyd George warned against deploying the army to rescue the navy. If the navy failed, said Lloyd George, the War Council ought to try something else. They were committed to action in the East, but not necessarily the Dardanelles. Kitchener disagreed, 'The effect of defeat in the Orient would be very serious,' he said, 'There could be no going back. The publicity of the announcement had committed us'. 'Failure would be morally equivalent to a great defeat on land,' said another minister.[160] Even so, the 29th Division remained at home. Churchill was dismayed but won a small concession. The War Council agreed to send General William Birdwood to give a military opinion on the Dardanelles.[160]

On 26 February the War Council met again. Churchill argued that the 29th Division 'Would not make the difference between failure and success in France, but might well make the difference in the East.'[160] Kitchener said that he recognised the responsibility he was taking in retaining the 29th Division but he was not to be persuaded.

'I am very doubtful'

On 25 February the outer forts were silenced. Sensing impending victory, the elated War Council pored over the division of the spoils. Moreover, when the War Council met on 10 March they learned that the bombardment was creating panic in Turkey.

Yet the hardest part of the task lay ahead – not helped by the onset of bad weather and unknown enemy firepower. 'I am very doubtful if the Navy can force a passage unassisted,' Birdwood telegraphed to Kitchener.[160] Shortly after receiving Birdwood's telegram Kitchener released the 29th division. Hankey observed:

> Until now the only officially recorded object in sending out our military forces was to help the Navy reap the fruits of success. Actually we were drifting inevitably into a major military campaign.[158]

'Is that all?'

Churchill sat up all night to plot the route of General Sir Ian Hamilton, the appointed commander, to the Dardanelles. In Churchill's view, too much time had already been lost for nothing. Kitchener, however, insisted upon briefing Hamilton first.

In fact, Hamilton's orders were concise. Although there was no question of abandoning the venture, he was to act only if the navy failed. 'Is that all?' asked a colleague when the instructions were read aloud at a conference. 'Everyone looked a little blank' noted Hamilton when he replied that it was indeed all.[153]

By now Hankey was becoming alarmed. Although he believed that that the operation was brilliantly conceived, he now realised that troops should have been there from the outset. There should have been no press announcement, the troops should have come in as a complete surprise instead of giving the Turks time to prepare. On 20 March, Hankey sent a memorandum to Asquith warning of the dangers that lay ahead, 'A joint military operation has not been thought through in any detail .... The opportunity for a *coup de main* has now been lost. ... We have merely said that so many troops are available and that they ought to be enough.[158]

On 18 March just as the naval squadron was approaching the final set of forts three ships exploded in waters that had not been swept clear of mines. Replacement ships were despatched and Admiral de Robeck (Carden had fallen sick two days earlier) was notified to continue as he saw fit. De Robeck replied that he would resume the bombardment as soon as his damaged ships were repaired.[160]

Two days later, however, on 21 March, the weather broke. On 22 March de Robeck conferred with Hamilton. Afterwards de Robeck telegraphed Churchill with a new plan, 'The result of naval action alone might ... be a brilliant success or quite indecisive whereas a combined attack will effect decisive and overwhelming results'.[155]

Churchill was dismayed and drafted a telegram ordering de Robeck (subsequently nicknamed 'de Rowback')[154] to resume the attack. 'I believed then as I believe now that we were separated by very little from complete success,' he said.[157]

Fisher threatened to resign if the order was sent, forcing Churchill to moderate his tone. 'Why turn and change at this fateful hour ...?' he asked de Robeck, 'An attack by the Army ... would commit us irrevocably.'[162]

During the next six weeks, Churchill repeatedly urged de Robeck to try again. The Turks were short of ammunition, he told de Robeck, and might well surrender if the bombardment was resumed. Besides, Hamilton would not be ready to attack until 14 April.[159] Asquith and Kitchener agreed with Churchill, 'I hope this will be done,' wrote Asquith.[161] Yet Asquith would not order de Robeck to resume the attack. He had heard too many reports of seas riddled with mines and coasts bristling with concealed guns.

'He anticipated no difficulty'

On 6 April the War Council met informally to discuss whether the military attack should be postponed. The minutes of the meeting note that:

> The First Lord urged that the attack should be pressed home vigorously.
>
> LORD KITCHENER agreed that the attack would have to be made.
>
> LIEUTENANT-COLONEL HANKEY said that the difficulty would be to land troops at all, owing to the opposition of howitzers in the ravines which intersect the Gallipoli Peninsula.
>
> MR CHURCHILL did not agree. He anticipated no difficulty in effecting a landing.[156]

Next day Hankey urged Asquith to postpone the attack. 'There is a great deal of force in this,' noted Asquith, 'It is one of the those cases in which military and diplomatic considerations are completely intertwined'.[161]

Churchill's views were clear, 'No operation ... cd [could] ever cloak the defeat of abandoning the effort against the Dlls [Dardanelles]' he wrote. 'I think there is nothing for it but to go through with the business.'[155]

The troops attacked on 25 April, almost six weeks after the bombardment was suspended. The Turks were ready and waiting. Churchill had forecast 5000 casualties. The final total was 120 000 including 41 000 killed or missing before the garrison was finally withdrawn, having failed to achieve its objective.[157]

'AN ACE OF SUCCESS'

Like many examples of escalation, the Dardanelles venture began with bright promises, that is, a possible end to the war risking only a few ships too old to be of service elsewhere. It was a tantalising prospect. Indeed, the idea of a naval bombardment was brilliantly conceived. It was the execution of the plan that was flawed. The risks of myopic vision are heightened when a solution suddenly appears after a long and arduous search. The effect of Churchill's presentation upon his tired and dejected colleagues was electrifying. Fatigue was forgotten, but so too were the practicalities for if the naval bombardment succeeded, a military force would be required to occupy Constantinople in order to reap the fruits of victory. This point was never discussed. Besides, although this war had brought many surprises there was no guarantee of success. The War Council saw only the advantages of the idea. No one probed the risks.

Collective myopia is not the full explanation, however. One question this book tries to answer is how we can become committed to a course of action without making a decision. The Dardanelles story shows how it can happen. Although the War Council was enthusiastic about the idea of a naval bombardment, the meeting on 14 January merely concluded with an instruction to the Admiralty to 'prepare' for a possible expedition. In other words, there was no actual decision to try Churchill's plan.

An important theme of this book is that ambiguity always lurks. During the intervening fortnight, Churchill uses the 'empty space' of ambiguity (see page 71) to turn the idea of a naval expedition into a reality by pushing the word 'prepare' to its semantic limits. Consequently when the War Council reconvenes a fortnight later the ships are almost ready to sail. Fisher, an experienced naval commander, has his doubts, but has negotiated the price of his silence with Asquith. No one else challenges the rising myth. Still the War Council sees only the advantages of the idea.

Yet collective myopia remains only a partial explanation. Even then, there was no formal decision to proceed with the expedition. No one stops Churchill so he subsequently presses on. Thus does the dish run away with the spoon.

Escalation

The prime attraction of the naval bombardment was that it could easily be broken off if unsuccessful. Yet before even a single shot has been fired, the War Council discovers that this assumption no longer applies. How does it happen?

It was suggested in Chapter 2 that we are only ever conscious of what we have done and never of doing it. Having tacitly allowed the Admiralty to publicise the bombardment, the War Council now realises that their credibility is at stake. A defeat would have serious implications. What follows is a textbook example of risk-seeking behaviour. That is, the War Council rejects the option that would involve a definite loss of prestige. Instead, they prefer the risk of incurring a much greater loss later on.

Yet was the War Council 'absolutely committed' at that stage? Lloyd George's point about only being committed to action in the East is ignored. Another important theme of this book is that reality exists as we define it. The Dardanelles story shows how we can create our realities and then act as if our creations were forcing us to. Specifically, by ignoring Lloyd George's point, the War Council commit *themselves* to seeing the business through. They then act out that commitment.

Shifting Sands

It was suggested in Chapter 3 that the decision process reflects a constant state of becoming as one state of affairs gives way to another. In the Dardanelles story the ships have not even left port when the ground begins to shift as Fisher's lobbying makes an impression. What follows is a paradox of consequences (see page 153) in that *a* becomes *b* by avoiding *b*. To be precise, the expedition becomes a fiasco thanks to the War Council's efforts to avoid fiasco.

Fiasco does not happen, it is created.

The Dardanelles venture enables us to see that events do not play themselves out randomly but are driven by an underlying *tension* between where the decision makers are and where they perceive they need to be. The War Council has half a million troops locked in stalemate in France while their hopes of achieving a swift victory now rest upon twelve old ships. It is an absurdity. The tension lies between the risks involved in diverting resources to an alternative theatre of war versus the opportunity cost of continuing stalemate.

Churchill heightens the tension by manipulating vividness effects (see Chapter 5). He makes success seem close by telling the War Council that events may move rapidly and that one division, a mere 30 000 troops, could make the difference between success and failure – a tantalising prospect. Yet Kitchener is unmoved. As far as he is concerned, there is not a man to be spared.

The official inquiry into the subsequent fiasco (known as the Dardanelles Commission) concluded that the War Council ought either to have accepted the loss of prestige and abandoned the naval expedition, or taken the risks involved in resourcing properly. Instead they vacillated.[157] Surely what they were trying to do was, in principle, much more defensible than merely dithering. That is, they tried to give the naval expedition a better chance of success by committing additional resources to it without seriously weakening the Western Front.

In other words, by doing what they could to improve the chances of success, paradoxically, the War Council ended up undermining the expedition. The first signs of the forthcoming massacre on the beaches are seen in the search for troops in that the provision of military support is not based on any estimate of what is needed but what can be 'scraped' together.

To stand any chance of success a military attack required speed and careful preparation. Not only were three weeks lost when Kitchener changed his mind about sending out the 29th Division, the decision also detracted from planning because the War

Council became preoccupied with procuring the means at the expense of considering the ends to which the troops would be put.

Fiasco Becomes Inevitable

The signs of the forthcoming massacre may be evident, but at what point does fiasco become inevitable? The decisive point in the story was the decision to transport large numbers of troops to within reach of the Dardanelles. The troops became a solution in search of a problem. Their very presence made it likely that they would be deployed, as indeed they were. From that moment, the venture underwent a profound change. The idea of a purely naval attack was receding in favour of a military expedition. In other words, the venture was becoming something *else*.

Yet the decision to transport the troops was taken casually at an informal gathering of key members of the War Council, and only subsequently minuted as an official meeting. In fact, it was not a decision at all in the sense that it was a deliberate, volitional choice between alternatives. There was no weighing up of the pros and cons, no deliberation or debate. When we create our realities we may then act as if our creations were forcing us to – which ultimately they are. That is basically what the War Council does, that is, the 'decision' to transport troops basically amounts to the acting out of a script that is already written.

The military expedition failed because it came to rely much more upon luck than planning. Reality is something that we negotiate. The Dardanelles story shows what can happen when negotiations lag behind events. Officially the troops are being sent to support the navy. The emerging reality is that the venture could well become a full-scale military campaign. Until that possibility is acknowledged, however, there can be no proper planning. The result is a confusion of purposes that is only resolved through the ripening of events, by muddling through in other words.

The most important decisions are sometimes the least obvious.

The decision to send General Birdwood to the Dardanelles shows how seemingly minor decisions can have important consequences. Birdwood's gloomy report contradicted the myth that the navy could force a passage unassisted. The receipt of this information coincided with Kitchener's decision to release the 29th Division. In addition, Birdwood's report seems to have been instrumental in dissuading Asquith from ordering de Robeck to resume the attack.

Trusting to Luck

As Hankey looks back over events he sees the mess that has been created thanks to the failure to plan the expedition properly and subsequently urges Asquith to cancel the attack. It was suggested in Chapter 4 that knowing is not the same as understanding. Although the War Council knew from earlier military analyses that a military attack on the Dardanelles would be a difficult undertaking, their maps conveyed little about the realities of the terrain, the steep cliffs and hidden machine-gun nests, the exposed beaches and the arid climate. Would they have paid more attention to Hankey if they had understood the risks involved?

Perhaps, but probably not because by now the loss of prestige

implied by cancellation was just too great. Asquith rationalises the
decision by telling himself that, depending upon whether the coin
turns up heads or tails, the war might be over in three months.
Churchill had every reason to press for persistence because he
knew he would be ruined if the venture failed. Indeed, the Gallipoli fiasco cast a shadow over his entire career. Yet was he as reckless as the minutes of the final meeting suggest, or did Colonel
Hankey compose these with an eye to posterity?

The Fortunes of War

Although fiasco was becoming inevitable, the massacre upon the
beaches might have been avoided if Asquith had ordered de
Robeck to resume the bombardment. Why did he hesitate when
success was within his grasp?

It was suggested in Chapter 6 that symbols can be more important than substance. Although the losses resulting from the sink-
ings were small compared with the daily carnage on the Western
Front, the incident signified futility. Suddenly all the doubts about
the wisdom of relying on ships alone, including those expressed in
Birdwood's report, seemed to have been vindicated. The result
was a reverse vividness effect whereby dire images of ships going
to the bottom of the sea for nothing eclipsed factual data in the
form of intelligence intercepts suggesting that the strategy was
working.

It was more than that, however. The Dardanelles story also
shows us how destiny can be shaped by *indecision*. Asquith is in
charge but he is not in control. Moreover, while Asquith hesitates,
the ground shifts yet again as de Robeck and Hamilton get together.

De Robeck uses the conference as an opportunity to pass the buck to Hamilton. For although de Robeck mentions the possibility of a combined attack in his telegram to Churchill, the navy subsequently played only a minor role in operations.

Time was another factor. Would Asquith have acted differently if he had known that Hamilton's transports had been sent out in such disarray that he would need not three weeks to prepare but six?

Ultimately the failure to resume the bombardment reflects the paradox of consequences. The bombardment was halted because it had failed to silence the forts. Yet silencing the forts was only a means to an end. The end was to procure the surrender of Turkey. Churchill realised the mistake when he told de Robeck that there was every possibility that the opposition might suddenly crumple. In his defence Churchill said, 'I believed then as I believe now that we were separated by very little from complete success.' Churchill was right. Turkey was on the verge of surrender. In March 1915 the graveyards of the Somme, Arras and Ypres lay in the future. The decision makers were knocking on the door of fate. Just as fate was about to answer, they turned away.

Chapter 11

The point of no return

'Either he's dead or my watch has stopped.' (Groucho Marx)

When Harold Macmillan was asked what he found hardest about being prime minister he replied, 'events, dear boy, events'. We all know the trouble events can cause. Events disrupt the even tenor of our ways, they expose our weaknesses and shatter our illusions.

Yet what if nothing happens to shatter our illusions? We saw in Chapter 9 the dangers of escalation and how we can easily end up devoting ourselves to lost causes and ventures that are doomed to fail. The one good thing that can be said about escalation scenarios is that they are punctuated with crises. At each critical juncture there is a decision to be made, that is, do we reinvest in the hope of turning matters around or do we cut our losses?

Yet what happens if no decision is required? This chapter concerns a phenomenon known as entrapment. Entrapment is where we become locked into a particular course of action not because of any specific decision, but through the simple passage of time. As we shall see, entrapment is more invidious than escalation.

THE SCENE IS A DILAPIDATED HAIRDRESSER'S SHOP

One Saturday morning I arrived at my regular hairdresser to find a note on the door, 'Sorry: closed due to illness'. Desperate for a 'cut and blow dry' I tramped from shop to shop. The town supports eleven hairdressers. Yet every door I opened, the response was the same, 'Sorry, we've nothing at all today.'

Then I noticed 'Val's' emporium (a pseudonym), across the road, opposite the bus stop. I was not hopeful. The crumbling woodwork, peeling paint, and blackened net curtains suggested that the shop had been closed for many years. Drawing nearer I was surprised to see a light on inside. Any port in a storm, I thought, and pushed open the door.

One look at the interior and I almost ran away. An old electric water heater dangled from a wall streaming with condensation. The sink was split by a huge crack, filled with a black and green mould. The shop smelled damp and dank. Only Val's advancing smile stopped me from bolting. I was not sure who I expected to see emerge from the back shop. Certainly not the youngish person smartly attired in a red cotton 'dungaree' style suit. Val seemed surprised to see a new customer, but pleased. Yes she could do my hair, '... now if you like'.

Operations commenced. 'Is the water alright?' asked Val. The water felt cold and clammy and smelled as musty as the shop. Yet the heater, I decided, looked dangerous enough without inviting Val to adjust it, especially with me under it. 'Fine,' I replied.

As Val 'shampooed' I looked out of the window. It was one of those January days that never become properly light. Snow was beginning to fall. Passers-by huddled into their coats. Inside the salon, a propane gas fire burned. A dryer had been turned on to provide more heat.

'How long have you been here?' I asked. 'Oh now,' said Val, 'let me see. I've just turned forty-eight. I started here when I left school so what's that, thirty-three years?' 'A lifetime,' I said. 'I suppose it is a lifetime, replied Val, 'but I never think of it. All I ever wanted was to do people's hair. I just can't imagine doing anything else. Sometimes in the morning, when its dark, I think, "Have I got to get up?" But once I'm here, I enjoy it. I just love being a hairdresser.'

'So how did you come to be in this particular shop?' I asked. 'Kathy, that's the woman who owned the shop,' said Val, 'was looking for someone. In those days you did three years' apprenticeship and two years "improving"'. 'Improving' was said with a laugh. 'Can you remember your first wage?' I asked. 'Yes, two-pounds-fifty. My children say to me, "Mam, why do you always pick the poorest jobs?"'

'You must have seen some changes,' I said. 'A lot of the treatments aren't as harsh as they used to be because of the EEC,' replied Val. 'False curls were all the rage at one time but you never hear of them now.' 'Do you get to hear lots of gossip?' I asked. 'Not really,' said Val. 'My children come home from school knowing more than me.... It's more family problems you get to hear about.'

Val bought the business from Kathy (a pseudonym) in 1980. Val's father helped with the money. 'I always knew that I would own my own shop one day,' said Val, 'and it suited me not to have staff and all the bother of getting rid of them. My marriage was breaking up and I wanted a job where I could start early and finish early.'

The washing process over, I moved to the cutting chair. Glancing further around I realised that there was only one other client – an elderly lady ensconced under a drier, smoking a cigarette and reading *Bella*. 'When do you finish?' I asked. 'Saturday, dinner time,' replied Val. 'What time do you start?' I asked. 'Eight o'clock,' replied Val, 'I have one lady who works in a shop who has to be away by nine. A lot of my other customers like to get down early on a Saturday before the traffic gets busy. I have one lady [in the next village]. I go on to do her hair on a Saturday except its her golden wedding so I went yesterday. . . . Wednesday is a funny day. Sometimes I can be busy. Sometimes, I can be waiting for the phone to ring.'

Just then, the telephone did ring. It was a client seeking an appointment. 'What day are you coming down,' asked Val, 'and what bus are you getting?' The question was a flashback to 1963 when people living on the hill tops travelled into town just once a week. In 1963 the shop represented the ideal hairdressing salon. Four hair dryers lined in fixed positions with 'Pullman'-style seats. White paintwork and white net curtains offered a brief escape from the omnipresent soot and dirt of a mill town and its dark houses with cold taps, stone sinks, outside toilets and invasive damp. In 1963 the salon was a thriving business with both sinks and all four driers in regular commission. Now the upholstery of two of the chairs is split, foam erupting. The other sink resonates rust, grime and cobwebs. The towels look grubby. The white plastic 'curlers' stored on trays are covered in a grey film of grease and dirt. Black mould pervades the walls and surfaces.

'I've only myself to keep'

The salon is closed on Monday and Tuesday. Monday is a holiday. On Tuesday Val goes into a local sheltered housing complex. 'I had one lady go there and she asked me if it would still do her hair,' said Val, 'that's how it started.'

Val charges £4.60 for a 'shampoo and set' – her staple hair treatment. So, in accountants' parlance the recovery rate is barely £9 an hour. The rent alone is over £100 a week and how much, I wondered, does that perpetually humming hair drier cost to run? 'That's the trouble with renting from the council,' said Val, 'you can't negotiate with them. 'No, I imagine not,' I mumbled. '. . . but you see, I'm ideally situated, next to a bus stop, parking, you could even get a wheel chair in.' 'True,' I said. 'And,' added Val, 'I've only myself to keep.'

Val's main worry is the uncertainty over the future of the building as a whole. The council have been talking about demolishing it. 'At one time,' said Val, 'leases were for ten years. Now they're only for three.' 'What will you do if they don't renew it?' I asked. A shadow crossed Val's face. 'I don't know,' said Val, 'go completely mobile I suppose.'

My 'cut and blow dry' costs £5. Normally I would pay at least £15. As I hand over the money, the round yellow casing of the water heater catches my attention. A red light is shining. Val exchanges a few pleasantries with me as she rakes in her cash box for change. I am hardly listening; something about that malignant red eye disturbs me.

The transaction complete, Val unhooks my coat from the hanger and hands it to me. I open the door and stand poised between the fuggy warmth of one world and the icy coldness of another. It is snowing harder now. Cars are crawling by, their headlights dipped, just as they had in 1963. Saturday dinner time and almost dark. Reluctant to leave, I step out onto the pavement, 'Good morrow and good-day.'

'Don't Clap Too Loudly'

Val's story can teach us a lot about the potentially invidious nature of entrapment. In 1963 the salon was a thriving business. Now it is commercially worthless and living on borrowed time. Every year the client list diminishes as death and population movements take their toll. Every year, the fixtures and fittings get older and dirtier and there is no money to replace them for the business generates just enough money to keep Val above the poverty line. Most of Val's clients depend upon state pensions for their income. To raise prices would only drive them away. Yet without a complete refurbishment, there is little prospect of attracting new clients. In short, the business is past the point of no return. How has it happened?

When Val said, 'goodbye' and 'see you next week' to her last customer at 5.30 pm on Friday 22 November 1963 President Kennedy was still alive. Almost every Friday night since she has said 'goodbye' and 'see you next week' to the same customer. Meanwhile, wars have been fought, people have walked on the moon, and heart transplants have become commonplace. Yet in the salon, little has changed. Hair treatments may be less harsh, false curls may have fallen from view, Wednesdays may be ambiguous but the shape and rhythm of the business is basically as it was in 1963. Time has stood still.

Or has it? The popular management literature suggests that we live in a world characterised by constant upheaval, rapid obsolescence and where the only constant is change. Indeed, the last century has seen many changes. In 1999, Channel 4 screened a series about a family who had volunteered to live for three months as if the year was 1900. The programme dispelled all romantic ideas about living in a bygone age. Walls and doors were painted in oppressive shades of brown and dark green in order to hide the dirt caused by the coal fires in every room. In 1900, washday really did take all day because there were no machines, no detergents and no instant hot water. It was such an effort that top clothes were never washed, only brushed. Hair had to be washed in soap, teeth cleaned in bicarbonate of soda. Heating water for a bath was a major undertaking. In the absence of refrigeration, grocers and butchers called every day. Even so, the breakfast milk was usually sour. Letters had a special significance as telephones were rare and faxes and e-mails lay far into the future.

What is interesting, however, is not only how much has changed but also how *little*. The open-air museum at Beamish in the north of England contains an Edwardian Street also dating from around 1900. One house has an estate agent's board outside it. It looks exactly like a modern board, the only difference is the absence of telephone and fax numbers and an e-mail address. The dentist's surgery seems uncannily familiar. The origins of the modern 'B&Q' superstore are clearly visible in the Edwardian ironmongers. The Co-op too was selling its own branded goods. In the bank, the details are different. Ledgers, dip pens and pewter ink wells have given way to computers and chained biros. Yet the outline of the modern high street branch is clearly recognisable.

The turbulence perspective, like any other image, highlights certain things while obscuring others. If we see the fourteenth century through the optic of the Black Death and the Peasants' Revolt it looks as if the only constant is change. Yet to focus solely upon these dramatic events is to the miss the subtler movements of the period such as the developments in the English wool trade.

The turbulence perspective is also misleading because it implies that the importance of a particular event is directly proportional to the amount of noise it makes. Yet it may be the oblique, almost imperceptible, shifts that are actually the most important.[163] For instance, ostensibly the two acts of Samuel Beckett's play *Waiting for Godot* are almost identical. The play concerns two tramps, Vladimir and Estragon, who are waiting for a man called Godot. Godot never comes. Several times they resolve to leave, 'Let's go,' they say to one another, but they never move. In Act II one of the companions, Pozo, has lost his watch. This small development is highly significant because it means that Pozo no longer controls time. Moreover, although Act II ends like Act I, that is, 'Let's go,', this time when Vladimir and Estragon do not move it is clear that Godot is never going to come.[164]

In Val's case, it is the subtler almost imperceptible movements of decay that have transformed the business. The white wood that was once the epitome of luxury now seems cheap and tacky. The towels that were once fresh and luxurious have become harsh and grubby. The curtains that were once white are now black. The salon is no longer a place to escape *to*, but *from*.

The point is, it has all happened so gradually. Every Friday is the same except that it is a little different. Although nothing dramatic has happened during the last 33 years or so, time has not stood still. Val's story highlights a paradox. That is, the business has been destroyed by preserving it. The Chinese proverb teaches that no one can step into the same river twice. The river may look the same but it is different. In Val's case the deterioration has occurred so gradually that the mould, dirt and decay that are immediately obvious to a stranger are invisible to her. The deterioration may be just as invisible to her clients, they have all been there for so long. In Val's eyes, the salon looks almost exactly as it did in 1963. She sees the salon for what it *was*, and not for what it has *become*.

Organisations can fall into the same trap. When Gerry Robinson looked at the Forte empire he saw a latter-day Val, not as extreme perhaps, but an enterprise that was clearly failing to deliver best shareholder value – a prime candidate for takeover, in other words. The question is, what did Sir Rocco Forte see?

Gerry Robinson's subsequent hostile bid in 1995 for the Forte empire surprised the business world and the media alike. It was the last thing anyone expected – not least Sir Rocco Forte. Yet as Forte discovered:

'*A thousand years scarce serve to form a State;*
An hour may lay it in the dust.'[165]

In the Tarot, card sixteen of the Major Arcana depicts the tower destroyed by a single bolt of lightning. It warns what can happen when we lose touch with reality. Although the tower looks solid and enduring, the masonry that holds it together has deteriorated over the years. Consequently, faced with a major challenge it can *only* collapse.

As analysts mulled over developments it became apparent that

Robinson's bid was not quite as audacious as it first seemed. Forte was a respected organisation, unremarkable perhaps, but, like the tower, a seemingly solid and enduring enterprise. Moreover, Forte recognised that the business his father had controlled for 60 years was ripe for reform. He had begun the work of repointing, chipping out the old masonry by removing layers of management. In doing so, of course, he may have drawn attention to the very weakness of the empire.

As always, it is easy to say 'I would never let that happen'. Yet whether it is a house, a marriage, a mighty corporation, or a corner shop, decay is inevitable. The difficulty is arresting it before it reaches the point of no return. One reason we fail to notice decay is because it happens slowly. Research suggests that we are more sensitive to the relative magnitude of change than absolute magnitudes.[143,144] Consequently, Val is more likely to notice the latest tear in a chair, the latest crack in a sink, the latest hole in a towel and the latest client who dies or moves away than the sum total of decay and deterioration. Likewise, some universities take comfort in losing only half a point in the latest rating exercise. They fail to notice the cumulative impact of having lost half a point every year for a decade. It is like bits of masonry falling from the tower. The tower looks almost exactly the same, except that it is on the verge of collapse, hence the allusion 'Don't clap too loudly, this is a very old house'.

'Crisis, What Crisis?'

We saw in Chapter 3 that what we call reality is frequently a figment of our imagination. Yet we also saw in Chapter 5 that the reverse is possible, that is, our perceptions of reality can be dangerously biased. When it comes to entrapment the complex twists and turns of the human imagination can lead us to deny the existence of an impending crisis – even when it is staring us in the face. In other words, we may end up refusing to see the future *after* it has arrived.

Instead we cling to what we have, even though what we have is fast slipping away. In Val's case the future resides in the young people with money to spend on haircuts who are literally passing by on the other side of the road. Val refuses to think about it. Likewise, near Val's salon stands an Italian restaurant. Fifteen years ago, when it first opened, tables were reserved up to three weeks in advance. Now, most nights, it stands almost empty. In this case, the future has arrived in the shape of competition plus a large gay community in the town. The dinner/dance floor now stands virtually redundant. The background music that might once have been romantic now seems sexist. As for the 'specials' board, it has not changed in seven years! Surveying the empty seats the owner sighed, 'There is always Fridays and Saturdays I suppose'.

The point is, sophisticated organisations may be just as reactionary. IBM refused to see the future after it had arrived, preferring to cling to its vision of mainframe computing. The London Stock Exchange continues to behave as a private gentlemen's club, clinging to its traditional pre-eminence while other organisations are cutting the ground from under it. Ironically, some Ivy League business schools have become so steeped in their traditional syllabi of strategic management, operations research and the like, that the new demand for courses in e-commerce is passing them by, despite falling rolls. Indeed, they could become one of the case studies they issue to students!

'Drifting Idly Towards Eternity'

You might say how can this possibly happen when organisations employ legions of analysts who spend their days doing nothing else except modelling the future?

Tom Stoppard's play *Rosencrantz and Guildenstern are Dead* encapsulates the spirit of entrapment:

> *We've travelled too far, and our momentum has taken over; we move idly towards eternity.*[11]

In a sense, Val's salon *has* been closed for years. The business is now driven by its own momentum. Organisations too can become closed off and begin drifting idly towards eternity. Moreover, organisations are very good at making sure that nothing happens to disturb the idyll. What happens is that all analysis and all prediction becomes a fixed game based upon the unspoken presumption of continuity.

An American company known as Facit specialised in making mechanical calculators. Facit's management were determined that their mechanical calculators should be the best in the world. They borrowed heavily in order to invest in research and upgrade production facilities. The whole organisation was reconfigured to enable Facit to lead from what it saw as its key strength.

Although electronic calculators were fast becoming a commercial possibility, Facit relegated the research and development engineers in this field to a subsidiary company in order to concentrate upon mechanical technology:

> Facit understood those technologies well. Top, middle and lower level managers agreed how a mechanical calculator factory should look and operate, what mechanical-calculator customers wanted

what was the key to success and what was unimportant or silly. . . .
Costs were low, service fast, glitches rare, understanding high and
expertise great.

But only within the programmed domain.[166]

Notice the words 'programmed domain'. Facit's communication
channels were programmed for mechanical calculators. Top management lived and breathed mechanical calculators. They knew
little about the advent of electronics. Lower-ranking staff were
better informed but lacked the means of communicating with the
highest echelons. Besides, Facit's management were in no mood
to listen. We saw in Chapter 9 that forecasting, however scientific-
ally sophisticated, may reflect wishful thinking particularly when
matters are turning against us. Facit's top management foresaw
customers would be slow to switch to electronic calculators. Moreover, as Facit had no organisational arrangements for gathering
information from people who were buying electronic calculators,
there was little to contradict this comforting assumption.[166]

Organisational momentum is sustained by all the routines and
protocols that are observed automatically and therefore unthinkingly. If you were asked to define the priorities of your organisation what would you say?

The danger is that we so easily become actors in a play that is
already written. A small amount of improvisation is permitted but
we inevitably fall back on the script because it does our thinking
for us.

It is more than that, however. Entrapment becomes a tale told
by an idiot in pinstripes as everyone in the organisation creates
their realities around the script and the myths embodied in the
script. Ultimately the whole organisational infrastructure comes to

reflect those myths just as Facit became geared to the myth that the future lay in mechanical calculators. Even the premises for decision making, the cues that elicit attention and the filters used to examine events and actions will be controlled by routines, the organisation becomes more and more detached from reality as:

yesterday's protocols shape today's perceptions and determine tomorrow's action.

It is like the butler in the Gothic horror story who tells the visitor enquiring at the door for the master of the house, 'The master of the house has been dead for fifteen years. But if you wait I'll get him for you.'

What makes such entrapment all the more insidious is that everything has the appearance of a well-managed organisation. There is a coherent strategy supported by integrated programmes of education, training, research and development. The result is a Maginot Line, brilliantly constructed, utterly unassailable, and pointing in the wrong direction.

Will the Microsoft of today become the Facit of tomorrow? It seems unthinkable – and yet just as Val's emporium has become a shadow of its former self, an organisation's perceptions of its core competence can become a dangerous illusion. To mix metaphors, they can become like antique chairs in a museum. Antiques can be preserved by scooping out the wood, leaving the outer shape and form visible. The danger is that the chair looks sturdy enough.

Red Light Spells Danger

Let us return to that red light. It was suggested in Chapter 4 that information is not reality but a ghost that is forever in danger of becoming real through being taken literally. The red light means that the water heater is 'on'. The risk is that Val gets so used to seeing the light that every time it comes on she takes it as confirmation that the business is sound. It is like the couple who take the ritual dinner-time exchange ('Hullo, had a pleasant day dear?') as confirmation that the marriage is working.

In Facit's case, the red light appeared in the seemingly healthy sales and profit figures. Facit saw the figures and concluded that the business was sound when in fact its typewriter and office furnishings businesses were subsidising the 'flagship' product.

Some day that red light must fail just as Facit eventually failed. When the bulb begins to flicker organisations often make matters worse by driving their time-served procedures and protocols harder and harder. All efforts become focused upon racing 'new improved' mechanical calculators to market. It is like replacing the light bulb and tightening the wiring. Even if those measures work for a while, any chance that might have existed to retrieve the situation is thrown away in a last-ditch effort that can only postpone the inevitable.

That red light is ambiguous because it also warns against interfering. Although the fixtures and fittings are worthless, for Val they are still serviceable items of equipment. To start tinkering with the water heater may actually make things worse by exposing the whole lot as rotten – like the married couple, who when they decide to try to brush up their marriage by taking a holiday or arranging a candle-lit dinner, discover that they have nothing to say to one another.

Val could probably buy some new equipment but it would be throwing good money after bad because the only hope of turning the business around is full-scale refurbishment. Sometimes moderation does indeed ruin all. In the early 1970s the British government gave authority for research and development to begin on the Advanced Passenger Train. The tilting train, as it became known, promised speeds of 150 mph. What made the concept unique, however, was the train's ability to run at that speed on existing track and within the limits of existing signalling. Four years and millions of pounds of taxpayers' money later, the prototype was towed to the museum. The project failed because the requirement to use existing track and existing signalling systems meant superimposing highly sophisticated technology upon a Victorian infrastructure.

Imagine participating in a competition to solve a crossword puzzle. The first person to arrive at the correct answers wins a prize. A dictionary that will enable you to work faster is available. Although there is a queue for this valuable resource, you are next in line. Is it worth waiting for the dictionary to arrive bearing in mind that you do not know exactly when the dictionary will arrive?[167]

It is a trap because, like Godot, the dictionary is destined never to arrive. When this experiment is performed in the laboratory competitors invariably discover that after having waited so long for this valuable resource, they have no option but to go on waiting. The same applies to decisions about careers, jobs, and relationships. As time goes on, it can become more and more expensive to change direction because of all the extraneous investments we end up making along the way.[168]

The danger is that we end up footling around with half-measures. The aviation industry recently launched a programme to modify the rudder on Boeing 737 planes. Rudder failure has been linked to at least two catastrophic accidents involving 737s. Like the DC-10s of a generation earlier with their suspect floors and baggage doors – the question is whether these modifications can make safe a suspect design. Some aviation experts are arguing that the whole fleet should be withdrawn. They may well be right. The point is, once a large investment is made we end up having to live with the consequences for a long time.

Polishing the Chains

Val's story conveys the spirit of entrapment. It shows how we can reach a point where the only thing left is our own momentum. Yet what sustains the momentum?

We saw in Chapter 2 that all understanding comes from a backwards glance. It was also suggested, however, that when we look back we may see different things at different times. In other words, the past does not exist 'out there' in any objective sense, but is something that we create and re-create in our imagination.

The future is the past entered by another door, said Poincaré. The same applies to the present. Past and present mingle like dancing shadows because we *create* the past so that we can live with the present.

Val looks back and decides that all she ever wanted to be was a hairdresser. The knowledge that she now has all she ever wanted enables her to live with her present poverty. In Val's mind, her poverty does not signify failure but success. The same self-defensiveness is seen in Val's attitude towards her expensive premises. Val tells herself there is nowhere else as good. The reality is that because Val cannot afford to transfer to new premises, there is nowhere else.

Interestingly, the results of attitude surveys into why people stay with a particular employer echo Val's story. Logically we might expect that as time goes on we would end up needing to stay because of pension rights and the like, and because it tends to become more difficult to obtain employment as one gets older. Yet research consistently shows that the feeling of wanting to stay grows stronger with time whereas needing to stay becomes less important.

What these results may really be saying is that because we *have* stayed, we tell ourselves it is because we want to stay. If this surmise is correct it means that although entrapment results from the passage of time, ultimately we can end up imprisoning ourselves. For instance, you might expect that solicitors who fail to achieve partnership status would exhibit a certain amount of resentment towards their firm. Yet a survey of corporate law firms found that the opposite was true. So-called 'ageing assistants' scored just as high on wanting to stay as partners.[169] These results may simply mean that a good many assistant solicitors are content to remain assistants all their lives. A more subtle possibility is that because the goal of partnership has eluded them, they tell themselves they never wanted it anyway. What better way to buttress that conviction than to express pleasure with one's lot.

Indeed, evidence suggests that our commitment to a decision may be all the greater if the decision is more or less irreversible. In an experiment, supermarket customers were allowed to choose between obtaining scouring pads on a trial basis or as a final purchase. Those who opted to make a final purchase reported that they liked the brand more than those who took the pads on a trial basis.[33]

This may explain why people who buy a house and then discover that it needs extensive and expensive repairs often end up delighted with their purchase telling themselves and others, 'I would not wish to live anywhere else.'

In extreme circumstances we may take to writing fiction in order to close the gap between our past and present circumstances. When Willy Loman in Arthur Miller's *Death of a Salesman* realises his expendability he tells his manager, 'In 1928 I had a big year. I averaged a hundred and seventy dollars a week in commissions.'[170] It is nonsense, as Willy's manager points out. Willy, however, insists upon it. Likewise, the character known as Uncle Tom in John Mortimer's *Rumpole* stories who has not had a brief in living memory is forever telling his younger colleagues of the days when the mantlepiece was laden with papers tied in pink tape bearing his name. The reality is that Uncle Tom was a hopeless barrister who crowned his career by losing an undefended divorce. Recreating the past as a golden era makes Tom's present state bearable.

Further along the spectrum are the colourful individuals sitting in their bathchairs in residential homes convinced that they won the battles of Trafalgar, Waterloo and El-Alamein. We say they are mad. Yet how often does it occur to us, when we claim the credit for success, that we may be separated by very little from those old codgers?

Clutching the Pole

(HAMLET *blows out the lantern. The stage goes pitch black.*)
(*The black resolves itself to moonlight . . .*)
(Act III of *Rosencrantz and Guildenstern Are Dead*)[11]

At closing time, when Val switches off the light, the salon goes pitch black. The black resolves itself into another day of appointments or waiting for the phone to ring. The implication is that all events play themselves out, one way or another. Indeed the family problems that Val got to hear about in 1963 have long since been resolved. In 1963, the family problems of today lay far out into the future. Perhaps the resolution of 1963 is the problem of today. Time was before the salon existed. In the 1950s it was a sweet shop. The time will come when it no longer exists. But meantime?

Meantime Val is by no means hopelessly trapped in a dying business. The seemingly perpetual cycle of clients has been resolved into a new line of activity as a mobile hairdresser. Why not get rid of the shop that is draining her income and depriving her of opportunity? Why not go 'completely mobile'?

A hairdresser without a salon: it is like a dentist without a surgery, a priest without a church, an industrialist without a factory.

The ultimate trap is our identity. Identity is different from image. Image is how others see us. Identity is how we see ourselves. Our identity is so precious that we may cling to it at all costs. We saw in Chapter 1 how the Mann Gulch firecrew ignored an order to drop their tools. Instead most of the crew died trying to flee from the flames weighed down by their equipment. They clung to their tools as the symbol of their identity. The order to drop their tools created an identity crisis because if they relinquished their equipment they were no longer firefighters. If they were no longer firefighters, then who were they? Similarly, trapeze artists have been known to fall to their deaths clutching their poles instead of grasping the wire and saving themselves because the poles are the symbol of their identity.[17]

Margaret Thatcher fell to her political death clutching her pole of Thatcherism. Curiously enough, although the Peasant's Revolt was triggered by the poll tax, Thatcher ignored the lesson of history and reintroduced the measure. When it became apparent that the poll tax was as much an anathema in the twentieth century as it had been six hundred years earlier, Thatcher reacted with the same intransigence as the ill-advised Richard II, 'Serfs yea are, and serfs yea shall remain'.

When the time finally came for Thatcher to fight for her political leadership she discovered that she had become trapped by her own persona. Having risen so far above grassroots opinion, Thatcher felt she could hardly descend upon the Commons tea room and be seen fishing in her handbag for the price of a cup of tea on the eve of a crisis. It was too late.

A good many hairdressers are destined to finish up like Val because they are unwilling to do anything except cut peoples' hair. They become poor clutching their combs while their more business-orientated contemporaries start opening up franchises and the like. Similarly, some dentists refuse to see that running a practice means running a business. They try to survive by working harder and harder at dentistry, rushing from surgery to surgery until they collapse with heart attacks and die clutching their probes. In contrast, vets have shown themselves very willing to grasp the wire. Clinical fascination lasts for about ten years then the attitude becomes 'I want to make some money'.

Organisations are equally capable of clinging to their poles. When the demand for mechanical calculators suddenly plummeted, Facit could have grasped the wire by expanding their highly profitable typewriter business. The demand for typewriters was three times that for mechanical calculators. Staff had been turning down orders because the company could not produce enough. Instead, Facit sold their profitable typewriter and office furnishings factories in order to cling to the mechanical calculator business.[166]

Skeletons and Cobwebs

In the late 1950s the City of London was a very different place from what it is now:

> If a director was in the office before 10 am it was assumed the bank was going bust, and normal directorial hours in the City were from 11 am to 4 pm. Most messages travelled within the Square Mile by hand; only the most urgent were sent by telegraph . . . . Directors . . . could still park their cars with ease under London Wall . . . took dry sherry before lunch in the Partners' Room where they all sat together. . . . In the afternoon they were served with tea and biscuits from a silver service.[171]

The angel of change was an outsider called Siegmund Warburg. Warburg's tactics horrified the City establishment. In an interview given towards the end of his life, Warburg said:

> I remember some people in very good houses talked very nastily behind my back: 'Do you know this fellow Warburg? He starts in the

office at *eight o'clock* in the morning!' That was considered contemptible.[172]

Even more contemptible, Warburg broke all the rules of gentlemanly conduct in order to drive through the union of British Aluminium with TI-Reynolds – the City's first hostile take-over bid. It was far from easy. The entire City establishment united against Warburg, but Warburg proved unstoppable.

Warburg's triumph over high City arrogance transformed the climate of competition. S. G. Warburg went on to become the UK's pre-eminent merchant bank. The rift with the City establishment eventually healed and Warburg was subsequently knighted. No one saw the dangers more clearly than Warburg who said:

> Being recognised as members of the British establishment is the most dangerous thing that could happen to us. . . . Because admittance to the establishment implies a temptation to become lazy and self-satisfied and complacent.[172]

In other words, Warburg saw that:

establishment does not mean efficient.

Warburg's interview was published in 1980. in the mid-1980s S. G. Warburg bought two broking firms and a firm of jobbers in anticipation of deregulation, known as the Big Bang. The public school ethos of Rowe and Pitman (one of the broking firms) sat uncomfortably with S. G. Warburg's tradition of meritocracy. Consequently, the dynamism and intensity that had characterised the organisational culture was sapped. The bank became bloated, and, in 1995, its unsustainable cost basis precipitated a crisis that cost Warburg's its independence.

The point is, whether it is a hairdressing salon or pre-eminent merchant bank, the potential for decay exists. It is not just the skeletons in our cupboards that should worry us, but also the skeletons sitting on boardroom chairs linked by a labyrinth of cobwebs. To be more precise, it is not the decay that does the damage but our failure to *see* ourselves and our organizations for what they are becoming – we have all been here for so long. Age may weary us, but it is the years that condemn.

Let's go.

Chapter 12

The art of decision making

'Jeeves … Your scheme has proved a bust'.
'Certainly it would appear that matters have not arranged themselves
quite as we anticipated, sir.' (Wodehouse, *Right Ho, Jeeves*)

So far, writing this book has been like lifting the bonnet of a car, pointing inside the engine and saying, 'there's your problem'. There is an important difference, however, between repairing a car engine and decision making. There is a way to fix an engine whereas the purpose of this book has been to been to suggest that the art of decision making rests not in prescription but in insight. Above all, the intention has been to show that real power is an ability to sense doubt and uncertainty, a feel for the risks and dangers that surround us, and an awareness of the limits of our ability to exert control and to predict the future. So what can we learn from the failures and fiascos described in the foregoing chapters?

Rising to the Level of Events

As this book was nearing completion I picked up Emily Brontë's novel *Wuthering Heights*. Reading about the snow-bound house and the ghost of Catherine it struck me as almost incredible that the manuscript was written by hand, without the aid of a computer and word-processing software.

The Mann Gulch firecrew perished because they refused to drop their tools. As decision makers, we run the same danger. Our textbooks emphasise the tools of analysis and computation. Rarely do we see the word *reflection*. As Queen Elizabeth I lay dying:

> Meanwhile, in an inner chamber, at his table, alone, the Secretary sat writing. All eventualities had been foreseen, everything was arranged, only the last soft touches remained to be given.... As the hand moved, the mind flowed too, ranging sadly upon the vicissitudes of mortal beings, reflecting ... with quiet clarity, on what the hours, even then, were bringing.[173]

Notice what is happening here. The death of a sovereign is a momentous event but there is no crisis. The pace may be slow but nothing has been left to chance. Everything is in place, all eventualities have been foreseen and still there is time to deliberate and take stock of events.

I am not suggesting that decision makers retreat into a world of candlelight, quill pens and messengers on horseback. My point is that reflection is the key to generating insight.

'The Torah speaks about four sons: one who is wise and one who is contrary; one who is simple and one who does not even know how to ask a question.'[174] The first son who is wise should be good at decision making. The son who is contrary might possess the virtues of flexibility and creativity. The son who is simple might prove single-minded and decisive. The real liability is the son who does not know how to ask a question.

*The art of decision making is **knowing** the questions to ask.*

Asking questions is important. Even more important, however, is asking the right questions.

From an early age we are encouraged to ask 'why'. Yet if we are to make sense of events, and indeed rise to the level of events, that is, distinguish the wood from the trees, we must also ask *'what'*. We know why many rural pubs, post offices, banks and shops have closed down but what are the larger forces driving events? The recent mergers in the financial services industry may represent the last act in the playing out of the forces generated by deregulation ('Big Bang') in 1986.

We are most at risk of failing to rise to the level of events when facing an unprecedented situation. The danger is that we anchor our judgements in the past and fail to see the situation for what it has become or will become. Rising to the level of events means asking:

What does it all mean?

'The lamps are going out all over Europe,' said Sir Edward Grey as the First World War started.

The next step is matching mindset and action to the situation. This is what the Stock Exchange singularly failed to do with Taurus. Those leading the venture failed to grasp that Taurus was bigger than the Stock Exchange. A member of the monitoring group said:

> There are plenty of projects that are large and complicated. That's no reason not to do them but you have to think, 'large and compli- cated and we are going to have to work very hard to get it to the end'. Yet there was never a sense that this one [Taurus] was under control.[89]

Having gauged the level of events the next step is deciding how to respond. As decision makers we are frequently bombarded by conflicting views about what should be done. Moreover, there is always a danger that those who shout loudest succeed regardless of the merits of their case. Another question to be posed is:

What is the force of the argument?[77]

The playwright Arthur Miller was often asked what was in those bags carried by Willie Loman in *Death of a Salesman*. what was he selling? Was it samples of rope, spoons, dog meat or what? 'Himself,' replied Miller.[170] Another important question is:

What are the emotional forces driving the decision?[77]

Decision science assumes that we can function like computers devoid of emotion. In contrast, the art of decision making lies in recognising what is in the bags, that is, the presence of emotional forces. Whatever our business plans, position papers and the like contain, ultimately they contain us. Moreover, we need to know what those forces are. How far was McDonald's ill-fated decision to sue for libel driven by policy considerations, and how far by personal hurt?

Almost all decisions require us to predict the future. Science and mathematics have provided us with highly sophisticated tools of forecasting. In contrast, the decision maker's art lies not in scientific certainty but is imbued with doubt and the knowledge that whatever their scientific authority, all projections are ultimately guesses.

Moreover, our guesses are frequently wishful thinking. There was nothing in the history of the Taurus project to justify the technical team's habitual optimism in predicting completion dates for various phases of the project. The question is what makes you believe that a certain thing will happen? No one asked what made the planners of 'Expo 86' believe that every man, woman and child in Canada would visit the exhibition.

In assessing the progress of any project it is useful to examine what has been achieved. An equally important question, however, is:

What remains to be done?

One of the mistakes in building Taurus was a tendency to focus upon progress as distinct from considering the challenges that still lay ahead. The next stage is to analyse whether a project can be completed within an acceptable timeframe and budget; whether it is still worth completing and what risks are involved.

Such analysis is only useful, however, if it is scrupulously objective. There is always the possibility that pressure from vested interests results in an overly optimistic assessment of the prospects. In judging the worth of any such analysis the question of authorship and influence over the conclusions is just as important as the quality of the work.

If objectives cannot be met can the project be redesigned? Colonel Hankey had the right idea when the Dardanelles expedition began to unravel. He wanted a small committee to review and replan the project. History might have been different if he had pressed the point.

Many decision failure are failures of imagination. We must accept that those whose task it is to answer our questions may be careful with the truth. Requirements are always 'virtually finished'; all projects are 'almost on time', all problems are 'minor glitches'. imagine if the roles were reversed, what would you say in order to get what you want? If I could ask only one question it would be:

> *What might this person know that I would be very interested to know too?*

A Dog is for Life

The first lesson of escalation is that it is easier to get into a mess than to get out of it. Cats have whiskers to keep them safe from being trapped in a hole too narrow for them. Decision makers must rely upon their imagination. It is not what a decision is that matters so much as what it might become. While all understanding comes from a backwards glance, we can also look forwards before becoming involved in a particular course of action and consider what might happen.

George Ball, the US Under-secretary of State, had the right idea when he warned President Lyndon Johnson of the dangers of becoming embroiled in Vietnam:

> The decision you now face is crucial. Once large numbers of US troops are committed to direct combat, they will begin to take heavy casualties in a war they are ill-equipped to fight in a non-cooperative if not downright hostile countryside. Once we suffer large casualties, we will have started a well-nigh irreversible process. Our involvement will be so great that we cannot – without national humiliation – stop short of achieving our complete objectives. Of the two possibilities I think humiliation will be more likely than the achievement of our objectives – even after we have paid terrible costs.[175]

This prophetic memo is dated 1 July 1965. The lesson for decision makers is that before becoming involved in anything ask yourself:

What are we getting into?

Research by psychologists into accidents in flight operations off nuclear carriers suggests that people who survive in dangerous situations do so because they live by the credo of never getting into anything without first making sure there is a way out.[17] It is a good precept for avoiding the pitfalls of escalation. We may not know what the future holds but we can at least check whether there is a way out if things turn out badly. In the words of the aviation industry we do well to remember that:

Take-off is optional, landing is compulsory.

Ball saw the dangers because he thought ahead. In contrast, much of the time our thinking is reactive, riveted to the here and now. Like the man who jumped from a twenty-storey building and as he reached the tenth floor muttered, 'alright so far'.[176]

Obviously we cannot foresee all the consequences of our actions. What we can do, however, is to use our imagination. For instance, force works by cutting off the other party's options. The problem is that it cuts off yours as well because once force has been applied, persuasion is useless. If circumstances permit, why not try persuasion first?

The correct time to withdraw from a course of action is when it has become clear that expectations cannot be met. Obviously it may be sensible to persist for a while and invest addditional resources in order to give the venture a chance to work but not when it has become obvious that persistence is futile. Escalation scenarios can present us with a dilemma in that there is always the hope of turning matters around. What is needed are:

Facts, not optimism.

If a decision begins to turn out badly someone needs to analyse whether expectations can be achieved. This was one of the mistakes of Vietnam, that is, the government continued pouring in troops without considering, in the light of experience, whether they were fighting a war that was unwinnable. For instance, part of the military strategy relied upon bombing roads in order to sever communications. Yet the roads were so poor to begin with that bombing them made hardly any difference. When Peter Rawlins took a closer look at Taurus he realised there was no hope of expectations being met. Yet right at the very outset a member of the Taurus monitoring group drew some graphs plotting deliverables against actuals and discovered that they were showing delivery at infinity! Even when the graphs started to converge they showed delivery in 1995 – that is, nowhere near the official deadline of mid-1991.[89]

Another possibility for limiting the effects of escalation is to set limits on your involvement. The important thing is to stick to them. There is always the temptation to 'give it another week' or another tranche of funding.

As regards our psychological attachment to past costs, there is a saying in poker:

If the odds are against you, quit.

No matter how high the stakes, the inescapable logic is that if the odds are against you, persistence only makes matters worse.

Liars Serving Truth

Decision science suggests that power accrues to those with the most information. Yet information can affect our ability to make decisions just as alcohol affects our ability to drive. Specifically, research by psychologists suggests that the more information we have, the greater our confidence in it. Yet the more information we have at our disposal the greater the likelihood of losing sight of reality because of the sheer confusion.

Although it can be dangerous to simplify, it can also be dangerous *not* to simplify. One technique is to stand back and ask yourself:

What does it all mean?

Just as barristers know that many seemingly complex legal cases turn upon a single point, you can reduce the risks of becoming confused by searching for the simple idea that lies behind the mass of information. For instance, although we can examine reams and reams of financial data, the issue may boil down to the following equation: 'In: £100 000; Out: £110 000.' Seen that way, we know at once what the problem is!

More importantly, although knowledge is power:

*ultimate mastery is not about having the most information but understanding the **limits** of one's information.*

Sensing the limits of one's data is largely a matter of attitude and expectation. Science is a search for truth. In this view information is either 'right' or 'wrong'. In contrast, the art of decision making is to see information as liars in service of truth.[49]

The most plausible liar is the single uncontradicted data source. Its appeal is that it makes us feel in control precisely because it seems certain. Recall, it is not what our information reveals that matters but what it conceals. It is risky to consider only the information that can be collected and processed through machines. For although we can vary the parameters of a spreadsheet, all we are doing is varying what the program allows us to vary and forgetting everything else.[64]

The key to reducing risk rests in consulting different sources of information. Machine-generated graphs and charts may indicate that a construction project has slipped by 10%. Does that mean a problem exists? Supposing you visit the site and see work in progress. Does the project seem well organised? Do the staff appear to be motivated and taking pride in work? When do they think the job will be finished? Likewise, in addition to reading a reassuring report prepared by a middle manager upon food safety practices in a motorway service station, you can take breakfast one morning and watch how the eggs are fried.

Take a Walk on the Wild Side

To learn something new about music buy a compact disc of an unfamiliar composer. The same precept applies to information for decision making. Although a sense of purpose is generally a 'good thing' there is something to be said for looking around at random. The graffiti in the toilets tells you something about the organisation and the people who work there. The so-called 'gutter press' offers a different perspective on life. So might the interior of a rough-looking bar. Even the noise of an ice-cream van can be the precursor to a flash of insight. The benefits of this kind of exercise may not be realised immediately but one day they could be significant. If you happen to take a job in the music industry you may just recall a tune blaring from an upstairs window during a trip to the backstreets ...

There's a Rumour Going Round

Rumour is an interesting source of information. It is frequently dismissed as unreliable precisely because it is information that cannot be verified. Yet it is not the content of a rumour that is significant so much as its *existence*. Although there were multifarious rumours during the final months of BCCI's existence they all pointed to the same conclusion. That is, it was not that BCCI contained one or two bad apples but that the barrel itself was rotten.

Rumour is special because it reflects more *intimate* contact with reality than machine-processed information. During the last fortnight of Barings' existence, according to computer printouts Leeson's profits were increasing exponentially. Yet reputable investment houses were warning their customers to be careful about using Barings as a counterparty because of the rumours circulating in the financial markets of the Far East suggesting massive exposure to risk.

Opposites

Expectations are powerful realities.

We saw in Chapter 1 that expectations become reality. We can reduce the risk of succumbing to our information filters by reminding ourselves that what we know and believe to be true is by definition a partial view of reality. We can reduce the risk of becoming seduced by counterpoising opposites. Where a decision rests heavily upon analysis pay particular attention to what experience and intuition say. Analysis may suggest that the risk of contracting food poisoning from eggs is very low. Yet how would you feel about feeding your child a dessert made with a raw egg?

Where a decision is intuitively appealing pay particular attention to analytical rigour. This was the mistake in the Dardanelles campaign. Although the idea of a naval bombardment was brilliant, its execution fell short. Likewise, where similarities are evident look for differences. Conversely, where differences are salient look for points of comparison. Incidentally if, having weighed up two alternative courses of action, you discover that they are virtually equal, it may be wise to choose the option with most intuitive appeal as your emotions are telling you something.

An important theme of this book is that everything exists in a constant state of flux and transformation, as forever becoming. To avoid the trap of our perceptions becoming rooted in the past, start from the assumption that things *must* have changed. In considering how things have changed, pay particular attention to the tiny shifts, the seemingly trivial breaks in the pattern. The subtle developments can signal a profound change that is not immediately obvious.

Triangulation is a good test of the reliability of one's information. This exists where three different sources of information all point to the same conclusion. There is one vital caveat, however. That is, everything may be pointing in the same direction because of what you have unconsciously chosen to see and hear.

Good judgement is usually the result of experience. And experience is frequently the result of bad judgement.[78]

All our information may point to the same conclusion, but what does experience say? Experience teaches us that what looks easy in theory may be difficult or even impossible in practice. Consider a large caravan mounted on a trailer. The load measures 10 feet wide. In theory it will pass through a gate measuring 10 feet and 3 inches. Yet no experienced site manager would attempt the exercise.

This was the mistake in the decision to utilise a software package to drive Taurus. On paper the decision made sense in that it would enable the ambitious timescale to be met by supplying part of the functionality. Experience and intuition suggested otherwise: 'I have been building systems for twenty-five years and you get a feel.'

Incidentally, experience can teach us that what is impossible in theory *is* achievable in practice. In theory certain spinning machines cannot handle low-grade cotton. In practice they can produce a serviceable yarn.

That said, experience can be a trap if it leads to a closed mind. A closed mind is rarely conducive to good judgement because it does not invite doubt. In contrast, wisdom is a combination of experience, curiosity, humility and respect for the perceptions and beliefs of other people. The Tenerife air crash might have been avoided if the pilot had behaved differently. He had a reputation as a martinet that did not encourage correction from subordinates. This may be one reason why the co-pilot failed to speak up although he was almost certain the pilot had made a mistake.

Look Hard and Look Twice

Decisions prove a bust when assumptions unravel. Yet it is virtually impossible to avoid making assumptions in decision making. What does the damage is not the making of assumptions so much as the illusion of control, the belief that we cannot fail. The first danger is that we forget we are making assumptions. We switch the kettle on and automatically assume that it will heat the water. When the military commanders said that the Bay of Pigs invasion force could hide in the caves, President Kennedy and his advisors automatically assumed that caves were close to the beach.

Assumptions can be identified by analysing your information according to the following categories:[177]

* *Known*
* *Unclear*
* *Assumed.*

Generally, the fewer assumptions, the better. Imagine a decision as a cart piled high with pottery. Every assumption represents a rut on the road to success. The second danger is that such is our belief in our own efficacy that we underestimate the risks and difficulties that may lie ahead. We know that the success of a particular project depends upon getting, say, ten customers to sign contracts within the space of three months. We know that there have already been expressions of interest from four organisations. It is easy to read too much into those expressions of interest and to forget that everything depends upon getting no fewer than ten organisations from an almost cold start, through all the decision procedures to committing themselves to a major undertaking within a short timescale. Such decisions are what is known as a 'real squeak' as there is so little room for failure.

The question that we need to ask ourselves is, what makes us believe that we can meet the challenge, apart from transcendant optimism?

Yet of the three categories of information:

Most dangerous are the **knowns**.

Assumptions frequently shade into fact. Once something achieves the status of fact it is like throwing a blanket over an accident victim who is presumed dead. No one will ever lift the blanket again. This is precisely what happened in the case of the lethal DC10s. Once the paperwork had been issued confirming that the requisite modifications had been made, no one thought to 'lift the blanket' and check. If there is a motto for decision making it is 'to doubt that which we are most sure of'.

Quacks Bawling

Another important theme of this book is that what we call reality frequently emerges as the product of negotiation. In other words, it is a myth. The notion of myth implies that what may seem rock-solid certain, such as notions of core competence, is basically an invention. It is also worth remembering that what may appear to be the best course of action may owe more to political adroitness than the substantive merits of the case.

It is safest to imagine ruling myths and competing myths then as eighteenth-century quacks bawling from their booths. Recall that all myths are partly true. It is the part that is untrue that should engage our attention. Moreover, the fact that everyone is doing something does not necessarily make it the right thing to do. The pub landlords who retained their hand-pulled ales and coal fires during the era of modernisation in the late 1960s created a market niche for themselves. Likewise, the brokers Cazenove stood virtually aloof from the merger mania in the City in the run-up to deregulation. Analysts doubted they would remain independent for long. The partners, however, decided that there would be a market for truly independent advice. Time has vindicated their judgement. More recently when the UK clearing banks were busy subscribing to the myth that the future lay in creating integrated investment houses like Barclays with BZW, LloydsTSB studiously concentrated upon the dull business of domestic banking and profited as a result.

Just as it is necessary to examine the emotional impulses driving a particular decision, it is also important to consider the political forces. Power and self-interest are almost invariably cloaked. Doctors talk about quality of patient care when what they really mean is 'what's in it for us?' Lawyers talk about the public interest when what they are really interested in is preserving the privileges of the profession. The critical question in identifying vested interests is to ask:

Who benefits?

Myths are ultimately promulgated by people. The best way of handling harebrained ideas is to let them expose themselves by asking questions. In other words:

instead of telling others they are wrong, get them to explain why they think they are right.

That said, decision makers are frequently honourable men and women trying to do their best to avoid mistakes. In the Dardanelles fiasco Fisher had little to gain personally from contradicting the proposal to rely upon ships alone. Asquith's first mistake was a failure to listen and to probe the force of Fisher's argument. The second mistake was to suppress the conflict. Recall, conflict is a trans*action*. Conflict can be conducive to good decision making because it enables perspectives to be shared, risks to be probed and alternative courses of action to be considered.

Indeed, when it comes to chairing discussions there may be something to be said for stimulating conflict. One factor that distinguished the handling of the Cuban missile crisis was dividing the decision makers into two groups to examine the options with each group then acting as devil's advocate in challenging each other's recommendations.

Buying a 'Cut and Shut'

Recall, rationality is not a guide but an achievement. When it comes to persuasion:

we are all second-hand car dealers.

Moreover, the vehicles we supply, that is, policy statements, position papers, business plans and the like, setting out the rationale for a decision are best seen as potential 'cut and shuts'. 'Cut and shuts' are cars that have been welded together from vehicles that have been involved in accidents. They look the part but are extremely dangerous because they tend to crumple in a collision.

The art of decision making is feeling for the joins. The place to look is the welding pertaining to costs and benefits. The rationale for the merger between Price Waterhouse and Coopers & Lybrand doubtless looked impeccable on paper. Yet after only a few months on the road the new organisation known as PwC collided with reality and was obliged to shed 10% of its UK partners when it discovered that the costs were higher than expected and the benefits rather less than had been promised.

Fortune Favours the Brave

Frequently it is not the problem itself that confounds us but how we approach the problem. More specifically, our decision making frequently reflects first-order thinking. This involves approaching within an existing framework whereas second-order thinking steps outside that framework. Consider a child that refuses to eat. First-order thinking would involve coaxing the child, and, when that fails, the anxious parent applies 'more of the same' perhaps offering a reward for cooperation, even pleading with the child to eat. What happens, of course, is that the child learns that refusing to eat is a good way of commanding attention. In contrast, second-order thinking involves changing the game by removing the food.

Second-order thinking can solve seemingly hopeless problems though at first sight it often involves doing something that seems stupid or even suicidal. For instance, a medieval castle had been under seige for weeks. The garrison were about to surrender as their food supplies were almost exhausted. The garrison commander then did something that his starving troops thought was madness. He had the last ox slaughtered, stuffed its belly with barley and tossed it over the castle wall. The besieging troops were dismayed by this contemptuous gesture for it suggested that the castle was set to hold out indefinitely. Consequently they gave up and moved on.[123]

The trick of second-order thinking is to examine the assumptions you are making about the problem. First-order thinking assumes that in war the problem is fighting the enemy. In contrast, second-order thinking recognises that fighting is only a means to an end. The real problem is to destroy the enemy's morale thus rendering them incapable of fighting. Throwing the ox from the battlements achieved precisely that. Another example of first-order thinking is to solve the problem of darkness by improving the lighting. Second-order thinking would be to alter the specification of what constitutes darkness. Likewise, in the 1970s research and development effort focused upon making computer hardware smaller. In contrast, Bill Gates recognised that if the software could be made smaller the hardware would automatically shrink. More recently, Unilever began a review of their long-term strategy having recognised that customers do not want washing powder but clean clothes.

First-order thinking focuses upon solving the problem. Second-order thinking involves questioning the question. Recall, decisions fail when expectations cannot be met. Second-order thinking recognises that we can create failure by entertaining unrealistic expectations. Most of us feel sad sometimes. Left to our own devices, the mood passes. Yet if someone says 'cheer up' they intensify the misery by making us feel guilty about our inability to feel constantly happy. This then is the depression – not the original sadness.[123] In other words, it is the expectation that we should be constantly happy that creates the problem. Likewise, the

THE ILLUSION OF ALTERNATIVES

success of Churchill's wartime premiership owed something to his ability to structure expectations – hence 'blood, toil, tears and sweat,' and as the bombs rained down 'I expect worse to come'.

'Don't hold onto,' counsels the Bhudda. An interesting case of second-order thinking concerns the restaurant Chez Nico in London's Park Lane. The restaurant had experienced a 14% drop in turnover. The owner Nico Ladenis responded by giving up the three Michelin stars. Explaining his decision to renounce the ambition of a lifetime, Ladenis said, 'It's like wearing a straitjacket. Constantly you have to conform. You have to have technique, flair, a sauce that is indefinable . . . . But sometimes you just want to do something simple like a poached lobster with a beautiful mayonnaise.'

Renouncing the risotto with black truffles and a warm escalope of foie gras with spinach salad enables Landenis to re-invent the business by giving it a more customer-focused orientation whereby the customer defines perfection. Gone is the sign outside the restaurant, 'We do not feel we have to produce our menu to show you how good we are. For your information, we do not serve prawn cocktails or well-done steaks'.[178]

The Illusion of Alternatives

Card seven of the Major Arcana of the Tarot depicts the knight. Two women, one older, one younger, tug his sleeve. First-order thinking sees the problem of decision making as choosing between alternatives. In this view, the knight must decide whether his destiny lies with the young woman or the older woman, he cannot have both. The knight solves the problem by dint of second-order thinking. That is, he jumps into his chariot and flees the scene. in other words, he solves the problem of choice by *rejecting choice*.

Likewise, first-order thinking focuses upon the costs of taking a risk. In contrast, second-order thinking asks if there may be more to lose by *not* taking the risk.

If At First You Don't Succeed . . .

Although the proverb urges us to persist in the face of failure, repeated failure usually tells us we are doing something wrong. Escalation is frequently perpetuated by first-order thinking. When first-order thinking fails to solve the problem the response is to try, try again by applying 'more of the same'. Consistency usually makes the problem worse. When Taurus ran into difficulties the technical team applied 'more of the same', that is, working longer and longer hours solving one problem after another. In contrast, second-order thinking would have entailed questioning the existence of so many problems.

One important factor that prevents us from engaging in second-order thinking is when the means eclipse the ends. Finishing Taurus became an end in itself. Likewise, the Dardanelles fiasco was ensured when the decision makers lost heart because the forts had not been demolished. Yet they were within an ace of procuring the surrender of Turkey – their real objective.

We can reduce the risk of the means eclipsing the ends by asking:

What are you trying to achieve?

One of British Rail's success stories was the decision to buy a small fleet of very fast and very powerful diesel locomotives known as the Deltics. These were introduced in the early 1960s and were intended to fill a ten-year gap between steam traction and electrification of the east coast main line. In fact, they exceeded expectations and remained in service for twenty years. What is interesting about the decision is that British Rail began by defining the problem before looking for a solution. In this case, the problem was to compete with air services which would in turn require an average speed of 75 mph. The Deltics were the means to this end.[179]

Being clear about what you are trying to achieve is important, otherwise, you may end up like the celebrated drunk who looks for his car keys not where he dropped them but under the lamp post because the light is good.[123]

It is not enough to say 'we want to expand' or 'we plan to increase turnover'. What are you actually trying to achieve?

Escaping *To* Reality

The next question is:

How can you be sure of achieving your objective?

Generally, the more 'ers,' 'buts', 'maybes' 'must look into that' and 'to be decided later', the greater the danger of plans going awry. Precision is all-important. If a project depends upon sponsorship, have sponsors been identified and what exactly have they committed themselves to?

Much has been said in this book about the dangers of means/ ends reversal. Yet the very essence of management is 'making do', that is, making the means fit the ends. Another lesson of the Dardanelles fiasco is that if the resources are seriously inadequate it may be better not to attempt something at all.

Another strategy for minimising the risk of failure is to engage in reality testing. In the novel *Jane Eyre* Rochester disguises himself as a fortune teller and informs his fiancé that there is a question mark over his fortune. The lady promptly vanishes, thereby confirming Rochester's doubts about her sincerity. One reason for the Deltics' success was that the design was extensively tested on a full-scale prototype before British Rail finally committed themselves to buying the locomotive. More recently, the success of the Inland Revenue's Self-Assessment project owes something to rigorous pre-testing not only within the Inland Revenue but also with taxpayers, accountants and other interested bodies. Likewise, unlike *Heaven's Gate*, the film *Titanic* was exposed to audience testing. The rapturous response suggested that the project was worth completing despite being hugely overbudget.

Catch a Falling Knife

To act or not to act? This is a basic dilemma of decision making to which there are no easy answers. Everything depends upon circumstances. One of the most dangerous things in an organisation is a loss of meaning where people are unable to make sense of events. This is what killed the Mann Gulch firecrew. We see the collapse of sense making in milder forms when people start running round like headless chickens devoid of direction or purpose. The argument for acting is that action generates feedback, it is a form of reality testing in other words.

Conversely, although the proverb suggests that they who hesitate are lost, in a situation of uncertainty they who hesitate may be ultimately more successful. They who succumb to the temptation to buy shares in a tumbling market (the 'wow! grab it! too good to lose!' syndrome may end up catching a falling knife, as the saying goes.

Those who hesitate keep their options open. In the Cold War-inspired film *Hunt for Red October* a Russian nuclear submarine is heading for America. Ostensibly the crew have decided to defect. Yet the real intent may be to launch a nuclear attack. The obvious response is to weigh up the situation, decide which of the two scenarios is the most probable and plan accordingly. A much wiser response to risk, however, is to:

know that you do not know.[180]

and plan for both eventualities.

Do No Harm

The cardinal rule of medicine is 'do no harm'. Again, frequently it is not the problem itself that creates risk and danger but how we react to it. The first question is:

Must you react?

Restraint is the hallmark of statesmanship. If McDonald's had ignored the leaflets distributed by the group of environmental activists the damage to their reputation would have been minimal compared with what followed. By reacting as they did McDonald's created the very situation that they were trying to avoid.

Sometimes the best way to respond to threats and other forms of provocation is to ignore them, feign deafness in other words. Otherwise you risk locking the other party into an escalating spiral. By demanding an apology McDonald's made it just as difficult for Steel and Morris to back down as it was for them.

Ill-judged reactions are frequently the result of becoming too preoccupied with the here and now. In order to regain a sense of perspective:

see near things as if they were distant.[181]

In other words, ask yourself how important today's problems will seem a year from now, three years from now and ten years from now.

Retaining a sense of proportion is also important. We saw in Chapter 6 that denigration is a cruel exercise whose purpose is to discredit the old myth by exaggerating its weaknesses. The exposé of practices relating to the sale and retention of organs at Liverpool's Alder Hey hospital has rightly attracted criticism. Such has been the uproar, however, that there is a danger of provoking a backlash that undermines research. It is one thing to criticise. It is another thing to demonise.

Another question that can prevent us from overreacting is to ask:

Is this a thorn in the side or a dagger through the heart?

Thorns tend to outnumber daggers by far.

Where a reaction is necessary then seek the subtle option that yields results without creating countervailing problems. In 1963 American intelligence discovered the existence of Russian-sponsored missile bases in Cuba. Since the missiles were aimed at the USA there could be no question of ignoring their existence. Two options were considered, a military strike aimed at eliminating the missiles or a naval blockade to prevent military supplies from reaching Cuba. A military strike held out the promise of firm, decisive action. In contrast, a blockade seemed a weak and uncertain response. Yet as the decision makers analysed the alternatives they realised that a military strike would invite retaliation, and if it missed the target – then what? In contrast, mounting a blockade enabled the American government to signify power and determination with minimal aggression and without raising the stakes. Moreover, the blockade could be tightened if necessary, and it still left open the option of a military attack.

Squeezing Hands

Another argument for calculated inaction is that those who poke and prod and demand answers may end up creating the very situation they were so anxious to avoid. If you think that you may not like the answer to a question:

Don't ask.

To ask is to lose the initiative. The art of decision making is to turn ambiguity into power by defining other people's realities. At the height of the Cuban missile crisis the American government received two letters from Russia. One was cold and uncompromising and had obviously been compiled by officials. The second was warm and conciliatory and had obviously been written by President Khrushchev himself.

It was unclear which of the two communications reflected the real position. Robert Kennedy is credited with a brilliant response known as the Trollope ploy. In Anthony Trollope's novels a squeeze of the hand was taken as a proposal of marriage. The American government decided to squeeze the hand of the Russians by responding to the second communication and ignoring the first. Responding to the more conciliatory communication enabled the Americans to create the reality they wanted. Imagine what might have happened, however, if the Americans had taken the seemingly logical step of asking the Russians for clarification![182]

Attila the Hun said the same thing in a different language, that is:

choose your enemies very carefully.

Much has been said in this book about the slippery nature of reality and how we create our realities and then act as if our creations were forcing us to – which ultimately they are. The point is, the potentially malleable nature of reality also implies freedom to create the world we want to live in. Moreover, although chance may have the last word, such freedom implies that we are not completely at the mercy of fate.

Blown Off-course

It is all very well to say that everything exists in a constant state of flux and transformation. How do we prevent a decision from becoming blown off-course?

One of the lessons of the Taurus project is that it is the *totality* of developments that matters. Small, seemingly inconsequential changes can add up to more than the sum of their parts. Another mistake was the failure to recognise that more is not necessarily better as consultation degenerated into interference. Likewise, a key lesson of the Dardanelles fiasco is that logical moves aimed at improving the prospects of success can have precisely the opposite effect. The same applies to making concessions piecemeal. Not only can the sum total undermine the cost/benefit structure of a venture, but, by the time decision makers realise what has happened, they may have become virtually committed to proceeding.

The answer lies in control. Although flexibility is usually seen as a virtue in management, sometimes it is necessary to be inflexible. In the case of Taurus that would have meant freezing the requirements on the understanding that it is always possible to make changes later, that is, once the system is up and running.

Besides, because we consult people this does not mean we have to comply with their demands. One way of avoiding a tragedy of the commons scenario is to say 'That may be your view but in the interests of the common good I ask you not to press the point'. It is a brave person indeed that holds out against such moral force.

An eye for paradox is also useful. One of the lessons of the Dardanelles fiasco is that there is nothing like common sense to undermine us. To be more precise, although Fisher had a valid point about the risks of relying upon ships alone, sometimes it is wise just to accept the risk and avoid the temptation to interfere and stop other people from interfering.

Creating Luck

Any decision that involves uncertainty implies the possibility of failure. The art of decision making is not about taking risks but minimising risk. Where a decision is necessarily risky consider whether unknowns can be counterbalanced with knowns. The Zurich Opera House took a highly risky decision to stage relatively unknown operas but balanced deep uncertainty by engaging well-known performers to help attract an audience.

It is also important to consider 'what if?' critical assumptions are not met and draw up a contingency plan. This may seem an obvious suggestion but it is surprising how often it is neglected. Contingency planning can also reduce the risks of escalation because:

alternatives are power.

Winner's curse arises because the winning party overestimates the value of the prize.[73] The question is, what makes one party believe that they need something so badly that they have no alternative but to pay the price? There are always alternatives if we are willing to look for them. It pays to have a choice and for other people to know that you have a choice – even if it is only to do without.

Show Some Emotion?

It was suggested earlier that all decisions are driven by emotion. Moreover, in situations of tension and crisis emotions frequently run high. It is not emotion that does the damage but the *connection* between emotion and action. In a nutshell, avoid the temptation to channel feelings and impulses into action.[77] Instead, allow emotion to subside before acting. Take your time, sleep on an idea, allow days or even weeks to pass before responding. Time acts as a solvent upon problems. It enables us to regain a sense of perspective, to see different possibilities and to avoid the dangers of responding to provocation. Time also enables the other party to cool down and reconsider.

A good trader has no ego.

The lucrative bonuses paid to traders in the financial services industry depend upon profits. If traders allow their egos to prevent them from cutting their losses they must pay for it.

Likewise, the art of decision making is being able to free oneself from the shackles of ego-defensiveness. The trick is to subtract your ego from the equation. What possibilities does that reveal? One option is to calculate the cost of intransigence bearing in mind that the price of anything is what you could have had instead. Relatedly you could consider what a detached observer might suggest. For example, what might the *Financial Times Lex* column say about what you should do?

'Should cut their losses';
'The offer may be disappointing but it is worth considering;'
'The loss is a psychological blow but even without it growth is forecast;'
'These may or may not turn out to be one-off expenses; probably not.'

Another possibility is to seek advice. Advice is only useful, however, if it is honest advice. As Machiavelli points out[183] the only way of disarming those who would tell us what we want to hear is by showing that honesty will not offend you.

Puzzled as Well as Beaten

Making a decision is easy. The hard part is implementing it. Any decision that threatens something of value to another party will almost certainly prompt resistance. Moreover, it is a mistake to underestimate peoples' capacity and determination to resist.

Ultimate genius is the stroke that leaves the enemy puzzled as well as beaten.[162]

The American military assumed that Japan would never dare attack Pearl Harbor, and that Saddam Hussain would never dare invade Kuwait. Likewise, did Coca-Cola ever imagine anyone daring to launch Virgin Cola? While other decision makers are busy working upon their probable scenarios the opportunity exists to launch an improbable one.

The bold stroke defeats resistance because it achieves surprise. Imagine a family being held hostage in a house by a group of terrorists. Suddenly SAS troops burst through a wall and shoot dead the terrorists before they have time to react. Surprise is achieved by entering the building from next door and quietly removing the bricks from the wall leaving only a thin layer of plaster between the troops and terrorists.

Many decisions succeed by dint of human will. Yet will has less to do with fanatical determination and more to do with picking out the bricks. Will rests in formulating a clear sense of purpose, considering how it might be achieved, what obstacles might emerge and how these might be overcome.

The good soldier avoids the battle. Decision making is partly the art of the possible in that no matter how technically brilliant something is, it only succeeds if it commands support. Taurus ultimately failed because, apart from the Stock Exchange, nobody wanted it. Decisions that go against the prevailing wind stand a high chance of failure because of all the contrary forces. Is it worth it? That said, the most lasting achievements are frequently secured by stealth. To proceed by stealth means removing the bricks from the wall by working informally and unobtrusively to create new realities and then using the decision-making process to formalise that which now exists.

Although it is fashionable for leaders to be portrayed as 'blasting their way through obstacles', patience is ultimately a more deadly force.

Small gains are within grasp.

One way of implementing a bold vision is to proceed bit by bit. The Conservative government used this strategy during the 1980s to emasculate trade union power by passing legislation in apparently piecemeal fashion. In contrast, earlier, much milder attempts by governments to curb trade union power failed precisely because decision makers tried to blast their way onto the statute book. A patient approach can mean to have *and* to hold.

If confrontation is unavoidable then try to avoid a full-frontal assault. Instead, focus upon the cornerstone. The aim of the Dardanelles campaign was to knock out the props from under Germany. Likewise, the precursor to deregulating the financial services industry was not an elaborate blueprint but the relatively simple move of forcing the Stock Exchange to abandon its rule on fixed commissions thus unleashing the forces of competition.

Ils Ne Passeront Pas

Some of the most determined fights in history have been fought over objectives that were strategically useless but symbolically significant – Verdun, for example. More recently merger talks between Chrysler and Daimler-Benz almost collapsed over the name of the company:

> 'Everything was going fine and the name came up,' says one participant. The Germans were adamant that the title should reflect Daimler-Benz's history, and the fact that their company was the bigger part of the merger. [Chrysler] . . . was equally determined [to be] . . . at the front. Neither side would budge.[184]

Eventually a compromise was agreed. It shows the importance of symbols, however. The barrister's wig, the superintendent's peaked cap, the leather desk diary and the like are important to those who possess them because they function as distancing mechanisms. They can also be used as bargaining chips in negotiations. It is surprising what people will concede in order to retain a piece of braid on a uniform. Why waste anything?

Loving to Death

It was suggested in Chapter 3 that the art of decision making involves seeing not one reality but many realities simultaneously. Resistance is a reflection of what your decision means to someone else. Instead of trying to sell another party your point of view it may be more effective to acknowledge their concerns. The magic words are:

'I understand'

Notice that you are not saying 'I agree'. The words 'I understand' signify sensitivity yet commit you to nothing. Sometimes they are all that is needed to mollify resistance. Sometimes all the other party wants is recognition that they have been wronged. An apology often works because it signifies recognition and restores the other person's esteem. Statements such as 'If I thought someone was doing that to me, I would be angry too' can be very effective in dealing with resistance. This is because they signify that the other party's response is legitimate, they *may* have good reason to be angry. I emphasise the word 'may' because words like 'if I thought' or 'if I believed' or 'if that were true' provide a springboard for reshaping the other party's perceptions. The intention is to suggest they are angry because they are misinterpreting the situation.

*Diplomacy is the art of letting someone else have **your** way.*[77]

Another option for dealing with resistance is to smother it by involving the potentially recalcitrant in the decision process. Involvement may not end resistance completely but it helps to nullify it because it implies ownership. This was the mistake in the decision to close the Victoria swimming pool. That is, since there was no consultation ('Go and say we're shutting') resistance became all the more dangerous because it was driven underground.

Another strategy for involving the potentially recalcitrant is to create an illusion of control by allowing them to make all the subsidiary decisions. Another possibility is to love them to death. The Taurus technical team supplied the monitoring group with copious information. The effect was to detract from the failure to meet any of the deadlines set out in the elaborate timetables. 'How do you control a group?' demanded a member of the monitoring group, 'You formalise it, bureaucratise it and give it lunch.'[89]

If the other party is in a hole, throw them a ladder.

The key to ending an escalatory spiral may be to do something that enables the other party to retract with dignity. At very least you must avoid taking any action that might humiliate them. When the Americans finally blockaded Cuba they made sure that the first ship to be stopped was not a Russian vessel thus signalling their determination while sparing the Russians outright embarrassment.

Why Ghosts Return to Haunt

The greatest gift, said the poet Robert Burns, is to see ourselves as the world sees us. A powerful precept for preventing our decisions from returning to haunt us is suggested by the lawyer who looked over the shoulder of his lovelorn son penning a letter to his beloved. The wise if unsympathetic father said:

think how would that sound read out in court.

The Hamiltons were horrified when the details of their expenses-paid weekend at the Ritz were subsequently 'read out' in court. Likewise, Peter Mandelson's ill-judged decision to accept a loan of more than £300 000 from a government colleague to enable him to buy a house cost him his cabinet post when it was later 'read out'.

The point is, whereas science deals in concrete reality calling a spade a spade, the art of decision making lies in recognising that realities can be rewritten.[185] 'Helping' can be rewritten as 'interfering'; 'enthusiastic' as 'carried away'; 'calculated risk' as 'recklessness'.

Rewriting reality can turn success into failure. This is precisely what happened to Marks & Spencer when their share price suddenly fell. Clothes that had been described by journalists only weeks earlier as the epitome of quality were redescribed by the same journalists as 'dowdy' and 'frumpy'. Likewise, Monica Lewinsky's revelations rewrote President Clinton's image.

According to George Bernard Shaw there are two tragedies in life. One is not getting what you want. The other is getting it. Yet it is not success that is dangerous but how we *react* to success. Siegmund Warburg did not say that becoming establishment leads automatically to idleness and complacency. He merely suggested that becoming part of the establishment creates the temptation to succumb.

More specifically, it is our desire to preserve success that undoes us. Val's hairdressing business rotted in front of her eyes. Likewise, when conductors of orchestras discover a style that audiences applaud they may adhere to it to such an extent that it descends into mannerisms. Organisations become complacent because all their rules and procedures are geared to preserving the status quo. In other words, like the child with its toys, they end up living in a world of make-believe.

To have one's world rewritten can be a cruel experience. 'The best way to cause people long-lasting pain is to humiliate them by making the things that seemed most important to them look futile, obsolete, and powerless'.[185] If Val were to imagine the fixtures and fittings of her salon piled into a skip, her world, the things that are most important to her, would look futile, obsolete and powerless.

Yet it might be the one thing that galvanised Val into action precisely because it would force her to see things differently.

(Incidentally in Val's case the issue is now academic. One weekend she finished at her usual Saturday lunch time. Twelve hours later the business wasn't there any more. That night there was a flood, the worst in living memory. I walked round the town on Monday night and found the fixtures and fittings, Val's livelihood, stacked on the pavement still dripping water. Shortly afterwards a notice went up in the window of the door: 'CLOSED DUE TO ILLNESS.' Then a few months later a 'To Let' board went up over the doorway followed by a notice in the local paper saying the salon was now closed permanently. I am unsure whether the illness or the flood came first. It makes little diffference as Val suffered kidney failure and will never work again. Perhaps some of those hair treatments were a lot harsher than she thought, to say nothing of years of exposure to passive smoking. It is the people she misses most.

The art of decision making lies in recognising that shared understandings are becoming untenable and renegotiating these before events shatter the myth. As decision makers we can guard against complacency by imagining how an inspector or investigative journalist would rewrite the operations for which we are responsible. The lift that you describe as 'creaky' might one day be seen as a 'death trap'. Likewise, there are currently no limits on the number of passengers that can be carried on trains operated by London Underground. If an accident occurred how might that non-decision be described? Rewriting reality can be an uncomfortable experience but it is better to do it for yourself and act upon what emerges from the exercise before someone does it for you.

The problem with organisations like Facit is that the whole organisational mindset becomes geared to continuity. The ruling myth is best seen as a kind of retaining wall straining to hold back reality.

Never offer a solution until someone recognises they have a problem.

It is futile to offer organisations like Facit a solution until they realise they have a problem. By then, of course, it may be too late. Crises occur when the forces of reality burst through the retaining wall. One way out of entrapment is to create a crisis and then solve it.

The Element of Surprise

Although 'what if?' – style questions offer a powerful technique for considering alternative scenarios, no matter how conscientiously we try to grapple with uncertainty, the unexpected happens. Many decision failures are failures of imagination. Rewriting reality can reduce the risk of being taken by surprise because it forces us to consider where our metaphorical fences and flood barriers are weakest and where misfortune might come gushing through.

Another reason we may be taken by surprise is that we never stop to imagine the possibility of a surprise, or, if we do, dismiss it too quickly. One way of reducing the risk of being taken by surprise is to consider the possibilities that are so audacious or so ridiculous they make us laugh – think again.

Seigmund Warburg offered us interesting advice:

> With mediocre people, you can usually calculate ... what their reaction will be. But with strong individuals, you must sometimes be prepared for some very surprising reactions.[172]

Sweet Are the Uses of Adversity

On a more optimistic note the art of rewriting can be used to create success. Again, the trick rests in cultivating an eye for paradox. In the words of the Tao it is to make use of what exists by capitalising upon:

what is not.[180]

A goblet is made useful by the empty space that enables us to pour in the wine. What makes a room useful is the empty space created by the four walls. 'Sweet are the uses of adversity,' said Shakespeare. The glory of being unable to attract sponsorship is freedom. Berni Steakhouses used 'what is not' to make a fortune. That is, by not offering extensive choices and complex dishes the organisation made huge savings in bulk buying and dispensed with the need to employ trained chefs. Removing the tablecloths alone saved £400 000 a year in laundry bills. More recently, easyJet and other cut-price airlines have built their success upon factors such as not using popular airports in order to save landing fees. Likewise, Carphone Warehouse owes part of its present success to having obtained sound business advice early on from Ernest Saunders. It was 'what was not' about Saunders through his association with the Guinness scandal that made him affordable to indigent entrepreneurs.

We can also apply 'what is not' to decisions about our own lives. In the words of the Rolling Stones you don't always get what you want. Sometimes it can be the best thing that happens to us. Would the physicist Stephen Hawking have been as eminent if he had not been struck down by illness, or was it that 'where his feet could not go, his mind would soar'?[186]

The Golden Chance

Much has been said in this book about failure. As we saw in the case of the Dardanelles fiasco, we invite failure when decisions owe more to luck than planning. Yet there is a saying in football that:

> *however badly we play, every game offers a golden chance.*

Just as past costs are irrelevant to decisions about the future, so too may be our mistakes. Situations can arise where although nothing has gone right from the start, there is still a chance of achieving our objectives. We are most likely to see it if our eyes are fixed upon the ends as distinct from the means. This was the mistake in the Dardanelles campaign. That is, although the bombardment had failed to silence the forts there was still a chance that the objective could have been achieved but the decision makers failed to see it. We know that many successes are a 'close-run thing'. No less disturbing is the possibility that some failures might have been turned to success if the decision makers had seized that golden moment.

Time and Tide

Most of us have experienced a run of luck at some time in our lives – periods where there does indeed seem to be a tide in our affairs carrying us on to greater things. Most of us are also familiar with the opposite, that is, periods when nothing seems to go right.

The key to understanding why this happens is positioning. Although there is rarely a perfect time to do anything, intuitively we know when something feels right, and when it feels wrong. although planning and control are important in decision making, success partly depends upon being sensitive to changing circumstances and having the patience to wait for a propitious time. No spreadsheet or graph can point the moment. Only intuition can tell us when the tide is running.

The word risk derives from the Italian *risicare* which means 'to dare', suggesting risk is a choice rather than a fate.[118] When the tide is running, there is more to be gained by being impetuous than cautious. To paraphrase Machiavelli, fortune is commanded by audacity.[183]

Epilogue: a dancing star

One must harbour chaos within oneself to give birth to a dancing star.
(Nietzsche)

A child reading this book might say if we are so bad at decision making, how have we managed to survive on this planet for so long? Surely, if we are so irrational, so consumed by our own pride we would have succumbed to catastrophe long ago?

Decisions, non-decisions, action and inaction rest ultimately with people. The answer may simply be that a book like this exaggerates human frailty because it mainly highlights decision fiascos, and that our successes far outnumber our failures.

Another, more interesting possibility is that although irrationality can be dangerous, it has its uses. An important theme of this book is that risk and danger enter in when we lose touch with reality. Does that mean that people with their feet firmly planted on the ground make the best decision makers?

It was suggested in Chapter 5 that one of the dangers of making decisions in a fit of depression is that we see things as worse than they really are. In this view, depression implies losing touch with reality. There is another perspective, however, namely:

depression is reality cutting in.[103]

The idea is frightening because since most of us are not depressed most of the time, it follows that most of the time we are out of touch with reality. Even more frightening is the implication that we cannot live without illusions. Indeed, when Florrie, the wife of the popular cartoon character Andy Capp, ventures out in the storm to go to work, Andy informs her that she should be glad she is able to go out to work, unlike Alice with her delusions. Florrie mutters, 'they can't be any worse than the realities'.

That said, although depression is unpleasant it may not be an entirely negative experience. Depression is synonymous with inactivity. By slowing down we are able to collect resources and ultimately re-energise ourselves. Pursuit of the unattainable is at the expense of the possible.[123] Since depression acts as a window on the world, it can prompt us to reflect upon where we are going and force us to be realistic about what we can and cannot achieve. In short, depressed people like the popular television character Blackadder may make good decision makers precisely because what may seem like habitual pessimism actually reflects realism.

The argument is intellectually defensible but it falls down intuitively for whatever virtues the fictional Blackadder may possess, he is not an inspiring figure. Yet why do we need inspiration?

It was suggested in Chapter 3 that our understanding reflects our choice of images. Decision science holds to the image of the mind as a machine. A child without any preconceptions might ask:

What are minds for?[187]

The notion of the mind as a machine obscures other possibilities, notably the mind's ability to protect us from reality in ways that we barely understand. Although many of us are terrified at the prospect of spending our last days paralysed and helpless, research suggests that people who actually suffer such deprivation do not experience anything like the intensity they might have anticipated.[188] People who touch the extremities of illness can end up occupying a world of fantasy where pain and despair cannot follow.

One of the things we lose as we progress from childhood to adulthood is the freedom to play. Instead it is drummed into us that achievement rests upon a planned, purposeful and orderly approach to everything that we do. The message is reinforced in business schools where we learn to prioritise our activities and manage our time down to the last five minutes. I wonder what our teachers would have made of the nineteenth-century scientist Henri Becquerel. Becquerel was a walking case of escalation, driven by the erroneous conviction that certain rocks emit X-rays. In order to prove his theory, Becquerel began devoting his life to carrying out experiments in order to test the effects of light upon minerals, convinced that his ideas would ultimately be vindicated.

One such experiment involved the following equipment: uranium, salt, a photographic plate, and a copper cross. Becquerel's luck was out because the experiment also needed sunlight and the Paris weather was dull and overcast. Becquerel threw the equipment in a drawer and forgot about it for five days.

For some reason, Becquerel then decided to develop the plate. The decision was completely irrational, because the plate had not been exposed to sunlight and Becquerel's theory assumed that the effects he was seeking were triggered by the sun. Even so, Becquerel went ahead:

And what he saw left him open-mouthed in disbelief. Shining out in brilliant white against the background was the image of the copper cross.[189]

Since these inextinguishable rays had nothing to do with sunlight, they suggested an infinite form of energy. In other words, shining out at Becquerel was the discovery of radioactivity.

Transcendent Optimism

We will never know what prompted Becquerel's extraordinary behaviour. Perhaps it was just the sheer frustration of being kept waiting, the desire to 'do something' regardless of whether it made sense or not, a desire born of a deep-seated commitment to the advancement of science.

Much has been said in this book about the dangers of escalation and unwarranted commitment. Yet without determination, without transcendent optimism what else is there to galvanise us into action and to sustain us when the going gets tough?

The pianist Alfred Brendel has described Beethoven's piano concertos as music that is better than it can be played. As decision makers our visions are almost invariably better than they can be realised in practice. That does not make them wrong, however. On the contrary, to dream may be to bring the impossible within grasp because we have seen it and experienced it.

Fantasy is the antithesis of rationality. Without fantasy, we are nowhere. Fantasy is the one means of resisting totalitarian fact and reason. Fantasy can be the mode for change and liberation. Moreover, fantasy is not within the purview of the elite or the oligarchy. Anyone can fantasise, about anything they like.[37] Martin Gilbert recounts the story of an inmate of the Dachau concentration camp washing dishes by a sink. He sees the door of the hut open and then resumes washing the dishes because he does not recognise the person who has entered, that is, his son. Even when the son embraces him, 'Daddy, I'm your son David!' he remains doubtful until someone produces pictures and family news. Then all the inmates start crying:

> Because Father had always told his friends in the camp when he lay ill with typhus that he had nightmares and also dreams of yearning, one of which was that his son came in an airplane, liberated the camp and said: 'Father, you can take ten people with you. Choose those who have been most kind to you and take them.' And as if the dream came true, his son came to liberate him.[190]

The dream of liberation, hopeless though it may have seemed, kept Yehiel Shmulei alive. Again, what are minds for?

Besides, what is planning if not dreaming with discipline? Plans do not have to be realistic or sensible for them to achieve something. Most plans are better than when played out in practice. The present National Health Service was once a dream. Yet it was only achieved by a willingness to water down ideals, that is, buying off the consultants, 'stuffing their mouths with gold' by allowing them to combine NHS work with private practice.

In the Victoria swimming pool there is a plaque commemorating the opening of the facilities in 1910. Perhaps the ghosts of those long-dead aldermen and councillors walked when the council tried to close the pool resenting the attempted destruction of their achievement. For that plaque signifies things accomplished, *done*. Many decisions are compromises or even shoddy compromises. Almost invariably there is a piece missing, a grand design that had to be pared down, something that never happened quite as planned because the money ran out. It is the accomplishments that we are left with that count.

Technically decisions fail when expectations are unrealised. Yet that implies a very narrow view of what constitutes success. Escalation, it has been suggested, frequently starts with bright promises. Yet if a decision does not start with bright promises it may never start at all.[33] This is because the exaggeration of goals, the process of myth making are the means by which decision makers create the ideal – that is, compose the music that is inevitably better than it can be played.

Dreams, fantasy and myth making are collectively important because they hold the potential to create the social cohesion, the sense of belonging and commitment necessary to move people to act. Without such optimism and the energy that comes from optimism, we would never dare attempt anything remotely ambitious far less strain to the best of our ability in order to achieve it. Obviously it is necessary to distinguish illusion from complete delusion. Illusions mean we see things as better than they are. Delusions are where we see things that are not there at all. Yet perhaps there is even room for delusion in decision making. Joan of Arc's visions may have stemmed from hallucinogens in the local grain, but she did produce one of history's miracles.

Let the French students of May 1968 have the last word: 'Soyons réalistes, demandons l'impossible!' So let us be realists, and ask for the impossible.[37]

References

1. Graham, G. (1999) 'Scientific certainties have taken a beating', *Financial Times*, 29 January, Survey of Global Investment Banking, 3.
2. Gardner, N. (2000) 'Property market ready for fall', *Sunday Times*, 7 May, Money 5.
3. Kay, J. (1999) 'Strategy and the delusion of grand designs', *Financial Times*: Survey: Mastering Strategy, 27 September, 2.
4. *Financial Times* (1995) Lex Column, Canary Wharf, 4 October, 20.
5. Cohen, N. (2000) 'Canary Wharf fulfils eastern promise', *Financial Times*, 7 July, 21.
6. Milner, C. (2000) 'Peak Rail banks more than £100 000 from Flying Scotsman nine-day visit', *The Railway Magazine*, October, 66.
7. *Financial Times* (1991) 'Behind closed doors. BCCI: the biggest bank fraud in history', FT Business Information.
8. *Inquiry into the Supervision of the Bank of Credit and Commerce International* (1992) (Bingham Report) London, HMSO.
9. Weick, K. E. (1995) *Sensemaking in Organizations*, Beverly Hills, CA, Sage.
10. Drummond, H. (1995) 'De-escalation in decision making: a case of a disastrous partnership', *Journal of Management Studies*, 32, 265–281.
11. Stoppard, T. (1980) *Rosencrantz and Guildenstern Are Dead*, London, Faber.
12. Tennyson-Jesse, F. (Ed.) (1957) *Trials of Timothy John Evans and John Reginald Halliday Christie*, London, Hodge.
13. Weir, A. (1999) *The Tombstone Imperative*, London, Simon and Schuster.
14. Weick, K. E. (1990) 'The vulnerable system: an analysis of the Tenerife air disaster', *Journal of Management*, 6, 571–593.
15. Watzlawick, P. (1976) *How Real is Real?* New York, Norton.

16. Janis, I. L. (1989) *Crucial Decisions: Leadership in Policy and Crisis Management*, New York, Free Press.

17. Weick, K. E. (1993) 'The collapse of sense making in organizations: the Mann Gulch disaster', *Administrative Science Quarterly*, 38, 628–652.

18. Mitroff, I. I. and Linstone, H. A. (1993) *The Unbounded Mind*, Oxford, Oxford University Press.

19. Weick, K. E. (1988) 'Enacted sensemaking in organizations', *Journal of Management Studies*, 25, 305–317.

20. Barthol, R. P. and Ku, N. D. (1959) 'Regression under stress to first learned behaviour', *Science*, 59, 134–136.

21. Manchester, W. (1996) *The Death of a President*, New York, Galahad.

22. Bryne, G. (2000) 'Flight into danger', *New Scientist*, 13 May, 24–27.

23. Clark, T. (1999) 'The mystery of flight 185', *Telegraph Magazine*, 7 August, 28–30.

24. Ministry for Finance, Singapore, (1995) *Baring Futures (Singapore) Pte Ltd: The Report of the Inspectors Appointed by the Minister for Finance*.

25. Gay, J. (1728/1986) *The Beggar's Opera*, Harmondsworth, Penguin.

26. Taylor, D. (1986) *The Roses of Eyam*, London, Heinemann.

27. Weick, K. E. (1979) *The Social Psychology of Organizing*, Reading, MA, Addison-Wesley.

28. Dickens, C. (1838/1985) *Oliver Twist*, Harmondsworth, Penguin.

29. Watzlawick, P. (1988) *Ultra-solutions*, New York, Norton.

30. Weyer, M. V. (2000) *Falling Eagle: the Decline of Barclays Bank*, London, Weidenfeld.

31. Burham, J. (1998) 'Political aftershocks rumble on after Turkish earthquake', *Financial Times*, 6 July.

32. Reid, T. (1999) 'There was no cash payment, says Mrs Hamilton', *The Times*, 14 December, 3.

33. Salancik, G. R. (1977) 'Commitment is too easy', *Organizational Dynamics*, 62–80.

34. Dickens, C. (1843) *A Christmas Carol* from *The Christmas Tales*, 1998, Oxford, Oxford University Press.

35. Bowen, M. G. and Power, F. C. (1993) 'The moral manager: com-

municative ethics and the *Exxon Valdez* disaster', *Business Ethics Quarterly*, 3, 97–115.

36. 'Concorde flown too far' (2000) *The Sunday Telegraph*, 30 July, 19.

37. Brown, R. H. (1989) *Social Science as Civic Discourse*, Chicago, University of Chicago Press.

38. Robert, R. J. (Ed.) (1974) *Winston S. Churchil: His Complete Speeches*, 1897–1963, 8 vols, London.

39. Stern, C. (1997) *Dr Iain West's Casebook*, London, Warner.

40. *The Hillsborough Stadium Disaster* (15 April 1989) Inquiry by Rt Hon. Lord Justice Taylor, Final Report, London, HMSO, Cm. 962.

41. Morgan, G. (1980) 'Paradigms, metaphors and puzzle solving in organization theory', *Administrative Science Quarterly*, 25, 605–622.

42. Lakoff, G. and Johnson, M. (1980) *Metaphors We Live By*, Chicago, University of Chicago Press.

43. Cathcart, B. (1999) *The Case of Stephen Lawrence*, Harmondsworth, Penguin.

44. Knights, D. and Roberts, J. (1980) 'The power of organization and the organization of power', *Organization Studies*, 3, 47–63.

45. Dunmore, H. (1999) *Your Blue-eyed Boy*, Harmondsworth, Penguin.

46. Hawking, S. (1988) *A Brief History of Time*, London, Bantam.

47. Benson, J. K. (1977) 'Organizations: a dialectical view', *Administrative Science Quarterly*, 22, 1–21.

48. Pfeffer, J. (1982) *Power in Organizations*, Boston, Pitman.

49. Brown, R. H. (1977) *A Poetic for Sociology*, Cambridge, Cambridge University Press.

50. Shilts, R. (1988) *And the Band Played On*, Harmondsworth, Penguin.

51. Drummond, H. (1998) 'Go and say, "We're shutting": ju jitsu as a metaphor for analyzing resistance', *Human Relations*, 51, 741–759.

52. Giddens, A. (1979) *Central Problems in Social Theory*, London, Macmillan.

53. Hatch, M. (1999) 'Exploring the empty spaces of organization: how improvisational jazz helps redescribe organization studies', *Organization Studies*, 20, 75–101.

54. Katz, F. W. (1982) 'Implementation of the holocaust: the behaviour of Nazi officials', *Comparative Study of Society*, 24, 510–529.

55. Lammers, C. J. (1988) 'The inter-organizational control of an occupied country', *Administrative Science Quarterly*, 33, 438–457.

56. Evans, H. (1983) *Good Times, Bad Times*, London, Weidenfeld.

57. Holt, J. C. (1963) *King John*, London, Routledge.

58. Owen, H. and Bell, J. (1967) *Wilfred Owen: Collected Letters*, London, Oxford University Press.

59. Dyer, G. (1995) *The Missing of the Somme*, Harmondsworth, Penguin.

60. Gilbert, M. (1992) *Churchill: A Life*, London, Minerva.

61. Turner, M. (1999) 'Aids in Africa', *Financial Times*, September 24, XXXI.

62. Crooks, E. (2000) 'Counting the economic cost of Aids', *Financial Times*, 17 April, 10.

63. Strong, P. and Robinson, J. (1990) *The NHS Under New Management*, Milton Keynes, Open University.

64. Weick, K. E. (1985) 'Cosmos vs chaos: sense and nonsense in electronic contexts', *Organizational Dynamics*, 14, 50–64.

65. Dickens, C. (1854/1989) *Hard Times*, Oxford, Oxford University.

66. Vlahos, K. (1997) 'Taking the risk out of uncertainty', *Financial Times: Mastering Management,* London, Pitman, 142–147.

67. Wechsberg, J. (1967) *The Merchant Bankers*, London, Weidenfeld and Nicholson.

68. Branson, R. (1998) *Losing my Virginity*, London, Virgin.

69. Stallworthy, J. (1974) *Wilfred Owen*, Oxford, Oxford University Press.

70. Gapper, J. and Denton, N. (1996) *All that Glitters: the Fall of Barings*, Harmondsworth, Penguin.

71. Treasury Committee (1996) 15 May, p. 21.

72. Nisbett, R. and Ross, L. (1980) *Human Inference: Strategies and Shortcomings of Social Judgement,* Englewood Cliffs, NJ, Prentice Hall.

73. Bazerman, M. H. (1998) *Judgement in Managerial Decision Making*, New York, Wiley.

74. Schwenk, C. R. (1986) 'Information, cognitive biases and commit-

ment to a course of action', *Academy of Management Review*, 11, 290–310.

75. Leeson, N. (1997) *Rogue Trader*, London, Warner.

76. Goldman Sachs (1998) *Financial Times*, 8 June, 22.

77. Ury, W. (1991) *Getting Past No*, London, Century.

78. Schlesinger, A. M. (1978) *Robert Kennedy and His Times*, London, André Deutsch.

79. *The Aberdeen Typhoid Outbreak* (1964) Report of the Departmental Committee of Enquiry, HMSO, Cmnd. 2542.

80. Hedberg, B. and Jonsonn, S. (1977) 'Strategy formulation as a discontinuous process', *International Studies of Management and Organization*, 7, 88–1.

81. Parker, G. (1998) '"Scrooge"' Brown attacked on church pensions', *Financial Times*, 22 December, 3.

82. MacKenzie, D. (2000) 'Polio on the loose', *New Scientist*, 18 November, 7.

83. 'Mad about sheep' (2000) *New Scientist*, 16 December, 45–47.

84. Morison, J. and Leith, P. (1992) *The Barrister's World*, Milton Keynes, Open University Press.

85. Trice, H. M. and Beyer, J. M. (1992) *The Cultures of Work Organizations*, Englewood Cliffs, NJ, Prentice Hall.

86. Simmel, G. (1950) 'The secret and the secret society'. In K. H. Wolff (Ed. and Trans.), *The Sociology of Georg Simmel*, New York, Free Press, 307–376.

87. Barley, S. R. (1983) 'Semiotics and the study of occupational and organizational cultures', *Administrative Science Quarterly*, 28, 393–413.

88. Meyer, J. W. and Rowan, B. (1978) 'Institutionalized organizations: formal structure as myth and ceremony', *American Journal of Sociology*, 83, 340–363.

89. Drummond, H. (1996) *Escalation in Decision Making: The Tragedy of Taurus*, Oxford, Oxford University Press.

90. Wrong, D. H. (1979) *Power, its Forms, Bases and Uses*, Oxford, Blackwell.

91. *BSE Inquiry* (2000) (Vol. 1, Findings and Conclusions, 887–1), London, HMSO.

92. Strachey, L. (1921) *Queen Victoria*, London, Harcourt Brace.

93. Bacharach, P. and Baratz, M. S. (1970) *Power and Poverty: The Theory and Practice*, New York, Oxford University Press.

94. Lukes, S. (1974) *Power: A Radical View*, London, Macmillan.

95. Nock, O. S. (1978) *The Last Years of British Railways Steam*, London, David and Charles.

96. Yamba, C. B. (1997) 'Cosmologies in turmoil: witchfinding and aids in Chiawa, Zambia', *Africa*, 67, 200–223.

97. Ziegler, P. (1982) *The Black Death*, Harmondsworth, Penguin.

98. Gilbert, M. (1994) *The Churchill War Papers*, London, Heinemann.

99. Martin, P. (1998) 'Goldman's goose', *Financial Times*, 11 August, 14.

100. Morrison, R. (2000) 'In this terrible place, an Ode to Joy', *The Times*, 12 May, 18–19.

101. Langer, E. J. (1975) 'The illusion of control', *Journal of Personality and Social Psychology*, 33, 311–328.

102. Griffiths, M. D. (1990) 'The cognitive psychology of gambling', *Journal of Gambling Studies*, 6, 31–43.

103. Taylor, S. E. (1980) *Positive Illusions*, New York, Basic Books.

104. Sellar, W. C. and Yeatman, R. J. (1992) *1066 And All That*, London, Methuen.

105. 'Scrap this weapon' (2000) *The Daily Telegraph*, 31 July, 21.

106. 'The point of no return' (2000) *The Sunday Times*, 30 July, 15–18.

107. Staw, B. M., McKechine, P. I. and Puffer, S. M. (1983) 'The justification of organizational performance', *Administrative Science Quarterly*, 28, 582–600.

108. McCarthy, C. (1999) 'Carlsberg earnings fall', *Financial Times*, 19 June, 16.

109. Kay, J. (1999) 'Perennial hits hard times', *Financial Times*, 20 January, 13.

110. Starbuck, W. H. and Milken F. J. (1988) 'Challenger: fine-tuning the odds until something breaks', *Journal of Management Studies*, 25, 319–340.

111. Du Cann, J. (1993) *The Art of the Advocate*, Harmondsworth, Penguin.

112. *Investigation into the King's Cross Underground Fire*, Desmond Fennell (1988), HMSO, Cm. 499.

113. Fisher, S. (1983) 'The pull of the fruit machine: a sociological typology of young players', *Sociological Review*, 41, 446–474.

114. Gagliardi, P. (1996) 'Exploring the aesthetic side of organizational life'. In S. R. Clegg, C. Hardy, and W. R. Nord (Eds), *Handbook of Organization Studies*, London, Sage.

115. Holman, M. and Pilling, D. (1998) 'Africa's 500lb weakling', *Financial Times*, 10 June, 19.

116. Samuel, E. (2000) 'There's something about Mary', *New Scientist*, 12 August, 38–40.

117. Porter, R. (2000) 'Embracing country life may not be an actively healthy pursuit.' Review of Kavlen, A., 'The biography of a germ', *New Scientist*, 5 August, 50–51.

118. Bernstein, P. L. (1998) *Against the Gods*, Chichester, Wiley.

119. Kieser, A. (1987) 'From asceticism to administration of wealth. Medieval monasteries and the pitfalls of rationalization,' *Organization Studies*, 8, 103–123.

120. Janis, I. L. (1972) *Victims of Groupthink*, Boston, Houghton Mifflin.

121. Senge, P. (1990) *The Fifth Discipline*, New York, Random.

122. Cameron, K. S. and Quinn, R. E. (1988) 'Organizational paradox and transformation'. In R. E. Quinn and K. S. Cameron (Eds), *Paradox and Transformation: Toward a Theory of Change in Organization and Management*. Cambridge, MA, Ballinger.

123. Watzlawick, P., Weakland, J. H. and Frish, R. (1974) *Change: Principles of Problem Formation and Resolution*, New York, Norton.

124. Kieser, A. (1989) 'Organizational, institutional and societal evolution: medieval craft guilds and the genesis of formal organizations', *Administrative Science Quarterly*, 34, 540–464.

125. Wendlandt, A. (2000) 'When a gift is a cover up', *Financial Times*, 24 March, 17.

126. Rushe, D. (2000) 'Safeway chief steps up his guerrilla war', *The Sunday Times*, 16 July, 7.
127. *Financial Times* (2000) 20 April, 22.
128. Miller, D. (1992) *The Icarus Paradox*, New York, Harper Business.
129. Robinson, E. (1999) 'Culture under siege', *Financial Times*, Survey FT Director, 4.
130. Drummond, H. (1998) 'Is escalation always irrational?' *Organization Studies*, 19, 911–929.
131. Hardin, G. (1968) 'The tragedy of the commons', *Science*, 162, 1243–1248.
132. Waters, R. and Cane, A. (1993) 'Sudden death of a runaway bull', *Financial Times*, 19 March, 11.
133. Ferguson, N. (1998) *The Pity of War*, Harmondsworth, Penguin.
134. Vidal, J. (1997) *McLibel: Burger Culture on Trial*, London, Pan.
135. Drummond, H. (1997) 'Giving it a week and then another week: a case of escalation in decision making', *Personnel Review*, 26, 99–113.
136. Perrin, S. R. (2000) 'A critique of escalation theory exemplified from the domain of the film industry', Unpublished PhD thesis, University of Sheffield, UK.
137. Ross, J. and Staw, B. M. (1986) 'Expo 86: An escalation prototype', *Administrative Science Quarterly*, 32, 274–297.
138. Yallop, D. (1993) *Deliver Us from Evil*, London, Corgi.
139. Rolt, L. T. C. (1962) *Thomas Telford: A Biography*, London, Longman.
140. Staw, B. M. (1996) 'Escalation research: an update and appraisal'. In Z. Shapira (Ed.), *Organizational Decision Making*, Cambridge, Cambridge University Press.
141. Schoorman, F. D. (1988) 'Escalation bias in performance appraisals: an unintended consequence of supervisor participation in hiring decisions', *Journal of Applied Psychology*, 73, 58–62.
142. Kim, S. and Smith, R. H. (1993) 'Revenge and conflict escalation', *Negotiation Journal*, 9, 37–43.
143. Kahneman, D. and Tversky, A. (1979) 'Prospect theory: an analysis of decision under risk', *Econometrica*, 47, 263–291.

144. Kahneman, D. and Tversky, A. (1982) 'The psychology of preferences', *Scientific American*, 246, 162–170.
145. Drummond, H. (1994) 'Too little too late: a case study of escalation in decision making', *Organization Studies*, 15, 591–607.
146. Prebble, J. (1979) *The High Girders*, Harmondsworth, Penguin.
147. Clark, A. (1999) 'Old ghosts to haunt new house', *Financial Times*, 26 November, 20.
148. Arkes, H. R. and Blumer, C. (1985) 'The psychology of sunk costs', *Organizational Behaviour and Human Performance*, 35, 124–140.
149. Staw, B. M. and Hoang, H. (1995) 'Sunk costs in the NBA: why draft order affects playing time and survival in professional basketball', *Administrative Science Quarterly*, 40, 474–494.
150. Northcraft, G. B. and Wolfe, M. A. (1984) 'Dollars, sense and sunk costs; a life cycle model of resource allocation decisions', *Academy of Management Review*, 9, 225–234.
151. Batchelor, C. (1999) 'Mind the gaps in the Jubilee Line schedule', *Financial Times*, 23 February, 10.
152. Bowen, M. G. (1987) 'The escalation phenomenon reconsidered: decision dilemmas or decision errors,' *Academy of Management Review*, 12, 52–66.
153. Hamilton, I. (1920) *Gallipoli Diary* (Vol. 1), London, Edward Arnold.
154. Gilbert, M. (1994) *In Search of Churchill*, London, HarperCollins.
155. Gilbert, M. (1972) *Winston S. Churchill* (Vol. 3), *Companion, Part 1, Documents July 1914–April 1915*, London, Heinemann.
156. Meetings of the War Council, extracts from Secretary's notes (Cabinet papers, 22/1).
157. *Dardanelles Commission*, First Report and Supplement 1917, and Final Report and Appendices, 1919, HMSO, Cd. 8490: Cmd, 371.
158. Hankey, M. P. C. (1961) *The Supreme Command*, London, Allen & Unwin.
159. Gilbert, M. (1971) *Winston S. Churchill* (Vol. 3), London, Heinemann.
160. Meetings of the War Council, extracts from Secretary's notes (Churchill papers, 2/86).
161. Asquith, H. H. (1982) *Letters to Venetia Stanley*, M. Brock and E. Brock (Eds), Oxford, Oxford University Press.

162. Churchill, W. S. (1923) *The World Crisis*, London, Butterworth.
163. Mintzberg, H. (1993) 'Crafting strategy'. In H. Mintzberg and J. B. Quinn (Eds), *The Strategy Process*, Englewood Cliffs, NJ, Prentice Hall, 105–113.
164. Beckett, S. (1986) *The Complete Dramatic Works*, London, Faber and Faber.
165. Holley, D. (1987) *Churchill's Literary Allusions*, London, McFarland.
166. Starbuck, W. H. (1983) 'Organizations as action generators', *American Sociological Review*, 48, 91–102.
167. Rubin, J. Z. and Brockner, J. (1975) 'Factors affecting entrapment in waiting situations: the Rosencrantz and Guildenstern effect', *Journal of Personality and Social Psychology*, 31, 1054–1063.
168. Becker, H. S. (1960) 'Notes on the concept of commitment', *American Journal of Sociology*, 66, 32–40.
169. Dias De Oliveira, E. T. V. (1996) 'The development and inter-relations of organizational and professional commitment: an empirical study of solicitors in large law firms.' Unpublished PhD thesis, University of Liverpool.
170. Miller, A. (1961) *Collected Plays*, Crescent, London.
171. Hobson, D. (1991) *The Pride of Lucifer,* London, Mandarin.
172. Reich, C. (1980) 'The confessions of Siegmund Warburg', *Institutional Investor*, March, 167–201.
173. Strachey, L. (1971) *Elizabeth and Essex*, Harmondsworth, Penquin.
174. Wiesel, E. (1987) *The Fifth Son,* Harmondsworth, Penguin.
175. Staw, B. M. and Ross, J. (1989) 'Understanding behaviour in escalation situations', *Science*, 246, 216–246.
176. De Bono, E. (1990) *Future Positive*, Harmondsworth, Penguin.
177. Neustadt, R. E. and May, E. R. (1986) *Thinking in Time: The Uses of History for Decision Makers,* London, Free Press.
178. O'Brien C. (2000) 'The death of the gourmet restaurant', *The Times*, 9 March, 41.
179. Allen, C. J., Fiennes, G. F., Ford, R., Haresnape, B. A. and Perrin, B. (1972) *The Deltics: A Symposium*, London, Allen.
180. Wing, R. L. (1988) *The Tao of Power*, London, Thorson.

181. Musashi, M. (1984) *A Book of Five Rings*, London, Fontana.
182. Kennedy, R. F. (1965) *Thirteen Days: A Memoir of the Cuban Missile Crisis,* New York, Norton.
183. Machiavelli, N. (1532/1998) *The Prince*, Oxford, Oxford University Press.
184. Simonian, H. (1998) 'Daimler-Chrysler deal in final stages', *Financial Times,* 19 September, 17.
185. Rorty, R. (1989) *Contingency, Irony and Solidarity,* Cambridge, Cambridge University Press.
186. White, M. and Gribben, J. (1992) *Stephen Hawking: A Life in Science*, Harmondsworth, Penguin.
187. Penrose, R. (1990) *The Emperor's New Mind*, London, Vintage.
188. Brown, K. (1999) 'Feeling just fine', *New Scientist*, 4 September, 36–37.
189. Chown, M. (1996) 'What's logic got to do with it?' *New Scientist*, July, 40–42.
190. Gilbert, M. (1986) *The Holocaust*, London, Fontana.

Index